POPULATION PRESSURE AND
ECONOMIC LIFE IN JAPAN

POPULATION PRESSURE AND ECONOMIC LIFE IN JAPAN

BY

RYOICHI ISHII, Ph.D.

ドクトル オブ フキロソフキー

石 井 了 一 著

LONDON

P. S. KING & SON, LTD.

ORCHARD HOUSE, 14 GREAT SMITH STREET

WESTMINSTER, S.W.1

1937

PRINTED IN GREAT BRITAIN

ACKNOWLEDGEMENT

THE author wishes to express his deep obligation and appreciation to the following, without whose constant encouragement and assistance this volume would never have appeared :

Professor Samuel J. Brandenburg, Chairman of the Department of Economics and Sociology, Clark University, Worcester, Massachusetts.

Mr. Ryusaku Tsunoda, Curator of the Japanese Library and Lecturer in Japanese Arts and Civilization, Columbia University, New York City.

Mr. W. L. Holland, International Research Secretary, Institute of Pacific Relations.

Miss Ada S. Glickman, A.M., New York City.

February, 1937.

At the New York Office, Manchurian Agricultural Products Institute (*Manshu Tokusan Chuokai*), Fortieth Floor, Lincoln Building, New York City.

CONTENTS

CHAP.
                                                                    PAGE
STATISTICAL TABLES IN THE TEXT xi

STATISTICAL TABLES IN THE FOOTNOTES . . . xvii

WEIGHTS, MEASURES AND MONEY, WITH BRITISH AND
    AMERICAN EQUIVALENTS xix

I. A RÉSUMÉ OF THE TRENDS OF THE POPULATION
    BEFORE THE REFORMATION OF 1868 . . . 1
    A. From the Early Period in National Develop-
        ment to the Seventeenth Century . . 1
    B. From 1721 to 1868 5
    C. The Stationary Population in the Later Toku-
        gawa Era and its Causes . . . 11

II. ECONOMIC EFFECTS OF THE MEIJI REFORMATION OF
    1868 17
    A. Economic Aspects of the Reformation of 1868 17
    B. Industrial Revolution of Japan . . . 21
    C. National Industrial Development and Its Social
        Implications 23

III. DEVELOPMENT OF POPULATION POLICIES SINCE THE
    EARLY MEIJI PERIOD 31
    § 1. Movement for the Abolition of Abortion and
        Infanticide . . . : . . . 31
    § 2. Development of the Present-Day Population
        Problem 37
        A. Movements for Racial Amalgamation . 37
        B. Emergence of the Population Problem . 39
        C. Summary of Chapter III . . . 46

IV. DEVELOPMENT OF THE METHODS OF ESTIMATING THE
    POPULATION 48
    A. From 1872 to 1919 48
    B. Modernization of the Census System and its
        Adoption (1920) 50

Contents

CHAP.   PAGE

    C. Comparison and Re-estimation of Various Population Figures 51

    D. Development of Systems for Collection of Vital Statistics 54

V. REGIONAL AND OCCUPATIONAL DISTRIBUTION OF POPULATION 57

    § 1. Introductory : Population Growth since the Early Meiji Period 57

        A. Present Population of the Japanese Empire 57

        B. Population Statistics since 1872 . . 59

        C. Statistical Comparison with other Countries 61

    § 2. Regional Distribution of the Population. . 64

        A. Changes in the Regional Distribution . 64

        B. Comparison of Concentration of Population by Prefectures . . . 66

    § 3. Urban-Rural Distribution 68

        A. Local Administrative Units of Japan . 68

        B. Trend toward Urbanization . . 69

        C. Demographic Effects of Urbanization . 74

    § 4. Occupational Distribution 76

        A. Statistical Data of Occupations . . 76

        B. Trend of Occupational Distribution within the Population . . . 80

        C. Comparison with other Countries . 82

        Summary of Chapter V 85

VI. DEMOGRAPHIC ANALYSIS OF THE RECENT TREND OF THE JAPANESE POPULATION 87

    § 1. Sex and Age Distributions 87

        A. Sex Distribution 87

        B. Age Distribution. 89

    § 2. Marriage and Divorce 92

        A. Marriage Statistics in Japan . . 92

        B. Informal Marriages and Illegitimate Births 94

        C. Trend of Marriage Rates . . . 96

        D. Age of Marriages 97

        E. Divorces 99

        F. Relationship of Marriage to Fertility . 100

    § 3. Fertility 105

        A. Trend of Crude Birth Rates . . 105

        B. Trend of Refined Birth Rates . . 108

        C. Application of Kuczynski Methods of Computation of Net-Fertility . . 110

CHAP.   PAGE

§ 4. Mortality 113
    A. General Trend of Death Rates . . 113
    B. Specific and Adjusted Death Rates . 117
    C. Causes of Death 119
    D. Condition of the Public Health . . 121
    Appendix to § 4 124

§ 5. Estimate of Future General and Working Population 126
    A. Estimates by Various Writers . . 126
    B. Estimates by Dr. Ueda and Mr. Soda . 130
    C. Résumé of Estimates 134
    D. Outlook for the Working Population . 135
    Summary of Chapter VI 137

VII. RURAL ECONOMIC SITUATION AND POPULATION TREND 140
    A. Conditioning Factors in the Small-Farming System 140
    B. Farm Statistics 142
    C. Effects of the Small-Farming System on the Rural Economy 145
    D. Rural Economy considered in the Light of the Theory of Diminishing Returns . . 148
    E. Land Distribution and the Tenancy Problem . 153
    F. Fundamental Causes of Agrarian Discontent . 158

VIII. PROBLEMS OF FOOD SUPPLY 161
    A. Introduction 161
    B. Supply and Demand of Food . . . 162
    C. Supply and Demand of Rice . . . 164
    D. Characteristic Problems of Japanese Rice . 167
    E. Pressure of Colonial Production and Over-Supply of Rice in Japan 169
    F. Government Rice Policy 172
    G. Estimate of Future Supply and Demand of Food 178
    H. Nutritive Aspect of the Food Problem . . 184

IX. COLONIZATION AND IMMIGRATION 188
    A. Historical Background 188
    B. Japanese in Overseas Territories . . . 190
    C. Emigration Movement 194
    D. Important Outlets for Japanese Emigrants . 199
    E. Chinese and Chosenese Migration to Japan Proper 206
    F. Conclusions 209

CHAP.   PAGE
  X. INDUSTRIALIZATION AS A REMEDIAL MEASURE .   . 212
      A. Introduction   212
      B. Industrial Progress of Japan.   .   .   . 213
      C. Prospect of Foreign Trade   215
      D. Mineral Resources   219
      E. Prospect of Further Industrialization .   . 223
      F. Industrialization and Employment   .   . 226
      G. Problem of Unemployment 230
      H. Conclusions 235
 XI. BIRTH CONTROL AND THE DISTRIBUTIVE SYSTEM   . 237
      A. Introduction   237
      B. Movements for Birth Control, Legalization of
          Abortion, and Eugenic Sterilization   . 238
      C. Study of Differential Birth Rates .   .   . 241
      D. System of the Distribution of Wealth and its
          Significance on the Population Movement 246

    SUMMARY AND CONCLUSIONS 249

    INDEX OF SUBJECTS   255

    INDEX OF PERSONAL NAMES 258

STATISTICAL TABLES IN THE TEXT

TABLE   PAGE

    I. ESTIMATED POPULATIONS FROM EARLY TIMES TO THE MIDDLE OF THE TOKUGAWA ERA   4

   II. CENSUS POPULATION OF THE TOKUGAWA ERA   7

  III. POPULATION OF JAPAN AND SOME SELECTED WESTERN NATIONS IN THE NINETEENTH CENTURY 9

  IV. POPULATION TRENDS OF MAJOR CLANS IN THE EARLY TOKUGAWA ERA . . . 10

   V. FREQUENCY OF MAJOR NATURAL CALAMITIES DURING THE TOKUGAWA ERA . . 13

  VI. ECONOMIC DEVELOPMENT OF JAPAN, 1894–1930 24

 VII. AGE DISTRIBUTION OF MEMBERS OF PARLIAMENT IN 1904 AND 1930 28

VIII. BIRTH STATISTICS IN CHIBA PREFECTURE, 1872–9 35

  IX. TYPES OF POPULATION STATISTICS OF JAPAN, BY FIVE-YEAR INTERVALS . . . 53

   X. AREA AND CENSUS POPULATION OF THE JAPANESE EMPIRE, AS OF OCTOBER 1, 1930 58

  XI. NATIVITY CLASSIFICATION OF THE JAPANESE POPULATION, 1930 58

 XII. GENERAL TREND OF POPULATION IN JAPAN PROPER, 1872–1935 59

XIII. RATE OF ANNUAL INCREASE OF TOTAL POPULATION AND INDEX NUMBER OF TOTAL POPULATION, 1872–1935 . . . 60

XIV. POPULATION GROWTH OF JAPAN AND OF SOME SPECIFIED WESTERN NATIONS, 1820–70, 1870–1920 62

 XV. AREA, POPULATION, AND DENSITY OF POPULATION OF SPECIFIED COUNTRIES . . 63

XVI. REGIONAL DISTRIBUTION OF JAPAN'S POPULATION IN 1881–5 AND 1927–31 . . 65

XVII. CLASSIFICATION OF NATIVE JAPANESE ACCORDING TO PLACE OF BIRTH, 1920–30 . . 66

TABLE   PAGE

XVIII. LOCAL ORGANIZATIONS CLASSIFIED ACCORDING
        TO SIZE OF COMMUNITY, 1893–1925 .   70

XIX.   DISTRIBUTION OF POPULATION BY SIZE OF
        COMMUNITY, 1893–1925   71

XX.   INCREASE OF URBAN AND RURAL POPULATION,
        1893–1925   72

XXI.   INCREASE OF URBAN AND RURAL POPULATION
        DURING TWO PERIODS : 1898–1925, 1920–30   73

XXII.   POPULATION INCREASE IN INDUSTRIAL CENTRES
        AND OTHER AREAS, 1920–5 .   .   .   73

XXIII. DISTRIBUTION OF FIVE-YEAR AGE PERIODS IN
        CITY AND NON-CITY DISTRICTS, 1925   .   75

XXIV.   RATES OF MARRIAGE, DIVORCE, BIRTH AND
        DEATH, AND RATE OF NATURAL INCREASE,
        OF GREAT CITIES AND JAPAN PROPER, 1930   75

XXV.   OCCUPATIONAL DISTRIBUTION OF GAINFULLY
        EMPLOYED WORKERS, 1872–5 .   .   78

XXVI.   OCCUPATIONAL DIVISIONS OF JAPANESE POPU-
        LATION, 1920   79

XXVII. OCCUPATIONAL DISTRIBUTION OF GAINFULLY
        EMPLOYED WORKERS, 1930 .   .   .   77

XXVIII. OCCUPATIONAL DISTRIBUTION OF GAINFULLY
        EMPLOYED WORKERS, 1872, 1920, 1930
        (PERCENTAGES)   80

XXIX.   OCCUPATIONAL DISTRIBUTION OF GAINFULLY
        EMPLOYED WORKERS OF JAPAN AND OTHER
        SPECIFIED COUNTRIES IN RECENT COM-
        PARABLE CENSUS YEARS   .   .   .   83

XXX.   RATIO OF ALL GAINFULLY EMPLOYED WORKERS
        PER 100 POPULATION AGED 15 AND OVER IN
        JAPAN AND OTHER SPECIFIED COUNTRIES   84

XXXI.   SEX RATIO OF POPULATION BY SIZE OF COM-
        MUNITY, 1920   88

XXXII. DISTRIBUTION OF POPULATION BY FIVE-YEAR
        AGE PERIODS, 1884–1930 .   .   .   90

XXXIII. DISTRIBUTION OF THREE FUNCTIONAL AGE
        GROUPS, 1884–1930   90

XXXIV. DISTRIBUTION OF POPULATION BY FIVE-YEAR
        AGE PERIODS IN JAPAN AND OTHER SPECI-
        FIED COUNTRIES   91

XXXV.   MARITAL CONDITIONS, BY AGE AND SEX GROUPS,
        1925 (PER 1,000 OF SPECIFIED GROUPS) .   94

XXXVI. NUMBER OF MARRIAGES, RATE OF MARRIAGE
        PER 1,000 POPULATION, AND RATE OF
        MARRIAGE OF ALL AGES PER 1,000 POPU-
        LATION, AGED 15–34, 1898–1935 .   .   97

TABLE		PAGE
XXXVII.	AVERAGE AGE OF FIRST MARRIAGE, BY SEXES, 1908–30	98
XXXVIII.	DISTRIBUTION OF SPECIFIED GROUPS OF AGE OF MARRIAGE, 1909–30 (PER 1,000 FIRST MARRIAGES)	98
XXXIX.	NUMBER OF DIVORCES IN JAPAN, RATE OF DIVORCE PER 1,000 POPULATION AND PER 100 MARRIAGES OF JAPAN AND THE UNITED STATES, 1883–1935	100
XL.	MARRIAGE AND BIRTH RATES OF ENGLAND AND WALES AND GERMANY, 1886–90, 1906–10, 1926–30	101
XLI.	MARRIAGE AND BIRTH RATES OF JAPAN, 1886–1890, 1906–10, 1926–30	101
XLII.	SPECIFIC FERTILITY OF MARRIED MEN AND WOMEN (PER 1,000 OF SPECIFIC GROUPS)	103
XLIII.	PROBABLE DECLINE OF FERTILITY DUE TO DELAY OF ONE YEAR IN MARRIAGE PER 1,000 MARRIED MEN AND WOMEN AT SPECIFIED AGES	104
XLIV.	BIRTH RATES OF JAPAN AND NORTH-WESTERN EUROPE, 1871–1926	106
XLV.	NUMBER AND RATE OF BIRTHS PER 1,000 POPULATION, 1920–35	107
XLVI.	RATIO OF FEMALES AGED 14–49, PER 100 FEMALES, ANNUAL NUMBER OF BIRTHS PER FEMALE AGED 15–49, AND RATIO OF FEMALES UNDER 15 PER 100 FEMALES, OF JAPAN AND OTHER SPECIFIED NATIONS	109
XLVII.	BIRTH RATE PER 1,000 POPULATION AND ANNUAL RATE OF BIRTHS PER FEMALE AGED 15–44, 1898–1930	110
XLVIII.	BIRTH RATE PER 1,000 POPULATION AND GROSS REPRODUCTION RATE OF JAPAN AND OTHER SPECIFIED NATIONS, 1926	111
XLIX.	NET REPRODUCTION RATE OF NORTH-WESTERN AND SOUTH-EASTERN EUROPEAN NATIONS	112
L.	NUMBER AND RATE OF DEATHS PER 1,000 POPULATION, 1920–35	114
LI.	SPECIFIC AND ADJUSTED DEATH RATES, 1925	117
LII.	SPECIFIC DEATH RATES OF JAPAN AND THE UNITED STATES, 1925	118
LIII.	GENERAL CLASSIFICATION OF CAUSES OF DEATH, 1930	119
LIV.	DISEASES RESULTING IN MORE THAN 5,000 DEATHS, 1930	120

TABLE   PAGE

LV. (APPENDIX TO § 4, CHAPTER VI) BIRTH RATE, DEATH RATE, AND RATE OF NATURAL INCREASE OF JAPAN, 1872–1935 . . 124

LVI. POPULATION OF JAPAN FROM 1926 TO 1959 AS ESTIMATED BY THE BUREAU OF STATISTICS (BY FIVE-YEAR INTERVALS) . . . 128

LVII. POPULATION OF JAPAN FROM 1926 TO 1970 AS ESTIMATED BY DR. SHIMOJO (BY FIVE-YEAR INTERVALS) 129

LVIII. RATE OF SURVIVAL PER PERSON IN PERIOD 1925–30 (BY FIVE-YEAR AGE GROUPS) . 131

LIX. POPULATION OF JAPAN FROM 1930 TO 1950, AS ESTIMATED BY DR. UEDA . . . 131

LX. ANNUAL NUMBER OF BIRTHS PER 1,000 WOMEN IN SPECIFIED FIVE-YEAR AGE PERIODS . 132

LXI. TOTAL NUMBER OF BIRTHS AND GROSS POPULATION OF JAPAN IN 1925–60 AS ESTIMATED BY MR. T. SODA 133

LXII. COMPARISON OF JAPAN'S POPULATION IN 1950–60 AS ESTIMATED BY VARIOUS METHODS . 134

LXIII. DISTRIBUTION OF THREE FUNCTIONAL AGE CLASSES IN 1925–60, AS ESTIMATED BY MR. T. SODA 136

LXIV. POPULATION OF MIDDLE-AGED GROUP IN 1925–1960, AS ESTIMATED BY DR. UEDA AND MR. T. SODA 136

LXV. NUMBER OF FARMS, TOTAL AND PER FARM ACREAGE, 1910–30 142

LXVI. DISTRIBUTION OF SPECIFIED ACREAGE GROUPS, 1910–30 (PERCENTAGES) . . . 143

LXVII. AVERAGE SIZE OF FARMS IN JAPAN AND OTHER SPECIFIED COUNTRIES 144

LXVIII. CASH ESTIMATE OF AGRICULTURAL ACCOUNT PROPER, REPRESENTATIVE FARMS, 1929 . 146

LXIX. MONTHLY SURPLUS OR DEFICIT OF FARMERS GROUPED BY THE SIZE OF FARMS . . 147

LXX. CASH ESTIMATE OF AGRICULTURAL ACCOUNT PROPER OF REPRESENTATIVE FARMS, 1921–1929 149

LXXI. AGRICULTURAL FERTILIZATION AND PRODUCTION, 1921–34 150

LXXII. VALUES OF PADDY AND UPLAND FIELDS, 1905–1929 152

LXXIII. LAND AND PRODUCE VALUES, 1905–29 . . 152

LXXIV. ANNUAL AVERAGE SUPPLY AND DEMAND OF MAJOR FOOD CROPS, 1925–9 . . . 163

TABLE   PAGE

LXXV. ANNUAL AVERAGE *PER CAPITA* CONSUMPTION
OF MAJOR FOOD CROPS, 1912–30 . . 163

LXXVI. ANNUAL AVERAGE SUPPLY AND DEMAND, PER
CHO YIELD, AND *PER CAPITA* CONSUMP-
TION, OF RICE, 1880–1931 . . . 165

LXXVII. ANNUAL AVERAGE SUPPLY OF RICE, CLASSIFIED
BY SOURCES, 1925–9 167

LXXVIII. CONSUMPTION OF RICE, WHEAT, BARLEY, AND
RYE IN 1937, 1947, AND 1957, AS ESTI-
MATED BY DR. ANDO 179

LXXIX. ESTIMATED ACREAGE OF LAND RECLAIMABLE
FOR AGRICULTURAL PURPOSE . . . 181

LXXX. ANNUAL EXTENSION AND CONTRACTION OF
ARABLE LAND, 1918–30 182

LXXXI. STANDARD NUTRITIVE REQUIREMENTS FOR
JAPANESE AS ESTIMATED BY DRS. SAWA-
MURA, MORI, AND TAWARA . . . 184

LXXXII. NUTRITIVE VALUE OF FOOD CONSUMED BY
JAPANESE, AS ANALYSED BY THE BUREAU
OF STATISTICS AND DR. GREY . . 185

LXXXIII. ANNUAL AND DAILY *PER CAPITA* FOOD AVAIL-
ABLE IN JAPAN, 1925 186

LXXXIV. NUMBER OF JAPANESE IN COLONIES AND LEASED
AND MANDATED TERRITORIES, 1929 AND
1930 191

LXXXV. OCCUPATIONAL DIVISION OF JAPANESE IN
COLONIES AND LEASED AND MANDATED
TERRITORIES 193

LXXXVI. NUMBER OF EMIGRANTS, NUMBER OF JAPANESE
RETURNING TO JAPAN, AND AMOUNT OF
REMITTANCES FROM EMIGRANTS ABROAD . 196

LXXXVII. NUMBER OF JAPANESE IN FOREIGN COUNTRIES,
1930 197

LXXXVIII. OCCUPATIONAL DISTRIBUTION OF JAPANESE IN
FOREIGN COUNTRIES, BY CONTINENTS, 1930 198

LXXXIX. ARRIVAL, DEPARTURE, AND NET INCREASE OR
DECREASE OF CHOSENESE IN JAPAN PROPER,
1924–8 207

XC. FACTORY CONSUMPTION OF COAL AND ELECTRIC
POWER, INDEX NUMBERS OF INDUSTRIAL
OUTPUTS, AND ADJUSTED VALUES OF
MANUFACTURED PRODUCTS, 1914–33 . 214

XCI. FOREIGN TRADE COMMODITIES CLASSIFIED AC-
CORDING TO THE DEGREE OF MANUFACTURE,
1897 and 1933 216

XCII. VALUE OF IMPORTS WITH CLASSIFICATION OF
PRINCIPAL COMMODITIES, 1929, 1931, 1933 217

TABLE   PAGE

XCIII.   VALUE OF EXPORTS WITH CLASSIFICATION OF
         PRINCIPAL COMMODITIES, 1929, 1931, 1933   218

XCIV.   NUMBER OF FACTORIES AND OPERATIVES, 1900–
         1933   227

XCV.   AGE AND SEX COMPOSITION OF POPULATION
         GAINFULLY EMPLOYED IN MANUFACTURING
         INDUSTRIES, 1920 AND 1930 . . .   228

XCVI.   AVERAGE NUMBER OF OPERATIVES IN TEXTILE
         MILLS PER GIVEN NUMBER OF SPINDLES
         AND LOOMS, 1929–33   229

XCVII.   UNEMPLOYMENT FIGURES OF TWENTY-FOUR IN-
         DUSTRIAL CENTRES, OCTOBER 1, 1925 .   230

XCVIII. UNEMPLOYMENT ESTIMATES OF THE SOCIAL
         BUREAU, 1929–33   231

XCIX.   REPORT OF THE UNEMPLOYMENT CENSUS,
         OCTOBER 1, 1930   232

C.   DISMISSED FACTORY WORKERS CLASSIFIED AC-
         CORDING TO THEIR DESTINATIONS, 1923–31   233

CI.   NUMBER OF BIRTHS PER 100 MARRIED WOMEN
         GROUPED BY SOCIAL CLASSES AND DURA-
         TION OF MARRIED LIFE, 5,506 WOMEN,
         KOISHIKAWA BOROUGH, TOKYO, 1926 .   245

STATISTICAL TABLES IN THE FOOTNOTES

PAGE

AVERAGE AGE OF DEATH OF MALE AND FEMALE, 1886–1929   116

EXPECTANCY OF LIFE OF MALE AND FEMALE AT SPECIFIED
AGES, 1891–1925   116

EXPECTANCY OF LIFE OF MALE AND FEMALE IN GERMANY,
FRANCE AND JAPAN AT SPECIFIED AGES . . .   116

RATE OF DEATH FROM ALL TUBERCULOSIS, PULMONARY TUBER-
CULOSIS AND INFANT MORTALITY RATE OF JAPAN AND
OTHER SELECTED NATIONS, 1930   123

PERCENTAGE OF TENANT ACREAGE TO TOTAL FARM ACREAGE,
1905–30   154

DISTRIBUTION OF LANDED AND TENANT FARMERS, IN 1910,
1920 AND 1930   154

AVERAGE RATIOS OF RENT OF PADDY AND UPLAND FIELDS
TO TOTAL VALUE OF PRODUCTS, 1915–20 . . .   156

TOWNS AND VILLAGES GROUPED ACCORDING TO PREVALENT
RENT RATIO, 1915–20   156

AVERAGE PRICE OF JAPANESE, RANGOON, CHOSENESE, AND
TAIWANESE RICE IN TOKYO, OSAKA AND KOBE MARKETS,
1918   169

AVERAGE RETAIL PRICE OF JAPANESE AND COLONIAL RICE
IN PRINCIPAL CITIES, 1930   170

AVERAGE DAILY WAGES OF CHINESE AND JAPANESE WORKERS
IN SOUTH MANCHURIA (c. 1930)   205

AGE AT MARRIAGE OF HUSBANDS AND WIVES AND NUMBER
OF BIRTHS PER WIFE, GROUPED ACCORDING TO FAMILY
INCOME, 2,200 COUPLES, NIIGATA CITY, 1924. . .   243

NUMBER OF BIRTHS PER MARRIED WOMAN OVER FORTY,
CLASSIFIED BY INCOME LEVEL, 2,912 WOMEN, TOKYO
(c. 1933)   243

NUMBER OF BIRTHS PER 100 MARRIED WOMEN AGED 19–30,
CLASSIFIED ACCORDING TO SPACE OF LIVING QUARTERS,
YOTSUYA BOROUGH, TOKYO, 1925   244

WEIGHTS, MEASURES AND MONEY, WITH AMERICAN AND BRITISH EQUIVALENTS

WEIGHTS AND MEASURES

Japan legalized the metric system in 1921. The law was to have taken effect on July 1, 1924, but the system will be applied exclusively only after July 1, 1944. Some standard weights and measures, still in use and cited in this paper, are noted below with American and British equivalents:

Koku = 10 To = 100 Sho (1·80391 hectolitre)
        4·96005 bushels (Great Britain).
        47·65389 gallons, 5·11902 bushels (U.S.A.).

Cho = 10 Tan = 3,000 Tsubo (0·991735 hectare).
        2·45064 acres (Great Britain).
        2·45062 acres (U.S.A.).

Kwan = 1,000 Momme (3·75000 kilogram).
        8·26733 pounds (Avoir.).
        10·04711 pounds (Troy).

MONEY

Yen = 100 Sen

Since the World War Japan has been off the gold standard except for a short period from January 11, 1930, to December 13, 1931. The nominal par of yen against pound and dollar are as follows: 2s. 0·582d.; 0·49846 dollar (0·84321 dollar since January 3, 1934).

CHAPTER I

A RÉSUMÉ OF THE TRENDS OF THE POPULATION BEFORE THE REFORMATION OF 1868

A. FROM THE EARLY PERIOD IN NATIONAL DEVELOPMENT TO THE SEVENTEENTH CENTURY

THE early movements of the Japanese people are known to us only by tradition. According to popular belief, the ruling tribes of Japanese moved from Kyushu in Western Japan eastward to Yamato, near Osaka.[1] Although established tradition places the date of this migration as 660 B.C., some modern critical historians have dated it about the beginning of the Christian era.[2] The strength of the Yamato race or Japanese expanded steadily at the expense of the aboriginal Ainu race, whose members were pressed into remote parts of the islands or assimilated by the newcomers. By A.D. 710 the Japanese had become sufficiently sedentary to have a permanent seat for their capital, which they established at Nara, Yamato. More fertile land for prospective colonization by their own prolific people was sought, and Ou or the North-Eastern Region was regarded as suitable for this project.[3] Within a century, soon after the capital was moved to Kyoto, where it remained

---

[1] For a theory of the economic cause of this migration see Kuroita, Shobi, *Kokushi no Kenkyu* (A Study of the National History), Tokyo, Iwanami Co., Revised edition, 1932, p. 33.

[2] Cf. ——, *Kokushi no Kenkyu* (A Study of the National History), Introductory volume, Revised edition, 1931, pp. 422–35; Dr. Naka Memorial Society, *Naka-Tsusei Isho* (Posthumous Works of Tsusei Naka), Tokyo, Dai-Nihon Tosho Co., 1915, pp. 1–35 text; Kume, K., *Kokushi no Hachimenkan* (The Manifold Views of the National History), Volume of Iwayocho, Tokyo, Isobe Koyodo, 1915, pp. 319–22.

[3] Uchida, G., *Nihon Keizaishi no Kenkyu* (A Study of Japanese Economic History), Tokyo, Dobunkan, 1921, Vol. I, p. 4.

until 1868, the last bulwarks of the power of the Ainu were broken, and all parts of present Japan proper except Hokkaido in the north, and Okinawa or Lacco Islands in the south, came under the control of the Yamato people.[1]

We have evidence that census returns were taken in Japan from ancient times. Historical traditions frequently tell about partial censuses after A.D. 86. In the era of recorded history, the Imperial order of A.D. 645 first provided for this task in a systematic manner and arranged to have the census taken every six years. The famous codification of Taiho in 701 regulated the census precisely.[2] However, the figures of these censuses, which included the population of the entire nation, are unknown to us. The remoteness of the date is not the sole reason for this dearth of information ; there were actual obstacles to the preservation of population records due to the attitude of the officials toward the census returns. For instance, each one of the records of the twenty-two censuses carried out between A.D. 645 and 790, except that of 670 which was preserved as a model, was burned by the Government after preserving it for thirty years.[3] The codification of Engishiki of 947 forbids transcription of the number of the gross population of the kingdom without Imperial sanction.[4]

In the early Heian (Kyoto) Era, about the end of the eighth and beginning of the ninth century, the Imperial prerogative declined and locally influential families began to usurp the power of the central authorities. The execution of the census laws then became difficult and they were gradually abandoned, due to the fact that a strong official central body was lacking. By about the end of the twelfth century feudalism was actually in operation, and now,

---

[1] *Encyclopædia Japonica*, Tokyo, Encyclopædia Japonica Co., 1919, Vol. I, p. 1176, "Ezo."

[2] Department of Agriculture and Commerce, Japan, *Japan in the Beginning of Twentieth Century*, Tokyo, The Japan Times Co., 1903, p. 47 ; Kanno, W., " The Increase of the Population in Japan in Earlier Times," *Keizaishi Kenkyu*, No. 7, May, 1930, p. 1.

[3] Nishioka, T., Nara Era, *Sogo Nihonshi Taikei* (The System of a Synthetic History of Japan), Tokyo, Naigai Shoseki Co., Vol. II, 1926, p. 187.

[4] Yokoyama, Y., " A Study of Japanese Population Since Ancient Times," *Gakugei Shirin*, 5 : 26, Sept. 1879.

because of military considerations, unbiased estimates of even local population became unobtainable.[1]

A number of old and modern estimates of the population of Japan from early times to the middle of the Tokugawa Era,[2] covering practically all estimates of importance, are given on page 4.

These estimates are too numerous and conflicting to give a fair idea of the chronological growth of the Japanese population. For this reason, and because of the probable greater degree of accuracy of their data, we may select the estimates of Yoshikiyo Yokoyama and Dr. Togo Yoshida in order to get a consistent view of the trend, although an attempt to obtain clear-cut knowledge on such a subject as we have under consideration is apt to involve the danger of hasty conclusions.   The sources from which these students derive their data are threefold : they include the preserved records of periodically distributed acreages [3] in certain districts, applied to the number of districts which are known to us ; the recorded size of the family and the number of towns and villages ; and, in other cases, the recorded amount of rice crops of feudal domains in the Middle Ages.   The estimates of Yokoyama and Yoshida, cited from the list in the Table I, are as follows :

Date.					Population.
823	.	.	.	.	3,694,331
859–922	.	.	.	.	3,762,000
990–1080	.	.	.	.	4,416,650
1185–1333	.	.	.	.	9,750,000
1572–1591	.	.	.	.	18,000,000

Assuming that these figures approach the truth,[4] we may conclude that Japan was rather thickly populated in comparison with other countries even in the early periods of her history.   The Japanese population in the latter part of the

[1] Kawakami, T., Heian Era, *Sogo Nihonshi Taikei*, cited, Vol. III, 1930, pp. 61, 274 ; Honjo, E., *Jinko Oyobi Jinko Mondai* (Population and the Population Problem), Tokyo, Nihon Hyoronsha, 1930, p. 2.

[2] The Tokugawa Era extended from 1603 to 1868, the year of the Reformation.   Cf. *infra*, pp. 11 ff.

[3] From 645 to about the middle of the ninth century, land was periodically redistributed (normally every six years) according to the sex and age of the people.

[4] The accuracy of Dr. Yoshida's estimate is corroborated by evidence to be mentioned on p. 8.

TABLE I

ESTIMATED POPULATIONS FROM THE EARLY TIMES TO THE MIDDLE
OF THE TOKUGAWA ERA [1]

Date. A.D.	Population.	Authorities.
589	3,931,151	*Shotoku Taishi Denki*
,,	4,031,050	*Taishi Denki*
,,	4,988,842	*Taishiden*
610	4,990,000	*Jugan-iko* ; Nishikawa-Korinsai, *Nihon Suidoko*
,,	4,969,699 *	Jurei Suzuki, *Kofutaii*
650–1150 [2]	8,833,290 *	M. Kimura
710–48 [3]	5–6 millions *	G. Sawada
721	4,584,893	*Gyoki Bosatsu Gyojoki*
724–48	2 millions	*Gyoki Shikimoku*
,,	4,508,551	*Ibid.*, Differently quoted
,,	4,899,620	*Ibid.*, Differently quoted
,,	8 millions	*Jugen-Iko* and Nishikawa, *op. cit.*
,,	6,631,074	Arai-Hakuseki, *Oritakushiba no Ki*
736	8,631,770 *	Ishihara
823	3,694,331 *	Y. Yokoyama, *Nihon Denseishi*
859–922 [4]	3,762,000 *	*Ibid.*
901–22 [5]	2 millions *	Hidenori Ino
923	1,128,167 *	*Chirikyoku Zasshi*
986–1010 [6]	22,083,325 *	Hidenori Ino
990–1080 [7]	4,416,650 *	Yokoyama, *op. cit.*
c. 1155	24–25 millions *	Hidenori Ino
1185–1333 [8]	9,750,000 *	
1278–87 [9]	4,984,828	*Kongyoku Satsuyoshu* and *Ruiju Meibutsuko*
1528	4,916,652	Bishop Shuntei, *Zakkishu*
1553	2,330,996 *	*Chirikyoku Zasshi*
1562	4,994,808	Katori Bunsho
1573–91 [10]	18 millions *	T. Yoshida, *Ishinshi Nachiko*
1673–83 [11]	24 millions	Nishikawa, *op. cit.*
1688–1703 [12]	26 millions *	Yoshida, *op. cit.*
1702	24,994,600 *	*Chirikyoku Zasshi*

* Indicates estimates by present-day writers. Date : [2] The Later Ancient Period. [3] The Nara Era. [4] Jyokan-Engi Period. [5] Engi Period. [6] During the reign of Emperor Ichijo. [7] Tenreki-Shoreki Period. [8] Bunji-Genko Period. [9] Koan Period. [10] Tensho Period. [11] Empo-Tenwa Period. [12] Genroku Period.

[1] Yugi, J., and Horie, Y., " Population Tables of Japan," *Keizaishi Kenkyu*, No. 7, May, 1930, pp. 168–90 ; Hanjo, E., *op. cit.*, pp. 15–16 ; *Population du Japon depuis 1872*, Bureau of Statistics, Japan, 1930, Appendix ; Yokoyama, *loc. cit.* ; Ino, Hidenori, " A Study of the Former and Present Population Figures," *Nyoranshawa*, Later Series, No. 14, July, 1915 ; Nishikawa-Kyurinsai (1648–1724), *Nihon Suidoko* (Studies of the Nature of Japan), Collected in Takimoto, S., Editor, *Nihon Keizai Daiten* (Grand Collection of Japanese Economic Documents), Tokyo,

sixteenth century may be compared with the population of a few nations in Europe about 1580, as cited by James Murdoch.[1]

Country.						Population.
Japan	.	.	.	.	.	18,000,000
Austria*	.	.	.	.	.	16,500,000
France	.	.	.	.	.	14,300,000
Spain	.	.	.	.	.	8,150,000
England	.	.	.	.	.	4,600,000

* Domain of the House of Austria.

If we make due allowance for the inaccuracies inevitable in estimating the population at this period, we are still justified in concluding that, compared to other countries of a similar geographical area, Japan possessed a relatively large population.[2]

B. FROM 1721 TO 1868

Local registration was in practice in Japan from the early days of the Tokugawa Era.[3] The census on a national scale, however, was carried into effect for the first time under the rule of the eighth *Shogun* (military regent), Tokugawa-Yoshimune, a celebrated ruler, who was in office from 1716 to 1744. On the 29th of June, the sixth year of Kyoho or 1721, the eighth *Shogun* ordered a count of the population according to existing registers, and in February, 1726, he ordered a census enumerating the actual population in that year and one every six years thereafter. Hence the census in the Tokugawa Era was begun in a strict sense in 1726. The order of 1726 read :

As promulgated in the last Ox year [1721], peasants, merchants, Shinto priests, Buddhist priests and nuns and all others of every

Shishi Shippansha, 1928–30, Vol. IV, p. 545 ; *Keizai Daijisho* (Grand Dictionary of Economics), Tokyo, Dobunkan, 1916, pp. 2085–9 ; *Taguchi-Ukichi Zenshu* (Collected Works of Ukichi Taguchi), Tokyo, Taguchi-Ukichi Zenshu Co., 1928, Vol. III, p. 457 ; Sawada, G., *Naracho Jidai Minsei Keizai no Suteki Kosatsu* (The Numerical Studies of Political Economy of the Nara Era), Tokyo, Fuzanbo, 1927, p. 152 ; Yoshida, T., *Ishinshi Hachiko* (Eight Lectures of the Meiji Reformation), Tokyo, Fuzanbo, 1911, pp. 25–6.

[1] Murdoch, J., *A History of Japan*, London, Kegan Paul, Trench, Trubner & Co., 1925, Vol. II, p. 70.

[2] The small farming system as one of the causes of Japan's large population will be considered later. *Infra*, Chapter VI, pp. 140–2.

[3] *Keizai Daijisho*, Cited, pp. 2085–9, Uchida, G., " Population."

domain must be examined this year without omission. The
result must be submitted by each lord with totals made according to districts. It is needless to examine this time the acreage
of the paddy-field and upland farms. The enumeration may be
made at any time desired, between the 4th and 11th month,
provided the date of examination and the age over which the
enumeration was made be mentioned. Enumeration of servants
under the Samurai class and enumeration of rear-vassals is not
required.

Hereafter without special notice the same thing shall be
observed every Rat and Horse year.[1]

The above order states that the enumeration must include
" others . . . without omission." Nevertheless, since the
population was divided into rather distinct classes, it was
quite possible tacitly to eliminate court nobles and *samurai*
in upper strata, and out-casts, beggars, and people without
domicile in the lower strata.[2] In other words, the census
objective was commoners only. Possibly for military purposes the *samurai* class as a group was excluded. Apparently, however, the census had no direct relation to tax levy,
for the census included people and places which were
exempted from levy, e.g. the priests and other elements of
the population in territories granted to shrines and temples.[3]
With regard to minors under fifteen,[4] the age limit of
inclusion in each case was left to the discretion of the clan,
provided the lords specified which rule was followed.[5]

It is to be regretted that the centralized censuses in the
Tokugawa Era were so defective. Were it not for these
defects they could claim the position of some of the earliest

---

[1] Cf. Honjo, E., *op. cit.*, p. 18 (trans. by author). Twelve signs make
one zodiac cycle and every Rat and Horse year means every sixth year.

[2] Tatsui, M., Edo Era, Series II, *Sogo Nihonshi Taikei*, Cited, Vol. X,
1926, p. 598.

[3] Honjo, E., *op. cit.*, p. 21.

[4] According to Oriental custom, age is computed by calendar years,
not according to actual years lived. Thus, a child born in December,
1934, is said to be two years old in January, 1935. However, the concept
of actual age was not entirely lacking. The writer has not ascertained
which system of age designation was followed by the Tokugawa regime.

[5] With regard to the geographical limit of the census, it was generally
believed that Okinawa, which was annexed in 1872, was excluded from
the count, as was also Hokkaido. However, some writers maintain that
after 1750 population of Hokkaido was as a rule included. Cf. Yugi, J.,
Horie, Y., *loc. cit.*

censuses in the modern world.[1] However, for our practical
purpose the Tokugawa censuses are quite satisfactory ; we
are primarily interested not so much in the accuracy of the
detailed figures of the population as in the general trend of
its movements ; and the censuses show such general trend
as the constancy of the census method was fairly well
established.[2]

From the documented work of Count Katsu and the
population tables of Dr. Honjo, and Messrs. Yugi and
Horie, the following table of census returns, with index
numbers taking 1726 as a basis, has been compiled :

TABLE II

THE CENSUS POPULATION OF THE TOKUGAWA ERA [3]

Year.	Male.	Female.	Total.	Index No.
c. 1721 . .	—	—	26,065,425	98·18
1726 . . .	—	—	26,548,998	100·00
1732 . . .	14,407,107	12,514,709	26,921,816	101·02
1744 . . .	—	—	26,153,450	96·51
1750 . . .	13,818,654	12,099,176	25,917,830	97·24
1756 . . .	13,833,311	12,228,919	26,062,230	98·16
1762 . . .	13,785,400	12,136,058	25,921,458	97·25
1768 . . .	—	—	26,252,057	98·88
1774 . . .	—	—	25,990,451	97·51
1780 . . .	—	—	26,010,600	97·57
1786 . . .	—	—	25,086,466	94·49
1792 . . .	—	—	24,891,441	93·71
1798 . . .	—	—	25,471,033	95·93
1804 . . .	13,427,249	12,194,708	25,621,957	96·50
1834 . . .	14,053,455	13,010,452	27,063,907	101·93
1846 . . .	13,854,043	13,053,582	26,907,625	101·35
1852 . . .	14,160,736	13,040,064	27,200,800	102·45

To these figures certain estimated additions must be
made in order to arrive at the total population of Japan in
the several years indicated. The population of the classes
which were excluded from the Tokugawa censuses, except
non-domiciles and those minors who were excluded by some

[1] The first modern census was inaugurated in Sweden in 1749.
[2] Droppers, G., " The Population of Japan in the Tokugawa Period,"
Transactions of the Asiatic Society of Japan, No. 22, Sept., 1894, p. 261.
[3] *Ibid.*, passim ; Honjo, E., *op. cit.*, p. 38 ; Yugi, J., and Horie, Y.,
loc. cit.

clans, was estimated to be 2,620,000 in the first year of Meiji or 1868.[1] Count Kaishu Katsu estimated the population of those classes and minors who were omitted from enumeration by a few clans as about 1,860,000. Garrett Droppers regards this number as too small and proposes to double it for addition to the census figures, although he does not give any convincing reason for it.[2] After consideration of all the available data, Dr. Eijiro Honjo, of Kyoto Imperial University and the foremost authority on the population of the Tokugawa Era, concluded that about two to three millions must be added, making the total population of the country somewhere between 28 millions and 30 millions. The late Dr. Togo Yoshida, a great scholar of Japan, basing his estimates upon a study of the rice crop, reached much the same conclusion, viz. that the population would be in the neighbourhood of 26 millions during the period of Genroku, 1688–1703, and about 30 millions in the period of Tempo, 1830–43.[3]

Dr. Honjo's estimate, however, does not include the period from 1846 until the end of Tokugawa rule, December, 1867. The actual population on March 8, 1872, was estimated by the present-day census authorities at 34·8 millions.[4] These same authorities estimate the average annual increase of the actual population from 1872 to 1875 at 180,000. From these data, it may be inferred that at the end of the Tokugawa regime in 1867 the population was about 33 millions.[5]

Assuming that 3 millions must be added to the census figures of the previous table, the Japanese population was about 28·5 millions at the beginning of the nineteenth century. This number shows again that Japan was densely populated in that period compared to many of the Occidental nations. In 1800 the estimated population of Japan ranked below that of Russia, but ranked above other leading nations of the West, such as the United States, England

[1] *Keizai Daijisho*, cited, pp. 2085–9, Uchida, G., " Population."
[2] Droppers, G., *op. cit.*, pp. 261–2.
[3] Yoshida, T., *op. cit.*, p. 26.   [4] Cf. *infra*, pp. 52–3.
[5] Cf. Andreades, A., " La Population du Japon," *Revue Economique Internationale*, Jan., 1931.

and Wales, France, Italy and Germany. The West was at
that time on the verge of the industrial revolution, which
was attended by a rapid expansion of the population.
The almost static Japanese population, therefore, was surpassed by France in 1820, by Germany in 1840, and by the
United States in 1870. As a result, the Japanese population
at the end of the Tokugawa Era, in 1867, estimated at
33 millions, exceeded that of none of the above-mentioned
countries, excepting only England and Wales and Italy.
A table showing the comparative trends of population of
the above-enumerated countries follows :

TABLE III

POPULATION OF JAPAN AND SOME SELECTED WESTERN NATIONS
IN THE NINETEENTH CENTURY [1]

(Unit—One Million)

Year.	Russia.	Japan.*	France.	Germany.	Italy.	England and Wales.	U.S.A.
1800 .	38·0	28·5	27·3	23·2	18·1	8·9	5·3
1820 .	46·0	30·0	30·9	27·0	19·1	12·0	9·6
1840 .	55·6	30·0	35·3	32·8	22·5	15·9	17·1
1860 .	69·1	32·0	37·4	38·1	25·0	20·1	31·4
1870 .	76·5	34·3	36·1	41·1	26·8	22·7	39·8

* The figures on the Japanese population, 1800 to 1860, are derived by adjusting the average annual increase or decrease to the census figures of Table II,
and adding 3 millions : the figure for 1870 is derived from the above data and
the estimated actual population in 1872.

Table II shows that during this period of about one and
a quarter centuries, the population surpassed that of the
year 1726, taken as the basis, only four times, viz. in 1732,
1834, 1846 and 1852. All the other twelve censuses show
decreases from the 1726 level. The number of 1852, which
is the last census enumerated and the highest in index,
102·45, shows an increase of just 652,402 compared to the
first census of 1726, taken 126 years before. If we take
only the first and last censuses enumerated, we get an
average annual increase of 5,178. The geometrical ratio of

[1] Cf. Chart of *Population Increase of 38 Countries, 1800–1930*, New
York, Population Reference Bureau, 1931.

increase is 0·193 per 1,000 per annum. On the whole the
entire table indicates a strikingly static situation. During
the entire period covering 131 years from the quasi-census
of 1721 to the last census enumerated, in 1852, the index
number was never lower than 93·71, the level of 1792, or
higher than 102·45, the level of 1852.

Estimates of the population prior to 1702 were enumerated in Table I. In view of the almost stationary state of
the population throughout the later Tokugawa Era, a more
detailed study of the immediately preceding period may be
of interest to students of the history of Japanese population.
For this period we have important data relating to this
study.

Encouraged by the results of the census which he had
instituted,[1] the eighth *Shogun* further ordered ten clans
with domains yielding over 100,000 koku (511,902 dry
bushels) of rice, to submit numbers of their registered
populations during the few decades just past. From the
reports of nine clans Dr. Honjo calculated the rates of
increase during the specified period as follows :

TABLE IV

POPULATION TRENDS OF MAJOR CLANS IN THE EARLY TOKUGAWA
ERA [2]

Clans (Chiefs of Clans).	Period.	Duration (Years).	Annual Increase (per 1,000).
Maeda . . .	1720–1732	12	3·77
Date . . .	1690–1702	12	2·51
,, . . .	1702–1732	30	1·62
Shimazu . .	1698–1732	34	15·66
Ikeda . . .	1686–1706	20	5·34
,, . . .	1706–1732	26	2·87
Todo . . .	1665–1690	25	4·52
,, . . .	1690–1732	42	·26
Hachisuka . .	1665–1688	23	10·82
,, . . .	1688–1732	44	4·98
Sakai . . .	1694–1732	38	·97
Niwa . . .	1685–1702	17	2·14
,, . . .	1702–1732	30	− 2·41
Nambu . . .	1669–1703	34	5·81
,, . . .	1703–1732	29	1·70

Judging from the above table, the population of the nine

[1] 1726. Cf. *supra*, p. 5.   [2] Honjo, E., *op. cit.*, pp. 44–6.

major feudal domains increased during the period from 1665 to 1732, except in one case only, that of Lord Niwa's, which decreased in the period 1702–32. It is a striking fact that where there were two periods of estimate in one domain, the earlier period, roughly from 1665 to 1702, shows, without a single exception, a very much more rapid rate of increase than the later period, roughly from 1702 to 1732. The stationary state of the population of the later Tokugawa Era after 1732 seems, therefore, to have been anticipated or prepared for by this diminution in the rate of increase. From these data, it can be fairly concluded that the turning point of the population trend in the Tokugawa Era lies somewhere near the 1702–32 period. Some attempt at interpretation must be added to the above statistical study of the trend of the population in the Tokugawa Era.

C. The Stationary Population in the Later Tokugawa Era and its Causes

After the period of internecine warfare, which continued incessantly for a century, but which culminated finally in external warfare of the great Korean Expedition of 1591–8, Tokugawa-Iyeyasu assumed the military regency in 1603, having defeated all opposing forces in the battle of Sekigahara (1600), the greatest battle ever fought in Japan. Thus emerged the Tokugawa Era, a period of peace and tranquillity ; in the words of Dr. John Orchard : " . . . no other nation has ever enjoyed so prolonged a freedom from both domestic and foreign warfare." [1] Consequently, for the first few generations national economy progressed rapidly and so did also the population. Inasmuch as the level of the economic arts and the standard of political justice remained practically stationary, this benefit of domestic peace, as reflected in the population trend, reached its maximum point in the early decades of the eighteenth century. A generation later the population became practically stationary, and in some instances showed declines.

[1] Orchard, J. E., *Japan's Economic Position*, New York, Whittlesey House, 1930, p. 8.

Kogai Tanaka declares that the prolonged peace of the Tokugawa Era was possible largely because of the stationary character of the population trend in the later half of the Era ; that is, the balance between numbers and food-producing capacity was maintained.[1] All the factors that Malthus enumerated as checks on population were in operation, with the single exception of war. A general historian observed after Droppers that : " The checks to any increase were famine, pestilence, calamities of flood, fire and earthquake, and sexual immorality. Prostitution was on a large scale and . . . pederasty was far from uncommon." [2]

Dr. Honjo and Dr. Tsuji pointed out that famines constituted the most important agent among these factors of population check. Droppers added to famines the factors of epidemic diseases.[3] Indeed, the effect of great famines is traceable in the census figures. For instance, the census of 1786 indicates a decrease of 920,000 compared with the figures of 1780 ; the census of 1792 shows a further decline of 200,000, a total decline of 1,100,000 in twelve years. This great fall was undoubtedly due largely to the disastrous famine of Tempei, which lasted from 1783 to 1787 and is popularly credited with the death of about half the population, or 1,200,000 people, in the north-eastern provinces alone.[4] After the great famine of 1836-7 the population returns of 1846 showed a decrease of 160,000 as compared with those of 1834. The destructive effects of epidemic diseases, which usually followed and enhanced the calamities caused by famines in those days when there were no scientific remedies, are also evidenced in the population trends.[5]

However, natural calamities, except some epidemics like

---

[1] Tanaka, K., *Edojidai no Danjo Kankei* (Sexual Relations of the Edo [Tokugawa] Era), Osaka, Reimeisha, 1926, p. 328.

[2] Longford, J. H., in Murdoch, *op. cit.*, Vol. III, p. 358.

[3] Honjo, E., *op. cit.*, p. 50 ; Tsuji, Z., *Kaigai Kotsu Shiwa* (Historical Episodes in the Foreign Intercourse of Japan), Tokyo, Naigai Shoseki Co., 1930, p. 634 ; Droppers, G., *op. cit.*, p. 265.

[4] Takekoshi, Y., *Nihon Keizaishi* (Economic History of Japan), Tokyo, Nihon Keizaishi Co., 1920, Vol. VI, p. 478.

[5] For the history of natural calamities in Japan see Gondo, Seikyo, *Nihon Shinsai Kyokinko* (Study of Earthquakes and Famines in Japan), Tokyo, Bungei Shunjusha, 1932 ; Okajima, H., *Nihon Saii Nenroku* (Annals of Destructive Natural Phenomena in Japan), Tokyo, 1894.

cholera, which was unknown in Japan prior to 1832,[1] were not new in Japan. Mr. Kamekichi Takahashi, a distinguished economist, contends that there were no periods in Japanese history when famines and epidemics occurred so frequently as in the later Tokugawa Era. He attributes this to the fact that both land and peasants in this epoch were so thoroughly exhausted that even a slight change in weather produced destructive results.[2] The following table, constructed by Professor Ichihashi of Stanford University, after the late Okajima's careful survey of destructive natural phenomena in Japan, attempts statistically to disprove this contention.

TABLE V
FREQUENCY OF MAJOR NATURAL CALAMITIES DURING THE TOKU-
GAWA ERA [3]

Calamity.	Number in Specified Period.		
	1601–1700.	1701–1800.	1801–50.
Earthquake . . .	45	22	41
Famine . . .	16	13	8
Epidemic . . .	9	26	6
Blizzard . . .	422	65	27
Long-continued rain .	9	12	6
Drought . . .	14	9	8
Volcanic eruption . .	26	35	9
Tidal wave . . .	9	14	3
Flood	433	38	6

This tabulation, if accepted as reasonably accurate, establishes one fact only, viz. that, aside from blizzards and floods, the frequency of calamities, despite the generally more complete records of the latter years, was no greater in the eighteenth and in the first half of the nineteenth centuries than in the seventeenth century. But frequency of calamities is not enough ; we must know also the nature and magnitude of damages caused by each of the several visitations. Since detailed knowledge of this type is not obtainable, it is not possible to reach definite conclusions as to the effect of the known calamities on population growth. It appears more fruitful to seek the chief causes

[1] Kawanishi, S., Editor, *Nihon Nominshi* (The History of Japanese Peasants), Tokyo, Kokon Shoin, 1930, p. 383.
[2] Takahashi, K., " Where does the Rural Village go ? " *Central Review*, Oct., 1930, p. 68.
[3] Ichihashi, Y., *Japanese Immigrants in the United States*, Stanford University Press, 1932, p. 381.

of the population check in the later Tokugawa Era among social and human factors rather than among natural ones. For example, the strengthening of the caste system, with its contingent restriction upon freedom of domicile and occupation, the formal prohibition of the disposal of land property (1643), and the frequent issues of sumptuary edicts,[1] even including the prohibition of "innovation" of commodities (1721),[2] which followed step by step the adoption of the seclusionist policy in 1634–9, all operated to retard population growth. In particular, the *samurai* were naturally inclined to refrain from raising large families since their incomes in form of rice annuities were fixed hereditarily, often at very low levels. Moreover, the extravagance among rulers and the poverty among the mass of commoners resulted in greater difficulty of marriage within both classes ; this led to an increase of prostitution, and to a general decline of sex morality, and encouraged the practice of abortion and infanticide.

Recent progress in the study of the social history of Japan has made it clear to us that among these human causes of population check, in the Tokugawa Era, abortion and infanticide were the most effective agents.[3] An exhaustive analysis of these agents was made by Dr. Honjo [4]

[1] From about the end of the seventeenth century sumptuary laws, issued from time to time throughout the Tokugawa Era, became more specific in character. This was in contrast to the terms of former laws, which were generally abstractive. A chronological table of sumptuary edicts proclaimed by the Tokugawa authorities was compiled by Messrs. Yugi, Eto, and Horie. Although this table is by no means complete, it shows that during the period from 1699 to 1867 200 such orders were proclaimed. Yugi, J., Eto, T., Horie, Y., "A Chronological Table of the Sumptuary Laws in the Tokugawa Era," *Keizaishi Kenkyu*, No. 1, Nov., 1929, pp. 204–22.

[2] The order of July 11, 1721, is read :

"I. Hereafter innovations in drapery, tools, books, and even other commodities and cakes are forbidden. In case there are necessary reasons for innovation, official sanction must be secured beforehand.

"II. It must be understood that commodities modified unnecessarily where traditional ones are sufficient for use, will be ordered, after investigations, to be relinquished." Cf. Takahashi, K., *Saikin no Nihon Keizaishi* (Economic History of Japan in Recent Period), Tokyo, Heibonsha, 1930, p. 31 (trans. by author).

[3] Tanaka, K., *op. cit.*, p. 331 ; Andreades, *loc. cit.*

[4] Honjo, E., *op. cit.*, pp. 109–57 ; *Nihon Shakai Keizaishi* (Social and Economic History of Japan), Tokyo, Kaizosha, 1928, *passim*, and numerous articles in the *Keizai Ronso*, *Keizaishi Kenkyu*, and other journals.

and supplemented by other students, notably Dr. Takeo Ono [1] and Professor T. Tsuchiya.[2] Here only one original document will be cited, for it throws considerable light on the turning point of the social custom concerning child-rearing.

In a memorial submitted by Ro-Tozan, a famous scholar of the Sendai Clan, to the clan authorities in 1754, the following remarks were made :

Up to fifty or sixty years ago a couple on the farm used to bring up five or six or even seven or eight children. Whether it is due to the prevalence of extinction of the family line or due to the prevalence of luxury, it has become the custom in recent years among the farmers for each married couple to rear no more than one or two children. As soon as a baby is born, its parents put it to death. This is an inconceivable act for men of noble character. But, as it is a custom followed by the ignorant populace, there is no question of humanity to be raised. In the final analysis it is due to their poverty ; they prefer to assure their own survival rather than to suffer hunger and penury with many children and so restrict the number of their children to two or three. Even rich families follow this evil custom, and deliberately restrict the number of their children.[3]

The memorial which has just been cited incidentally confirms the present writer's opinion, derived from statistical data, that the turning point of the population trend in the Tokugawa Era was sometime near the 1702–32 period.[4]

In view of the scope of this thesis, we must, for the present, be satisfied to accept certain conclusions from the original documents cited by Dr. Honjo and other scholars concerning the practice of abortion and infanticide. These conclusions follow :

1. Practices of abortion and infanticide were prevalent throughout all social classes. Records indicate that even some *Shogun* (military regents) and *Daimyo* (lords) restricted

[1] Ono, T., " Decrease of Rural Population in the Tokugawa Era," *Social Reform*, No. 77, Feb., 1927, pp. 127–39, and others.

[2] Tsuchiya, T., " Provisions for Child-Bearing in the Old Sendai Clan," *Keizaigaku Ronshu*, 3 : 1 ; " The Population Policy of the Akita and Kagoshima Clans," *Kokka Gakukai Zasshi*, 39 : 3, and others.

[3] Memorials of Ro-Tozan (1696–1776), collected in *Nihon Keizai Daiten*, cited, Vol. XI, pp. 477–8 (trans. by author).

[4] *Supra*, p. 11.

their families. Throughout society, families generally reared only one child, and in most cases no more than two or three.

2. In spite of the prevalence of the practice of abortion and infanticide, it never secured official sanction. Partially from political motives and partially from the ethical point of view, the governments resorted to three principal means of discouraging these practices : (*a*) Legal prohibition with punishment of offenders, upon which means the central authorities mainly relied ; (*b*) Direct subsidy to poor families to raise their offspring, usually according to the number of children they reared, and indirect subsidy encouraging the reclamation of land for internal colonization with the avowed purpose of child-rearing ; (*c*) Moral appeal with the distribution of pamphlets and dispatch of preachers. Most lords resorted to the (*b*) and (*c*) means of remedy. Also many public-minded people promoted the cause with unreserved devotion. Similar policies instituted by the reformed government after 1868 will be referred to in more detail in § 1, Chapter III.

The partial success of these policies is admitted, but they did not affect the general tendency. If the validity of Mr. Tanaka's observation be accepted, that the prolonged peace and the consequent prolonged sway of the Tokugawa regime was due to the stationary state of the population,[1] it follows, then, that the very failure of the rulers' population policy contributed to the prolongation of the government. A significant fact lying behind this paradox is found in the relation between the government and the population in the Tokugawa Era. That is, it was not the government but the economic condition under the given social circumstance, which was the controlling factor in the population trend of this period.

[1] *Supra*, p. 12.

CHAPTER II

ECONOMIC EFFECTS OF THE MEIJI REFORMATION OF 1868

A. Economic Aspects of the Reformation of 1868

THE Tokugawa *Shogunate* or Military Regency restored the governing power to the sovereign on December 9, 1867. Under the Tokugawas, the class system of Japan reached its apogee. This stringent class system placed on the shoulders of the helpless peasants the unbearable burden of supporting the vast parasitic ruling class.[1] This fact, together with the standstill of the rice economy under the policy of national seclusion and the gradual extension of money economy,[2] arrested the social and economic organization throughout the later Tokugawa Era. The fall of the Tokugawas, however, is directly attributable to the diplomatic difficulty brought on by the visit of Commodore Perry's American fleet in 1853.[3] This event occurred at the very time when the progress of historical study had awakened the pioneer leaders to questioning the right of the *Shogun*,[4] and at the time when the powers of the lords not in hereditary vassalage to the Tokugawas,[5] particularly

---

[1] Honda-Masaharu (1538–1616), one of the loyal retainers to the Tokugawa *Shogun*, ruled on the principle that the way to govern the peasants was to exploit them to such an extent that they barely survived. *Honsaroku* (Memoir of Honda-Masaharu), Collected in *Nihon Keizai Daiten*, cited, Vol. III, p. 21.

[2] Cf. Takizawa, M., *The Penetration of Money Economy in Japan*, New York, Columbia University Press, 1927, Chap. VIII *et passim*; Ishihama, Chiko, "Development of Japanese Capitalism," *Kaizo*, Oct., 1932, pp. 50–65; Okawa, Shumei, *Nihon Bunmeishi* (The History of the Japanese Civilization), Tokyo, Gyochisha, 1926, p. 286.

[3] Cf. *Ibid.*, p. 289.

[4] Cf. Hara, K., *An Introduction to the History of Japan*, New York and London, G. P. Putnam's Sons, 1920, p. 360 ff.

[5] There were two kinds of lords under the Tokugawa regime: hereditary and non-hereditary vassalages to Tokugawa. The latter were rivals of the Tokugawas before the Tokugawas assumed regency.

those of South-Western Japan, were becoming a rival force.

The fact that difficulties in foreign relations forced the Tokugawa *Shogunate* out of power indicated the course of the new Japan. The leaders knew the fate of the neighbouring lands in the South Seas and in India, and the destiny now facing even the great Chinese Empire under the mighty pressure of the Western powers. Menaced by the Occidental approach, Japan, smaller than most of the neighbouring countries, had no assurance that the Japanese were superior to the peoples already subjugated, or those in the process of being subjugated.[1] Under such circumstances it is quite natural for a homogeneous people with a pride of race to be united in an intense patriotism.[2] This patriotism stands out among the factors that helped to make the Meiji Reformation successful.[3]

To cope with the situation noted above, the Japanese had, among other things, to rebuild their economic and social systems. This was a task involving formidable difficulties. An idea of the problems which the leaders of the nation faced may be gained by reading the Charter Oath which was proclaimed by the fifteen-year-old Emperor Meiji on March 14th of the first year of Meiji, 1868. The main parts of the Oath are as follows :

[1] The precarious position of Japan was well pointed out by Herbert Spencer in correspondence between him and Baron—later Count—Kentaro Kaneko in 1892. Baron Kaneko, at the request of Premier Hirobumi Ito, wrote to Spencer for his opinion regarding the national policies of Japan. The letter, dated August 26, and quoted here in part, depicts the seriousness of Western pressure in the Orient even as late as 1892. It reads :
"... Apparently you are proposing by revision of the treaty powers with Europe and America ' to open the whole Empire to foreigners and foreign capital.' I regret this as a fatal policy. If you wish to see what is likely to happen, study the history of India. ... I believe that you will have great difficulty in avoiding this fate in any case, but you will make the process easier if you allow any privileges beyond those which I have indicated." Cf. Duncan, D., *The Life and Letters of Herbert Spencer*, London, Methuen & Co., 1908, p. 321.
[2] Knapp, A. M., *Feudal and Modern Japan*, Yokohama, Kelly and Walsh, revised edition, 1906, pp. 4–5.
[3] Cf. Takahashi, K., " Economic History of the Meiji-Taisho Period," *Taiyo*, 30 : 8, June 15, 1927, p. 21 ; Miura, Shuko, *Nihonshi no Kenkyu* (Studies of the History of Japan), Tokyo, Iwanami Co., 1930, Vol. II, p. 331.

I. An assembly widely convoked shall be established, and all affairs of state shall be decided by impartial discussion, and in the light of public opinion.

II. The civil and military powers shall be centred in a single whole, and, in order that the national mind may be satisfied, equal opportunity shall be assured to all classes.

III. The whole nation from the upper to the lower classes of the people shall be united and shall strive for the progress and welfare of the country.

IV. All outworn customs shall be abandoned and justice and righteousness shall regulate all actions.

V. Intelligence and learning shall be sought for throughout the world, in order to strengthen the foundations of the Empire.

The fundamental principle of the above Oath is the advancement of enlightenment, democracy, and nationalism, which later development of events in Japan proved to have been steadfastly pursued.

In the second year of Meiji, four leading clans of the Southwest petitioned the Emperor to take over their feudal authority. The rest of the 286 *Daimyo* or lords [1] followed suit and feudalism was thereby abolished in that year, 1869.[2] The radical reforms which followed accomplished, in the main, the establishment of freedom of domicile and occupation, freedom of contract, and affirmation of private property ; they also brought about the adoption, in their technical aspects, of modern educational, military, monetary and communication systems. These reforms naturally entailed the acceptance of a liberal economic policy. Such a policy Japan clearly recognized and utilized, as essential, if she was to meet the industrialized powers of the West on an even footing.[3] The motto of the reformists, " Sonno joi," or " reverence for the Emperor and expulsion of foreigners," was transformed, before anybody was aware, into " Fukoku Kyohei," or " enrichment and strengthening of the nation." [4]

However, in Japan, where there was no intervening period of commercial expansion between the fall of feudalism and

---

[1] *Encyclopædia Japonica,* cited, Vol. VI, pp. 683–94, " Daimyo."
[2] It may be said that feudalism was actually abolished in 1871, when the prefectural system was organized.
[3] Cf. Takahashi, K., *Saikin no Nihon Keizaishi,* cited, pp. 41–3.
[4] Cf. *Ibid.,* p. 5.

the rise of modern capitalism (which had prevailed in Europe for about two hundred years), and where 80 per cent of the occupied population were engaged in agriculture,[1] there were no trained leaders in business and no accumulated capital. Consequently, the foundations of modern industry were laid by the government, under the influence of young statesmen, most of whom came from the *samurai* class. These young leaders were assisted by foreign experts who numbered over five hundred in 1875,[2] and functioned either as advisers or as regular officials. Thus, according to Dr. T. Nagai, the Meiji statesmen were the last Mercantilists; and, according to Dr. H. G. Moulton, they were the first modern planners of national economy.[3]

The Government founded and operated a few model dockyards, cotton and silk factories, woollen mills, ironworks, machine factories, glass, brick, and cement plants, and printing shops. It also operated mines and foundries and established pastures and stallion pastures.[4]

Maintenance of these model establishments in the then unexplored fields of industries in Japan added to the burden of the new Government, which was also involved in similarly extensive programs in almost all other spheres of economic and social life. Further expenses were incurred in putting down the Kagoshima Rebellion in 1877. Thereafter, the credit of the Government began to decline, and in 1881 the government notes depreciated to an average for the year of 54·3 per cent of their face value.[5] Under such economic pressure the Government decided to liquidate its interests in the model factories and other industrial establishments, and after 1885 it transferred most of them to civilian hands

---

[1] See *infra*, p. 78.

[2] Address on the advisability of the recognition of Manchoukuo by the Foreign Minister, Count Uchida, before the 63rd session of the Imperial Diet of Japan. Cf. *The New York Times*, Aug. 25, 1932, p. 6.

[3] Nagai, T., *Nihon Jinkoron* (Japanese Population), Tokyo, Ganshodo, 1929, p. 322; Moulton, H. G., *Japan*, Washington, Brooking Institution, 1931, p. 328.

[4] Cf. Takahashi, K., *Saikin no Nihon Keizaishi*, cited, pp. 86–97; *Saikin no Shakai Undo* (The Recent Social Movements), Tokyo, Kyocho-kai, 1929, p. 11.

[5] See the table of money depreciation in Takahashi, K., *Saikin no Nihon Keizaishi*, cited, p. 163.

as rapidly as it could assure itself of their continued operation on a business basis.[1]   Since then the Government has resorted to the policy of promoting enterprises like banking and transportation, and leaving other industries to capitalistic self-regulation, though protection has been extended whenever necessary and possible to these other industries.

B.   INDUSTRIAL REVOLUTION OF JAPAN

The above is a brief review of the economic aspects of the Reformation of 1868.   So far, reform had come mainly through legislation and the initiative of enlightened leaders of the government.   At first, however, the effects of their measures made themselves felt slowly.   It was only with the two victorious foreign wars of 1894–5 and 1904–5 that the nation was actually prepared for the transformation of economic life along industrial and capitalistic lines.   The acquisition of complete tariff autonomy in 1911 further stimulated these developments.

Particularly, the favourable conclusion of the war of 1904–5 in which Japan defeated Russian designs in the Far East strengthened confidence in the future development of the nation and thereby encouraged the influx of necessary capital from foreign countries.   At the end of 1903, in spite of the active efforts of the Government to induce foreign capitalists to invest in the country, foreign capital invested in Japan, including public and private loans, amounted to only 195 million yen.   Thereafter, during the war of 1904–5, it increased rapidly and by the end of 1907 had reached the substantial amount of 1,400 million yen.[2] Still another illustration of the progress of industrialization of the nation at this period was the rapid increase of the urban population.   During the five-year period of 1893–8 less than 40 per cent of the population increase was drawn to urban districts, that is, to communities of more than

---

[1] Cf. Kobayashi, U., " The Transition of Public and Private Industries," *Meiji Taishoshi* (History of the Meiji-Taisho Period), Tokyo, Jitsugyo no Sekaisha, Vol. VI, 1929, pp. 53–132.
[2] Takahashi, K., *Saikin no Nihon Keizaishi*, cited, p. 234.

10,000 population. During the next five-year period, from 1898 to 1903, this figure rose to 64 per cent.[1]

Thus fully prepared for any industrial expansion by the first decade of the twentieth century, Japan, during the period of the Great War, achieved an entirely new plane of industrial life. We are here more concerned, however, with the social transformations resulting from the economic changes of the post-war era than with these changes themselves.

The post-Great War economic dislocation was prolonged in Japan. The ill-advised postponement of the restoration of the gold standard and the great earthquake of 1923[2] individually and in combination were contributive to a delayed economic rehabilitation. Under these circumstances the nation experienced the most serious financial crisis in 1927. Japan, which in 1913 was a debtor nation to the extent of 1,224 million yen, became by 1919 a creditor nation to the extent of 1,399 million yen. However, in 1929 she was again a debtor nation, with a net debt of 810 million yen.[3]

The removal of the gold embargo early in 1930 at the old par of yen, when the exchange rate of the yen was greatly depreciated,[4] was, because of the consequent fall in prices, particularly disastrous to small merchants and manufacturers as well as to the general population. The official encouragement of the " rationalization " of industry under such circumstances afforded impetus to the progress of industrial efficiency. Nevertheless, it greatly facilitated the concentration of capital and enterprises, and rapid changes in the social and economic life of the nation inevitably followed. The most pertinent factors of this development of the ascendency of capitalism will be considered in later pages.[5]

In the above rather brief account of the history of the economic development of Japan since the Meiji Refor-

---

[1] See *infra*, p. 72.   [2] *Infra*, p. 41.
[3] Moulton, H. G., *op. cit.*, p. 308.
[4] Exchange rate of yen in American dollars (per $100) was $46.10 average for 1929, in contrast to $49.846 at par.
[5] See *infra*, p. 27 ff.

mation, two important facts must be emphasized : (1) the economic consequences of the Reformation which had been directed along the line of industrialization were finally realized at the beginning of the twentieth century following the two victorious foreign wars ; [1] (2) the social consequences of this industrialization have come since the end of the Great War because of the concentration of capital.

C. National Industrial Development and Its Social Implications

Some of the statistical aspects of these developments will be traced. Table VI on page 24 illustrates the trend of some of the chief factors in the development of national economy at the beginning of the Sino-Japanese War (1894), Russo-Japanese War (1904), and the Great War (1914), as well as later, in 1924 and 1930. In interpreting some of the salient facts in this table a few additional figures will be mentioned whenever appropriate.

The tendency toward industrialization can be judged from the statistics of manufacturing corporations. The ratio of their capital against that of all corporations rose from 18 per cent in 1894 to 40 per cent in 1930. In this connection, it must be added that while the exports of finished products increased from 23·03 per cent of the total value of exports in 1897 to 51·29 per cent of the total in 1932, imports of such products declined from 33·44 per cent of the total to 15·38 per cent of the total during the same period.[2]

The extent of the concentration of capital can be fairly estimated from the growth of large corporations. Of the total amount of corporation capital, corporations with a capital of over 1 million yen held 44 per cent at the time of the Russo-Japanese War, while by the close of the Great War they held 83 per cent. But the concentration of banking institutions was even more phenomenal. At the time of the Sino-Japanese War each of the 863 banks averaged a

[1] Cf. Takahashi, K., " Economic Revolution of the Meiji Reformation," *Kaizo*, Aug., 1928, p. 22.
[2] See *infra*, p. 216.

TABLE VI

ECONOMIC DEVELOPMENT OF JAPAN, 1894–1930 [1]

(All figures marked Y express as evaluation in single yen; other values are expressed in 1,000 yen.)

Items.	1894.	1904.	1914.	1924.	1930.
Population (Unit 1,000)	41,142	46,135	52,093	58,281	63,319
Price index.	100	156	182	393	260
All Corporations, Number	2,844	7,621	16,858	33,567	51,910
Capital	254,252	1,262,688	2,068,786	10,849,329	13,946,640
,, *per capita*	Y6.18	Y27.37	Y39.75	Y186.16	Y220.26
Corporations of over 100,000 yen capital—					
Number	361	1,917	2,507	12,666	13,646
Capital	201,658	1,135,321	1,836,883	10,465,360	13,338,457
Ratios to the capital of all corporations (%)	79·3	89·91	88·79	96·46	95·64
Corporations of over 1,000,000 yen capital—					
Number	—	139 (1905)	358	2,768	2,950
Capital	—	554,511	1,299,847	8,966,049	11,525,274
Ratios to the capital of all corporations (%)	—	43·92	62·83	82·64	82·63
Corporations in Manufacturing, Number	778	2,384	5,266	13,251	18,205
Capital	44,560	162,836	833,569	4,055,517	5,518,936
Ratios to the capital of all corporations (%)	17·53	12·90	40·29	37·38	39·57
Banks, Number	863	2,227	2,153	1,799	898
Capital and reserve	131,641	466,060	882,223	2,868,571	2,739,804
Per bank capital and reserve	153	209	410	1,595	3,051

Factories—					
No. of Factories	—	9,234	17,062	48,394	*62,234
Factory Workers	—	526,215	853,964	1,789,618	1,683,563
Patents granted	326	1,253	1,824	1,928	4,976
Railways, mileage	2,118	4,693	7,074	10,414	13,357
Per mile passengers	17,273	22,427	30,178	81,021	93,773
Shipping, tonnage	169,419	797,366	1,593,404	3,564,867	3,968,596
Foreign Trade—					
Gross value	235,463	701,488	1,223,552	4,367,126	2,382,657
Per capita value	Y5.72	Y15.21	Y23.51	Y74.93	Y37.63
National Expenditure—					
Total	78,129	277,056	648,420	1,625,024	1,557,864
Per capita	Y1.90	Y6.01	Y12.46	Y27.88	Y24.60
National Wealth—					
Total	—	—	32,043,000	102,342,000	110,188,000
Per capita	—	—	Y615.75 (1913)	Y1,756.01 (1925)	Y1,740.20
National Income—					
Total	242,354	947,602	2,246,758	12,882,761	10,240,000
Per capita	Y5.89 (1892)	Y20.54 (1902)	Y43.17 (1912)	Y221.05	Y161.72

Population: estimated actual population at the beginning of the year; Price index: combination of the old and new index numbers of the Bank of Japan; Capital: paid in capital; Factories: prior to 1929 shops employing five or more workers, since then shops with capacity thereof are included; * excluded government factories in 1930; National wealth and income: estimates of the Bureau of Statistics.

[1] *Nihon Teikoku Tokei Zensho* (Statistical Encyclopedia of the Japanese Empire), Bureau of Statistics and Tokyo Statistical Association, 1928; *Nihon Teikoku Tokei Nenkan* (Statistical Year-Book of the Japanese Empire), Bureau of Statistics, Japan, No. 51, 1932; *1920–30 Seiji Keizai Nenkan* (Political and Economic Year-Book for 1920–30), Tokyo, Tokyo Seiji Keizai Kenkyujo, 1930; *Kinyujiko Sankosho* (The Financial Reference Book), Department of Finance, Japan, 1933; *Kigyo no Hatten to Shihon no Shuseki* (Development of Enterprises and Accumulation of Capital), Bureau of Statistics, Japan, 1929.

capital of 110,000 yen. The number of banking establishments rose to 2,227 in 1904. Since then it has decreased
to 2,153 in 1914 and to 1,799 in 1924. The control of the
banks by the big financial interests was extended still more
rapidly during the prolonged post-Great War liquidation.
By 1930 the number of banks declined to 898, but these
898 banks had 7,613 branches and 1,740 million yen in
capital plus 1,000 million yen in reserves. The per unit
average capital was close to two million yen, and capital
plus reserves exceeded three million yen. A great bank
merger further absorbed 99 banks during the course of a
two-year period which ended the latter part of 1932.[1]

The estimates of national wealth and income are subjected
to wide variation as there is no uniform method of calculation.
Therefore, extensive comment cannot be made on these
subjects in this brief survey. As stated by the Bureau of
Statistics, the national income in 1924 was 10,240 million
yen, or 221·05 yen per person. The above *per capita* income
of Japan in 1924 was very close to that of Italy, and was
about ten times that of India as given in the *Rekkoku
Kokusei Yoran*, or the " Brief International Statistics," published by the Bureau of Statistics of Japan.[2]

Shipping, an industry of which Japan can boast and
which already had 1·6 million gross tons in 1924, swelled
to 3·6 million tons ten years later. In 1930 Japan was
third in world tonnage, the tonnage being approximately
four million tons.[3] The nation's merchant marine lines
circle the globe.

By the time of the Sino-Japanese War Japan already felt
the need of external markets for her industry.[4] The subsequent territorial expansion of the nation is regarded by some
writers as simply an extension of militarism rather than

[1] *Kinyujiko Sankosho*, cited, 1933, p. 120.
[2] The *per capita* national income of Italy was given as 260 yen in 1925
and that of India in 1924 as 22 yen. Yano, T., and Shirosaki, K., *Nihon
Kokusei Zukai* (Graphic Interpretation of the National Trend of Japan),
Tokyo, Kokuseisha, 1933, p. 30.
[3] *Statistical Year-Book of the League of Nations*, Geneva, League of
Nations 1931–2, p. 210. This source gives the 1930 tonnage as 4,317,000
tons.
[4] Cf. Ota, K., " Fluctuation of the Price of Rice and the Economic
Factors Involved," *Social Reform*, No. 144, Sept., 1932, p. 59.

an example of modern imperialism. Nevertheless, the motivating force in Japanese expansion has been the necessity of protecting from foreign penetration, both the actual or prospective markets and sources of supply of raw materials in the adjoining territories. Since the Sino-Japanese War, Japan has acquired Taiwan (Formosa), Karafuto (Southern Sakhalin), and Chosen (Korea) ; if we add to these the territories under Japanese jurisdiction such as leased and mandated territories, Japan's territorial expansion has amounted to 78·1 per cent, all of this having fallen into Japanese hands in the course of twenty-four years from 1895 to 1919.[1]

Among the rather lengthy previous interpretations of the statistical figures of Table VI a point which shall be developed here is the high degree of concentration in finance and industry. Dr. Moulton observed that the extent to which both vertical and horizontal integration has been carried out in these enterprises is without parallel elsewhere in the world.[2] In spite of the fact that nearly 50 per cent of the gainfully employed people of Japan were engaged in agriculture in 1930, the large concentration of capital makes Japan a nation whose economic life is largely influenced by the big capitalists.

The field of politics is no less affected by the grip of financial and industrial interests. A Parliamentary campaign in Japan which, in spite of legal restrictions, resembles that of the pre-reformed British Parliament, costs in the vicinity of 20 million yen for about 1,000 candidates.[3] It is asserted that the major portion of the expenses are paid by a few big businesses. This political mechanism is

---

[1] *Tokei Nenkan*, cited, No. 51, 1932, p. 8.
[2] Moulton, H. G., *op. cit.*, p. 135.
[3] The expenses of the electoral campaigns of the 1920 and 1924 elections were reported by the Police Bureau of the Home Department as follows :

Year.	No. of Candidates.	Expenses per Candidate (Yen).	Total Expenses (Yen).
1920 . . .	900	24,248	21,823,000
1924 . . .	1,105	19,829	21,910,000

Since then the law has regulated the maximum amount of expenditure per candidate, but it is believed that additional sums are still spent in secret. Cf. *Jiji Nenkan* (Jiji Year-Book), Tokyo, Jiji Shimposha, 1930, p. 155.

reflected in the anomalous phenomenon that the rural districts, which still hold about one-half the votes by virtue of their vast population, are reduced to a status of being mere happy hunting ground for the spokesmen of the city interests. Statistics on the occupations of members of Parliament show that the farmers occupied 55 per cent and 34 per cent of the seats at the time of the Sino- and Russo-Japanese Wars respectively ; by 1914 this proportion had dropped to 21 per cent. In the election of February, 1930, among 466 members, only 73 farmers, or 16 per cent were returned.[1]

The transformation of national economy along capitalistic lines strengthened an already existing tendency toward stratification of economic classes with its consequent diminution of opportunity for individual initiative. This tendency is borne by the statistics of age composition of the members of the Parliament in 1904 and 1930, shown in Table VII. Clearly the old-age group is gaining in strength at the expense of other groups.

TABLE VII

AGE DISTRIBUTION OF MEMBERS OF PARLIAMENT IN 1904 AND 1930 [2]

Year.	No. of Members.	No. in each Age Period.						
		30–34.	35–39.	40–44.	45–49.	50–54.	55–59.	60 and Over.
1904	379	14	61	78	107	69	28	22
1930	466	2	18	62	106	95	71	112

Another development in this connection is the increasing unemployment among people of training and education. As a matter of fact, this diminution in the opportunities for the educated class has been the most important single factor in arousing the nation to an examination of the problem of population increase.

The essential points in the history of the economic develop-

[1] *Tokei Zensho,* cited, p. 260 ; *Tokei Nenkan,* cited, No. 51, 1932, p. 383.
[2] *Tokei Nenkan,* cited, No. 51, 1932, p. 393.

ment of Japan since 1868 have been traced in the preceding pages. Within half a century Japan experienced all the gradations through which great powers of the Occident passed only in the course of several centuries of modern history. From a medieval state of feudalism, Japan, in this remarkably short period, emerged as a modern capitalistic and colonizing nation.

All this shows the changed structure of Japanese society in recent decades. At the same time, the very fact that the nation emerged from a feudal state only a generation ago and that about half of the entire population is engaged in a single occupation, agriculture, is not without significance in the determination of the true characteristics of social trends in Japan. Now under the heavy stress of the rural depression and external friction the economic and political systems are severely criticized by the people, who feel no real loyalty to any authority and institution except the Emperor. A long series of assassination of financial and political leaders which followed is a mere outward expression of radical demand for reform, particularly to " restore " the rule of Emperor from the "financial and political usurpers." Thus now some question whether or not the power of the big business is more sham than real.[1]

So much so, from the above study one pertinent fact stands out : during this half-century, the material welfare of the nation was greatly enhanced both from *per capita* and national standpoints. This is true in spite of the rapid growth of population. However, her hasty introduction to modernization and industrialization was accompanied by a neglect of social development ; in this important aspect of healthy national life, Japan has hitherto remained backward. This fact was recognized by the Imperial Economic Conference sponsored by the Cabinet in 1924, which declared that :

The efforts of Japan, governmental and popular, have previously been devoted mainly to the strengthening of the national prestige and there is doubt as to whether we may not have

[1] Cf. Beard, Miriam, " Japan Reviews the Feudal Spirit," *New York Times*, Magazine Section, July 15, 1934, p. 11.

neglected due introspection for the furtherance of a well-balanced economic and social development.[1]

Our present study is an attempt at this much-needed introspection into Japan's social and economic development as reflected in the trend of the population movement. The following chapters will attempt to examine the factors inherent in the problem of Japan's socio-economic transformation.

[1] Cf. Nagai, T., *op. cit.*, p. 172. The delay in adopting a comprehensive modern census system due to the emergency of a great foreign war (*infra*, p. 50) may be regarded as a specific example of the situation noted above. Yusuke Tsurumi, one of the Japanese writers well known abroad, accounted for the retardation of social development in Japan thus : " . . . from the very beginning, the potential Russells, Gladstones, and Morleys of Japan have had to work under the thundering guns of the Western powers blowing their way to new territories, new empires of trade, new spheres of influence. It is not surprising that they made little headway. One cannot help asking where English democracy would have been if its growth had been conditioned by such circumstances." Tsurumi, Y., *Present Day Japan*, New York, Columbia University Press, 1926, pp. 13–14.

CHAPTER III

DEVELOPMENT OF POPULATION POLICIES SINCE THE EARLY MEIJI PERIOD

§ 1. MOVEMENT FOR THE ABOLITION OF ABORTION AND INFANTICIDE

FROM our study in Chapter I it may be fairly concluded that at the beginning of the Meiji Period, population growth was slow, and that the factor which chiefly contributed to this condition was the prevalence of abortion and infanticide. The report of the governor of Kisarazu Prefecture [1] to the Ministry of Finance in February, 1873, stated that " in the districts of Kazusa and Shimosa, abortion and *mabiki* [" thinning," i.e., infanticide] have prevailed for a long time and this evil custom is widespread not only among the poor but even among the well-to-do." [2]

An anonymous book entitled *Minkan Akushu Jojitsu*, or the " Conditions of Evil Customs Among the People," presents much interesting data. This book is believed to have been published sometime after 1871, because it contains certain new institutional terms, like *yen* (monetary unit) and ken (prefecture), introduced in that year. This book will be cited below in some detail because the present writer, in view of the scope of this thesis, has not attempted an exhaustive study of the conditions leading to abortion and *mabiki* or infanticide in the Tokugawa Era. The reasons for the practice which the " Conditions " enumerates are as follows :

1. People do not bring up their children because more than two male and one female offspring are considered too many.

---

[1] The Kisarazu Prefecture was incorporated in Chiba Prefecture in 1873.
[2] Yoshikawa, Shuzo, " The Child-Rearing Policy in the Early Meiji Period," *Keizaishi Kenkyu*, No. 7, May, 1930, p. 33.

2. It is a rule to abstain from rearing more children because too large a family results in a shortage of the means of subsistence both for the parents and the other children. Neighbours also despise for his short-sightedness a man impoverished by a large family.

3. Rich people must provide the feasts prescribed by social custom on certain occasions in their children's lives, else they incur a penalty for default or are regarded as misers. To avoid both these extremes, even rich people do not bring up all the children born to them.

4. There are people of advanced age who do not bring up their infants for several reasons : (*a*) because they feel ashamed of having born children at their age, (*b*) because they have sons who are married, and are therefore afraid of causing trouble to their daughters-in-law, (*c*) because they fear a disturbance of their rest in later years, or (*d*) because there is an actual difficulty in nursing.

5. There are people who do not bring up their infants because they already have adopted sons or daughters toward whom they feel sympathy. A man having divorced his wife during her pregnancy, usually does not raise the child born after the divorce because it would constitute an obstacle to his remarriage. A man adopted by a family [1] as the second husband of a daughter already the mother of children by her first marriage, does not bring up his own children born of this marriage, in order to avoid family complications.

6. There are people who abstain from rearing a second or later child because, in the event that their property is divided among many sons, all would be poor ; and the oldest son, who is regarded as the future head of the family, would suffer particularly.

7. There are families which abstain from child-rearing on account of zodiacal superstitions.[2]

---

[1] In Japan, it is a general custom for families without sons to adopt a male. The adopted son inherits the family but he may or may not marry a daughter of the family into which he has been adopted.

[2] Honjo, E., " Policy of Child-Bearing of the Tosa Clan," *Keizai Ronso*, 36 : 1, Jan., 1933, pp. 171–2. See the survival of the zodiacal superstitions in more recent period, *supra*, p. 61.

This enumeration listed in " Conditions " shows, incidentally, that abortion and infanticide were practised in Japan from the later Tokugawa Era to the early Meiji Period, for the same reasons that modern birth control is practised in the West. Sheer economic necessity was not the only cause, but problems of the standard of living, efforts for better living conditions, consideration of family complications, and concern for the future of the offspring were points involved.

The three major means of minimizing these ills, i.e. legal prohibition, subsidy, and moral appeal for child-rearing, practised under the Tokugawa regime,[1] were repeated in the Meiji Era. On December 24 of the first year of Meiji, 1868, midwives were forbidden thereafter to practise abortion.[2] The Revised Codes of 1873 imposed a penalty of one hundred days' imprisonment for abortion. The Codes also applied the penalty for deliberate murder to persons found guilty of infanticide.[3] The system of award for information leading to the apprehension of offenders was continued by the government. An announcement of the local government of Tosa reads :

Lower half of the corpse of an infant . . .
The above was discovered at five and half of the morning [5:00 A.M.] of the 27th of this month at . . ., being brought by a dog. Recently a strict order for the care of infants was proclaimed. It is a matter of great concern to society should anyone still practice strangling infants. The search for the present offender will be continued, and to any body who will inform the authorities of the identity of the offender, two hundred ryo [*c.* 500 yen] will be awarded immediately.[4]

Other time-honoured means, the registration of pregnant women and midwives, and the solidarity in responsibility of community leaders, were frequently resorted to by prefectual governments. Chiba Prefecture, which was organized in 1873, even established special community officers for the supervision of child-rearing.[5]

[1] *Supra*, p. 16. [2] Cf. Tanaka, K., *op. cit.*, p. 337. [3] Acts 114 and 164.
[4] Honjo, E., " Policy of Child-Bearing of the Tosa Clan," *op. cit.*, p. 165 (trans. by author).
[5] Yoshikawa, S., *op. cit.*, p. 39.

D

There were many types of pamphlets which resorted to moral appeal in an effort to discourage the reckless practice of infanticide. These were circulated all over Japan from the later Tokugawa Era on. The one which Dr. Honjo cites for us was printed in the summer of 1873 at Fukushima. The cover of the pamphlet pictures a woman with a fiend's face strangling a baby ; and the text maintains that poverty is not due to a large family, the proof being that there are many who are poor even though they have no children. It goes on to draw an analogy from the growth of the taro [1] with numerous baby taroes, and finally appeals to the feeling of maternal love, referring to the proverbial love of mother pheasants and so on.[2]

The seriousness with which some prefectual governments assumed the task of the abolition of these means of family restriction will be seen from the fact that in the Kisarazu Prefecture mentioned before, a contribution of 2 per cent of their monthly salaries for five years beginning in February, 1872, was imposed on all public officials ; besides, a contribution sponsored by the Government was collected from well-to-do people for a " child-rearing fund." For the distribution of such funds a very elaborate device was adopted after the example of many clans of the Tokugawa Era ; e.g. Chiba Prefecture made it a rule to subsidize by fifty sen the birth of a child to the poor, and to provide twenty-five sen per month for three years thereafter. This subsidy was extended to any family, regardless of class, after the sixth effective birth. But there was no subsidy for the first son and daughter and none for the second son or daughter in case the first died, and so on.[3] Undoubtedly this was because there was less danger of the first surviving infant being " thinned."

But even this serious effort to increase the number of effective births was not permanently successful ; considerable immediate gains appeared, but after a few years the

---

[1] Species of *Colocasia*. Their rootstock is a vegetable of ordinary use in Japan.

[2] Honjo, E., " Pamphlets Pleading for Child-Rearing," *Keizai Ronso*, 33 : 4, Oct., 1931, p. 603.

[3] Yoshikawa, S., *op. cit.*, p. 40.

old custom reasserted itself. For a venerable social institution, particularly one growing out of economic conditions, cannot change as quickly as the form of government. The following figures indicate the effects of the vigorous efforts for suppression of abortion and infanticide in the years immediately preceding and following the organization of Chiba Prefecture in 1873. It will be noted that since this period the influence of government effort in this direction seems to have weakened.

TABLE VIII

BIRTH STATISTICS IN CHIBA PREFECTURE, 1872–9 [1]

	1872.*	1873.	1876.	1877.	1878.	1879.
No. of births .	18,969	29,493	30,020	28,733	25,868	25,621
Birth rate (per 1,000) . . .	18·6	29·1	27·5	26·1	23·2	22·9

* Territory corresponding to the Chiba Prefecture.

The slowness with which the abolition of the old practice proceeded is attested by the fact that in 1898 the police ordinance of the same prefecture ruled that the still-births and deaths of infants under three months of age should be reported to the police as well as to the registrars.[2]

In the early years of Meiji many societies were founded with the intention of stimulating interest in and providing funds for child-rearing. Only one of them will be mentioned here. The Sensensha of Tosa was organized about 1873 with over 120 members, to take care of babies that would otherwise have been " thinned." By August, 1875, it was reported to have reared 356 infants.[3] For some time the prefectual government subsidized that body. In the course of a few more years, the Sensensha dissolved, and the

[1] *Dajoruiten* (Collected Documents of the Supreme Council), 2 : 137, and *Tokei Nenkan*, No. 1, 1882, pp. 65–77, cited in Yoshikawa, S., *op. cit.*, pp. 43–5.

[2] *Ibid.*, p. 45.

[3] *The Kochi Shimbun*, No. 50, Aug. 13, 1875. According to *Kochi Jizen Kyokai Enkakushi*, or " The History of Kochi Charity Association," only about twenty babies were reared. Cf. Honjo, E., " Policy of Child-Rearing of the Tosa Clan," *op. cit.*, pp. 166–70.

Kochi Ikujikai, or the Kochi Child-rearing Society, began to function about 1879 or 1880, with a subsidy from the Prefecture. The revised charter of 1891 of this society states that the society " was organized to abolish the evil customs of abortion and infanticide," and it enumerates as its main three additional activities, child-rearing, the education of midwives, and the subsidizing of those who adopt foundlings. The fact that the new charter of 1908 states that the main purpose of the organization thereafter was to be the support of orphanages and reformatories, similar to those of to-day, indicates that the undesirable practices were yielding to control.[1] The history of this organization may be regarded as a replica in miniature of the history of social and economic changes in Japan, as reflected in the population policies throughout the early decades of Meiji.

In 1921 Yasunori Nikaido, former director of the Bureau of Statistics, observed that abortion and infanticide were still practised in some districts, especially in Kwanto and Tohoku.[2] Dr. Takeo Ono, one of the foremost rural sociologists in Japan, said in 1927 that in Kawaguchiko, Yamanashi Prefecture, at the foot of the northern side of Mt. Fuji, the ratios of live-births and still-births fluctuated in response to the attitudes of the forester-policemen, the government agents for the enforcement of law in these mountainous districts, toward such practices as abortion and infanticide.[3]

However, during the twentieth century, which has witnessed Japan's rapid progress in the path of industrialization, the custom of family control by the crude means of abortion and infanticide has practically disappeared. To-day Japanese are quite offended when social historians refer to these reckless practices of the Tokugawa Era, and to their persistence among certain people until only a generation ago.

The prohibition of abortion and infanticide was instituted

---

[1] *The Kochi Shimbun*, No. 50, Aug. 13, 1875. According to *Kochi Jizen Kyokai Enkakushi*, or "The History of Kochi Charity Association," only about twenty babies were reared. Cf. Honjo, E., "Policy of Child-Rearing of the Tosa Clan," *op. cit.*, pp. 170–1.

[2] *Tokei Shushi*, No. 489, Nov., 1921, p. 223.

[3] Ono, T., "Decrease of the Rural Population in the Tokugawa Era," *op. cit.*, p. 138.

as a step in a national programme of modernization rather
than as a policy intended to increase the population. Its
effectiveness in recent decades has been largely due to the
modern rapid economic development which facilitated the
absorption of the increasing population.

The above history of family control in the early Meiji
period demonstrates, incidentally, the comparative ease
with which even such long-established customs may be
altered, not so much by pressure of governmental decrees
as in response to economic environmental changes. Even
trained observers like Professor G. C. Allen have contended
that large families are inherent in the family system of
Japan.[1] Yet the above short history proves that up to a
few decades ago, that same family system was a restraining
factor in the population increase of the nation.

§ 2. DEVELOPMENT OF THE PRESENT-DAY POPULATION PROBLEM

A. *Movements for Racial Amalgamation*

We have already referred to the devices which the reform regime of Meiji deliberately adopted in order to
withstand Western pressure in Asia.[2] One device which was
proposed was that of racial amalgamation. This subject
excited keen discussion among scholars and statesmen in the
second decade of Meiji. The motive and purpose of the
proposal are clearly stated by Yoshio Takahashi, the author
of the *Nihonjinshu Kairyoron*, or " The Improvement of the
Japanese Race," which was published in 1883. He says in
part :

Having accepted the hypothesis that the physical and mental
constitution of our Japanese is inferior to that of European
peoples, it follows that in the event that we persist on an inferior racial level there is a danger that we may soil the historical record of our blameless Empire. What, then, can we
do. The only solution is to improve our racial quality by means
of inter-marriage [with the Caucasian race]. . . . When we

[1] Cf. Allen, G. C., *Modern Japan and Its Problems*, New York, Dutton,
1927, p. 198.
[2] *Supra*, pp. 18–21.

marry European women there is an additional benefit in the custom of following a meat diet.[1]

The major objection raised against this proposal was that it would defeat its own purpose by neglecting the moral basis of the struggle for existence, i.e. should Japan become strong by this means there would be no Japanese.[2]

Due to its impracticability and to the antagonism which it aroused in many writers, the movement for racial amalgamation as a means of improving the Japanese race made no headway. However, agitation over the question of intermarriage persisted throughout the second and third decades of Meiji. This was perhaps due to the leaders' exaggerated anticipation of the imminence of inter-marriage, which, it was thought, would follow the abrogation of unequal treaties and abolition of foreign settlements, and the eventual admission of foreigners to residence.

Premier Hirobumi Ito requested Baron—later Count—K. Kaneko to write to Herbert Spencer for his opinion regarding this problem. Spencer's reply, which was negative, indicates the seriousness with which the leaders of Japan regarded this question of population. In his communication, which has been previously referred to,[3] Spencer quotes the Baron to the effect that the question of inter-marriage, " now very much agitated " among Japanese scholars and politicians, is one of the " most difficult problems " of the day. His advice against inter-marriage was based on his theory that amalgamation is detrimental because it destroys racial characteristics which are the result of century-long adaptation to environment, and because it breaks down the integrity of the personality.[4]

Additional evidence of the existence of a widespread desire, during the early decades of the Meiji period, for a

---

[1] Takahashi, Y., " A Reply to the Question concerning the Improvement of Race," *Kojun Zasshi*, No. 112, March 5, 1883, cited in Ishii, Kendo, *Meiji Jibutsu Kigen* (The Origin of Things in the Meiji Period), Tokyo, Shunyodo, revised edition, 1926, p. 69 (trans. by author).

[2] e.g. Dr. Hiroyuki Kato, cited in Koyama, E., *Jinshugaku* (Ethnology), Tokyo, Oka Shoin, 1929, p. 386.

[3] *Supra*, p. 18, footnote.

[4] This view was also maintained by such students as Joseph Arthur de Gobineau, and more recently by A. M. Carr-Saunders.

larger and better population, is seen in the attitude of the Government and the people. Both, as we have noted,[1] were resolved to suppress the prevalent practices of family restriction such as abortion and infanticide. Though advocated as one of several policies included in a programme of modernization promulgated by the Reformation, this movement for the suppression of abortion and infanticide soon supplemented the movement toward an improvement in the racial stock. Both were conducive toward a larger population.

B. *Emergence of the Population Problem*

When the quinquennial average annual rate of population increase jumped from 9·4 per 1,000 (1892–6) to 12·51 (1897–1901) and the nation definitely became a rice importer (1897), apprehension in regard to the source of the future food supply arose in some quarters. However, acceleration in economic as well as in territorial expansion followed the Sino-Japanese War, and the militaristic and imperialistic turn of mind generally justified an even laiger and ever-increasing population. Mr. Tokugoro Nakabashi wrote in 1907 that the requisite for a world power is a great population. Thirty to fifty million were enough to constitute a great power in the nineteenth century, but at the end of the present century it would, he claimed, require eighty to a hundred million to maintain a strong position.[2] Nakabashi was a politician rather than a scholar. Nevertheless, his opinion reflects the current thought of that period. A number of notable writers faithfully interpreted the Malthusian theory, but such writers unanimously avoided taking up the question of the actual population of Japan in the light of this theory.[3]

Even among the more critical writers of this period, this problem of population presented an enigma. Mr. Miyakuni

[1] *Supra*, § 1, Chap. III.
[2] Collected in Nakabashi, T., *Kokoku Sakuron* (Policies of National Expansion), Tokyo, Seikyosha, 1913, p. 94.
[3] Cf. Kato, H., *Nihyakunengo no Gojin* (Japanese Two Hundred Years Hence), 1894 ; Taguchi, U., *Jinkoron* (The Population), 1902, collected in *Taguchi-Ukichi Zenshu*, cited, Vol. III, pp. 442–68.

said in the *Encyclopædia Japonica*, edited in 1911, that
Japan was then actually feeling the injurious effects of over-
population, but he contented himself by concluding that the
encouragement of agriculture and emigration would be a
sufficient remedy.   In 1912, Councillor T. Egi, of the Colonial
Bureau, found that " it is hardly necessary to say that, at
our present rate of increase, it is only a matter of time
when Japan will be confronted with the problem of surplus
population."   Nevertheless, Egi was also content to propose
as remedies industrialization and colonization.   He says
(English original) :

The possibilities of commercial and industrial development
in the Far East are immeasurable. . . .   And if our commercial
and industrial development goes at a healthy rate, employment
may be found at home for many of the millions yet unborn.
I am in the opinion, however, that our main hope lies in the
fullest utilization of the colonial territory already at our disposal.[1]

The serious disturbance in food distribution during the
Great War was not in general regarded as being related with
the problem of population.   The militaristic enthusiasm and
economic prosperity of the war period encouraged the idea
of a large population.   That this optimism survived for
some time after the war was indicated in the hostile attitude
of the Japanese government toward Mrs. Margaret Sanger
when she visited Japan in March, 1922.

However, the series of events which followed the post-
war depression hastened the change which was taking place
in the Japanese attitude toward population.   The restoration to China of Kiauchau, Shantung, and relinquishment
of many other claims in China at the Washington Conference
(1921–2) were blows to Japanese expansionist efforts, and
revived sad memories of the fruitless joint expedition to
Siberia (1918–22), which cost Japan one billion yen.[2]   The
Washington Conference was instrumental for the first time
in Japan, in bringing on unemployment among skilled

[1] Egi, T., " The Population Problem of Japan," *Japan Magazine*,
Aug., 1912, pp. 231–3.
[2] Cf. *1920–30 Seiji Keizai Nenkan*, cited, p. 199.

workers, due to the suspension of shipbuilding. The pessimism caused by these events was further aggravated by the loss of from 3·1 to 5·5 billion yen [1] in the great earthquake of September 1, 1923.

These events suggested limitations to the possibilities of Japan's economic expansion. The final blow which aroused the Japanese to a re-examination of the population situation was destined, however, to fall in 1924. In May of that year, the American Government, in spite of the strenuous efforts of the Government and people of Japan to avert it, enacted the Immigration Bill of 1924, with the so-called Japanese Exclusion Clause. This came as the final step in the prolonged antagonism to Japanese immigrants, an antagonism which in 1920 had been expressed in the Alien Land Law of California.

This blow was a particularly keen one for the Japan of that day. As evidenced by the sentiment which prevailed at the Imperial Economic Conference sponsored by the Cabinet in 1924, the Japanese regarded emigration as the veritable panacea of all their country's social problems. This attitude is well illustrated by the following passage in the Government's draft of problems submitted for the consideration of the Immigration and Colonization Section of the Conference.

Protection and encouragement of emigration and colonization contribute toward a reasonable distribution of the population and the natural resources ; emigration and colonization are the most important factors in the solution of our various social problems.[2]

[1] Estimates of the Bureau Statistics and Tokyo Municipality, respectively. Cf. *The Great Earthquake of 1923 in Japan*, Social Bureau, Home Department, Japan, 1926, Vol. I, p. 467.

[2] Cf. Nagai, T., *op. cit.*, pp. 171–2 (trans. by author). However, it was not the actual number of immigrants with which the Japanese were concerned in the American exclusion law, but it was the moral question of open, statutory discrimination, when they believed the same end could have been achieved by other means. Even if Japan were to enjoy a quota equal to that of European nations, the annual entry would be only 246. Cf. Letter of Secretary Hughes to Chairman Albert Johnson of the Committee on Immigration of the House of Representatives. Cited in Taft, H. W., *Japan and America*, New York, Macmillan, 1932, p. 150. It is estimated that this number of 246 would be reduced to less than 200 by the " national origins plan " which, provided for in the Immigration Law of 1924, took effect in 1928.

The exclusion law affected not only the problem of emigration, but also involved the relative racial and political position of Japan as well. An incurable tone of pessimism was thus cast over the future of racial and international co-operation.[1]

At this time when, in the eyes of her people, the position of Japan among the nations of the world was under a cloud, internal pressure due to the increasing population became even more serious. While the present writer cannot share the common view which confuses the two problems of food supply and population, he does admit that the relationship between the two is close ; indeed, this phase of the subject is of sufficient importance to warrant more extended treatment than can be accorded it in this study.[2] Here we may note merely that the problem of food supply played not the least significant rôle in the awakening of the national consciousness to a new interpretation of the population question.

In 1919, the year following the famous rice riots, a law for the promotion of the reclamation of land was passed. Three years later, in 1922, the first rice price control law was enacted. The annual net import of rice increased from the two million koku mark to 5·92 million during the five-year period, 1918–22, and to 9·35 million koku during the next five-year period, 1923–7.[3] Further, the price index of rice, which, with 1900 as 100, reached an annual average of 156·20 during the war period, 1914–18, leaped to an average of 319·02 and 314·22, respectively, for the two five-year periods of 1918–22 and 1923–7. The general price indices for the above three five-year averages were 166·72, 285·80,

[1] Typical of the Japanese view of the significance of the Exclusion Law is the following declaration of Yusuke Tsurumi : " It [the far-reaching effect of the Japanese reactions] does mean that an explosive force has been lodged in the Japanese mind—an explosive force that those who seek ways of international peace and progressive democracy in Japan will have to reckon with for decades to come. Who can fail to regret that troublesome forces have been stored up by processes that could have been avoided without crossing in the slightest the natural desire of the American Government to preserve the integrity of American society and the standards of American labour ? " Tsurumi, Y., *op. cit.*, p. 105.
[2] For a discussion of the variations in the two problems see pp. 40, 166.
[3] *Kome Tokeihyo* (Statistical Tables on Rice), Statistical Section, Department of Agriculture and Forestry, Japan, 1931, p. 37.

and 253·72 respectively.[1] Thus, the price index of rice was in considerable excess of the general price index.

The birth rate, which had declined from the peak of 34·1 per thousand in 1911 to 31·6 in 1919, suddenly jumped to 36·2 in 1920,[2] and remained above 34 for the next few years. At this time the general public manifested great concern over the fact that the natural increase expanded from 682,000 in 1922 to 944,000 in 1926. This latter figure is equal to the population of a prefecture of moderate size, and is greater than the peaks of natural increase of any European power except Russia.[3]

In view of the progressive increase of both the population and the food imports at a period when the expansion of the national economy was at a standstill, the rise of alarmist views concerning the future of the Japanese population was only natural. Professor R. Minami, a noted writer on population, observed in December, 1926 :

The most acute problem which Japan to-day is facing and which government and civil circles are one and all debating, is the question of the population. And, if I am not mistaken, the concensus of opinion is that the nation is over-populated.[4]

As influential a newspaper as the *Tokyo Asahi* on July 26, 1927, published the population report of the Bureau of Statistics for the year 1926 under the headline :

LOOK AT THIS FIGURE !

Two million and one hundred thousands were born in the past year,
The natural increase really amounts to nine hundred and forty-three thousands.[5]

The two great papers of Osaka—the *Mainichi* and the *Asahi*

---

[1] *Beikoku Yoran* (Brief Report on Rice), Bureau of Agriculture, Department of Agriculture and Forestry, Japan, 1930, pp. 18–19.
[2] The great rise in birth rate in 1920 was partly due to a change in the method of calculating the population. See *infra*, p. 56, *et passim*.
[3] e.g. The highest point reached by Germany was 910,000 in 1906, Italy 498,000 in 1912, and the United Kingdom 593,000 in 1920. Cf. *Nihon Teikoku Jinko Dotai Tokei Kijutsuhen* (Analytic Section of the Statistics of the Population Movement of the Japanese Empire), Bureau of Statistics, Japan, 1930, p. 110.
[4] Minami, R., " Population Problems in Japan," *Social Reform*, Dec., 1926, p. 49 (trans. by author).
[5] Translated by the author.

—both dealt with the question of population in their editorials [1] on August 1, 1927. It is interesting to note that a question of such academic interest as the population increase created such a stir of interest among the Japanese general public. This fact may be regarded as an indication of the seriousness of the problem itself, as well as of the increasing alertness of the enlightened public to such issues.

Under these circumstances, political parties advocated the policy of industrialization as a means of relieving the pressure of population increase. The Tanaka Cabinet which came into power in April, 1927, adopted this policy as the first plank in its platform, under the name of " Sangyo rikkoku," or " Founding the nation upon industry." [2] The establishment by this Cabinet of a department of overseas affairs, designed to encourage emigration and colonization, as well as to unify policies of colonial governments, met with enthusiastic national approval. The new Cabinet also realized the cherished desire of the preceding Cabinet by organizing in July, 1927, the Commission for the Study of the Problems of Population and Food Supply.

At this point the question of the Japanese population became the focus of world-wide attention. An American student of population problems regarded it as the foremost " danger spot " of world peace. [3] It even became a subject for editorials in American newspapers [4] and a feature topic of popular magazines. [5]

The anxiety of the Japanese people at this time over the population increase is well illustrated by the reaction of the *Tokyo Asahi* to the opening address delivered by Premier General Tanaka before the Population Commission. The

[1] Editorials of Japanese newspapers usually deal with only one topic on any single day. They are necessarily confined, therefore, to a discussion of only the most urgent problems.

[2] Cf. Harada, S., *Labour Condition in Japan*, New York, Columbia University Press, 1928, p. 98 ; Ayusawa, I., " The Population Problem and Industrialization in Japan," *International Labour Review*, Oct., 1927, p. 524.

[3] Thompson, W. S., *Danger Spots in World Population*, New York, Knopf, 1929, Chap. II.

[4] Cf. " Japan's Prolific Millions," *The New York Times*, Editorial, Sept. 16, 1928.

[5] Cf. " Japan's Mounting Millions," *Literary Digest*, Feb. 13, 1926 ; " Japan Growing a Million a Year," *ibid.*, July 5, 1930.

Premier said, among other things, that the increasing population was one symbol of the expanding national strength. The *Asahi* took up this statement and commented as follows :

The reason why the population is a national problem to-day rather than at the period of imperialistic expansion is that increase in population now means increase in over-population. In other words, it is based on the recognition of the fundamental fact that there exists a threat of an increasing difficulty in effectively absorbing the new increment of our population under the present state of national economy.[1]

The *Asahi* went one step further and concluded that under the leadership of a scion of the old militarist school like Premier Tanaka nothing could be expected from the work of the Commission.

Fortunately, however, the Commission embraced well qualified experts, and proved to be an important milestone along the path of the development of population thought in Japan. The draft placed before the Commission for deliberation by the Government stated that :

Japan, which is not blessed by Heaven in unlimited natural resources, and where industry is not yet fully developed, the intensification of the density of population disturbs the balance of the supply and demand of labour, and results in unrest in our national life. . . .[2]

On superficial examination, this statement seems to indicate that the Government regarded the population problem as an unemployment problem. We must endeavour to see the meaning underlying these words, however. The Government did not suggest that the solution of the problem of the food supply was the solution of the population problem, but showed an intelligent understanding of the importance of food in the complex socio-economic problem of population. Furthermore, the report of the Commission defined the limitations of emigration and colonization in the field of population problems and urged the necessity of population control.

[1] *The Tokyo Asahi*, Editorial, July 22, 1927 (trans. by author).
[2] *Jinkobu Toshin Setsumei* (Reports of the Population Section), Population and Food Commission, Japan, 1930 (trans. by author).

By March, 1930, the Commission had submitted eight outline reports to the Government and then disbanded. The subjects of the eight reports are as follows : Internal and external colonization ; Adjustment of labour supply ; Population policy in the colonies ; Population control ; Promotion of industry ; Improvement of the distribution and consumption of the national wealth ; Advisability of the establishment of a permanent population research organization ; Advisability of establishment of a social department.

The Government favoured the recommendation of the Commission for the establishment of permanent institutions to conduct research studies in the various aspects of population, but failed to act from purely financial reasons. In November, 1932, however, a research institute was organized by the most active members of the old Population Commission and by leaders in the related departments and bureaus of the government. This body is to conduct scientific researches on such aspects of the population question as the phenomenon of differential birth rates, the eugenic phase of population movements, population theories, and similar aspects of the problem.[1]

The revival of nationalism since the Manchurian crisis of September, 1931, has not altered the new attitude of the enlightened public in Japan toward its population problems. Even recently the Chief of the Court Physicians published an article on methods of contraception, and a Minister of Education has openly advocated the advisability of well-balanced practice of birth control.[2]

C. *Summary of Chapter III*

In this chapter the trend of the population problems in Japan since the Reformation of 1868 has been traced. It has been noted that prior to the period of the Sino-Japanese War, the population problem involved only two aspects : the effort to break the custom of abortion and infanticide

---

[1] *The Midorigaoka*, Otaru Commercial College Organ, Jan. 26, 1933 ; *Shokumin*, Jan., 1933, p. 172.
[2] *Infra*, p. 239.

inherited from the feudal era, and the demand for the improvement of the racial stock. Although the national economy expanded under the Meiji regime, it took about three decades to abolish the medieval practice of family restriction.

After the Sino-Japanese War the national economy expanded more rapidly along the line of industrialization. In this period the population began to increase rapidly and the nation turned from being a food exporter to a food importer. Throughout this period a larger population was favoured. The problem of population numbers, as expressed by Malthus, i.e. population growth to be regarded as an essentially antagonistic factor in economic welfare, was not introduced in Japan until the conclusion of the Great War. The change in attitude toward the population problem in Japan coincided, incidentally, with a similar change among Western nations. As Robert R. Kuczynski observed, prior to the Great War every government and the majority of its people regarded a large population as an economic asset and favoured an increasing population, whereas after the war the opposite view came into favour.[1]

[1] Kuczynski, R. R., " Population Growth and Economic Pressure," *Annals*, American Academy of Political and Social Science, July, 1930, p. 1. See also Wolfe, A. B., " The Population Problem since the World War : a Survey of Literature and Research," Series I, *Journal of Political Economy*, Oct., 1928, pp. 530–7.

CHAPTER IV

DEVELOPMENT OF THE METHODS OF ESTIMATING THE POPULATION

BEFORE entering upon a study of the movements of the Japanese population since the Meiji period, some attention must be given to the history of population estimates and to that of vital statistics in the corresponding period ; for some knowledge of this subject is essential to a proper understanding of the figures bearing upon the Japanese population.

A. FROM 1872 TO 1919

The Meiji regime enacted a registration law in April of the fourth year of Meiji, 1871, requiring registration of citizens. As a result, the system of registering each household unit was established through actual investigation in each case.[1] The first enumeration of the domicile population was conducted on March 8, 1872.[2] From 1873 to 1886 enumerations of the domicile population were conducted at the beginning of every year, and after 1886, at the end of every year. This enumeration of domicile population is continued at present, even though a comprehensive census system was introduced in 1920.

From 1873 to 1897 the tabulation of the domicile population was made by adjusting births, deaths, and acquisition and loss of domiciles annually to the basic figure of 1872. Beginning with 1898, the domicile population was calculated

---

[1] Cf. *Keizai Daijisho*, cited, p. 2096, Ishizawa, " Census."
[2] Jan. 28, 1872 (the last day of January), according to the calendar of that time. This old calendar system was abandoned on Dec. 3, 1872, when the present solar calendar was introduced. Cf. Honjo, E., *Jinko Oyobi Jinko Mondai*, cited, p. 193.

every five years through the actual enumeration of figures listed in the registers. The domicile population of inter-censual years was estimated by adjusting births, deaths, and other factors to the basic figure of every five years. After 1919 the old method for the estimate of domicile population was resumed.[1]

It must be noted that the domicile population embraces all Japanese citizens even though a considerable number of them live abroad. On the other hand, it excludes both foreigners living in Japan and, naturally, people without a domicile. To rectify partially the inconvenience of such statistics, in 1886, a system was introduced to estimate the actual number of Japanese subjects in each administration area. This system records the registration of temporary transfers of residence, and recruiting and retirement of soldiers and sailors to and from barracks or warships, the imprisonment and dismissal from prisons, and emigration to colonies and foreign countries.

This method of computing the actual population of Japanese subjects proved a failure. Theoretically, the registrations of temporary residence, covering removal in one place and entry in another, balance ; also the actual population in Japan proper is smaller than the domicile population by the number of emigrants who stay abroad. The "actual population" in 1913 was reported, however, to be 55,131,270, or 1,769,081[2] in excess of the domicile population of the same year, 53,362,189. It is evident, therefore, that the new system was both inadequate and inaccurate.

There was a great number of omissions in the registration of the temporary removals from residences. For example, in 1913 the registration of entries into temporary residences was 8,266,306, and that of temporary removals 6,052,020, an excess of entries over removals of 2,214,286.[3] Therefore, by adjusting the calculated average ratio of omissions to

---

[1] Ueda, T., Editor, *Nihon Jinko Mondai Kenkyu* (Studies of Japanese Population Problem), Tokyo, Kyochokai, 1933, p. 199.
[2] Takano, I., *Honpo Jinko no Genzai Oyobi Shorai* (Present and Future of Japanese Population), Tokyo, Tsuzoku Daigakukai, 1916, p. 17.
[3] *Ibid.*, p. 19 ; *Tokei Nenkan*, cited, No. 27, 1908, pp. 44–5.

the number of temporary registrations in each locality,[1] the Bureau of Statistics estimated a new " actual population." These revised figures were termed " B " and the original ones " A " in " actual population." Reports of the " actual population " were discontinued after 1919.

B. MODERNIZATION OF THE CENSUS SYSTEM AND ITS ADOPTION (1920)

The census in its modern sense, based upon the actual enumeration of individuals at a fixed date, was provided for by legislation enacted in 1902 ; the first census under this new law was to be taken in 1905, the thirty-eighth year of Meiji, again in 1910, and every ten years thereafter.[2] The date was undoubtedly so fixed in order to conform to the decimal system of the European calendar. Unfortunately, however, the inauguration of the new system was postponed indefinitely, due to the national emergency arising from the Russo-Japanese War of 1904–5 ; this determination to postpone was reached despite the efforts of the House of Peers to allow only the first census, that of 1905, to be abandoned. Only Taiwan conducted a census as of October 1, 1905, but this was in the form of an extraordinary census.[3] In 1918 the fervent hope of the statistically conscious public was realized at last, and it was ordered that the first census be taken on October 1, 1920. In 1922 the census law was amended to provide for a brief census to be taken between the two regular censuses.[4]

In Japan the census is still limited almost wholly to the

---

[1] Formula of calculation of " B actual population " is : " B actual population " of a given prefecture = " A actual population " of that prefecture—

$$\frac{\text{Temporary entries of all Japan} - \text{Temporary removals of all Japan}}{\text{Temporary entries of all Japan} + \text{Temporary removals of all Japan}}$$

$\times$ Temporary entries of that prefecture

+ Temporary removals of that prefecture.

Cf. *Tokei Nenkan*, cited, No. 27, 1908, p. 45.

[2] Takano, I., *Tokeigaku Kenkyu* (A Study of Statistics), Tokyo, Okura Shoten, 1915, p. 277.

[3] *Ibid.*, p. 278.

[4] Okazaki, F., " On the Terminology ' Census,' " *Keizai Ronso*, 33 : 1, June, 1931, pp. 153–6 ; A leaflet on how the tables of the census returns are made up, Bureau of Statistics, July, 1931.

TABLE IX

TYPES OF POPULATION STATISTICS OF JAPAN, BY FIVE-YEAR INTERVALS [1]

I Year.	II Domicile Population.	III " B Actual Population."	IV " Estimated Actual Population."	V Census Population.
1872 . .	33,110,796	—	34,806,000	—
1875 . .	33,997,415	—	35,316,000	—
1880 . .	35,929,023	—	36,649,000	—
1885 . .	37,868,949	37,975,069	38,313,000	—
1890 . .	40,453,461	40,968,835	39,902,000	—
1895 . .	42,270,620	43,048,226	41,557,000	—
1900 . .	44,825,597	44,813,300	43,847,000	—
1905 . .	47,678,396	47,641,500	46,620,000	—
1910 . .	50,984,844	50,504,900	49,184,000	—
1915 . .	54,935,755	54,448,200	52,752,000	—
1920 . .	57,918,671	—	—	55,963,053
1925 . .	62,044,649	—	—	59,736,822
1930 . .	65,892,183	—	—	64,450,005
1935 . .	—	—	—	69,254,148

Dates: II, IV, 1872—March 8; II, III, 1875–85—January 1, thereafter December 31; IV, after 1875—January 1; V, October 1.

the balance of domicile and estimated actual population up to 1920 will be considered. The excess or deficit of the domicile population over the estimated actual population is as follows :

Year.	Excess or Deficit (−) of Domicile Population.	Year.	Excess or Deficit (−) of Domicile Population.
1872 . . .	− 1,695,000	1900	979,000
1875 . . .	− 1,319,000	1905	1,058,000
1880 . . .	− 720,000	1910	1,801,000
1885 . . .	− 444,000	1915	2,184,000
1890 . . .	551,000	1920	2,446,000
1895 . . .	714,000		

The above table shows that although in 1872 the domicile population was short of the estimated actual population by about 1·7 millions, in 1920 the reverse was true with a

[1] II, V, *Tokei Zensho*, cited, p. 9; *Tokei Nenkan*, cited, No. 51, 1932, p. 18. III, 1885–90, Honjo, E., *Jinko Oyobi Jinko Mondai*, cited, pp. 223, 237, 1900–15, information from Director T. Hasegawa of the Bureau of Statistics given to the writer under the date of Sept. 7, 1933. IV, *Population du Japon depuis 1872*, cited, pp. 4–5.

difference of almost 2·5 millions. Such a shift of balance may be interpreted by considering that the early shortage of the domicile population was due mainly to the omissions in registrations. As time progressed the discrepant figures in registers due, for example, to negligence in reporting disappearances, accumulated.

Among the many types of population figures only the estimated actual population is, prior to 1920, logically comparable to the census population of other countries. Therefore the writer has relied on this estimate prior to 1920, and the census figures thereafter, for his study of the general trend of the growth of population, to be considered in the first section of the next chapter.

The weakness of the estimates prior to 1920 lies in the fact that they are merely estimates of the gross population by sexes in even thousands, with no detailed figures of age or geographical distribution. Furthermore, these estimates, by neglecting to include such details, provide no data whereby the figures given can be linked up with such points in the nation's demographic structure as the rate of marriage, the birth rate, and so forth.

For the base of calculations of demographic rates, the Bureau of Statistics used the domicile population up to 1898. Of course, such factors as the number of marriages, divorces, births, and deaths among Japanese residing abroad, were included in the census through the reports obtained from the official agents.[1] From 1899 to 1919 the " B actual population " was the basis of calculation ; after 1920 the census population and estimated population for inter-censual years formed the basis.[2]

D. DEVELOPMENT OF SYSTEMS FOR COLLECTION OF VITAL STATISTICS

While the demographic rates were calculated by the " B actual population " during the period from 1899 to 1919, this basis was not consistently used by the Government in

[1] Cf. *Tokei Nenkan*, cited, No. 43, 1924, p. 34.
[2] Cf. *Annual Report of the Sanitary Bureau*, Sanitary Bureau, Home Department, Japan, 1930, p. 86.

the calculation of other statistics. Instead of this, most departments and bureaus depended mainly upon the domicile population.[1] This basis, of course, had its defects; for instance, the domicile population living abroad should not be included in determining the average *per capita* value of imports or exports. Moreover, the several governmental departments were not consistent in their practices. For example, the *Beikoku Yoran*, or the " Abstract Statistics on Rice " of 1930, uses the " estimated actual population " for the calculation of the *per capita* consumption of rice prior to 1920.[2] Had the Government only adopted a comprehensive census system sooner, much of this confusion might have been avoided. At least, however, unification of statistical treatments and a greater utilization of the most adequate data might be achieved through an agreement between governmental officials. The writer has consistently relied on the " estimated actual population " prior to 1920 in his calculation of *per capita* figures relating to the study of economic development in Chapter II.

In contrast to the slowness which characterized the adoption of the census, the system for collection of data for vital statistics (or the statistics of the population movement, as the Japanese Government calls it) has made great progress since 1902. In that year, when the compilation of population statistics was made the exclusive business of the Bureau of Statistics, Japan adopted a centralized enumeration system after the German and Austrian models.[3] According to this system, each case of birth, still-birth, death, marriage, and divorce was entered, with all necessary information, on separate cards prepared by the Bureau of Statistics. These cards were sent quarterly from local registrars to the Bureau of Statistics, where they were counted and tabulated by statistical experts.

The progress in the collection of data was somewhat handicapped until 1919 by the ineffectual system of estimating the basic population which is essential for the calcu-

[1] e.g. *Tokei Nenkan*, cited, No. 43, 1924, p. 143 ; *Tokei Zensho*, cited, p. 234 ; *Kinyujiko Sankosho*, cited, 1932, p. 3.
[2] *Beikoku Yoran*, cited, 1930, p. 3.
[3] Takano, I., *Honpo Jinko no Genzai Oyobi Shorai*, cited, p. 24.

lation of all ratios, such as birth rate per 1,000 population, and so forth. For example, as discussed in detail in Chapter VI, the birth rate in 1920 jumped from 31·6 per 1,000 of the preceding year to 36·2, its peak in Japan. This sudden and considerable increase in the recorded birth rate was due partly to an actual increase in births, and partly to more accurate registration induced by the census publicity ; but it was chiefly due to the elimination of a huge discrepancy which was contained in the previous base population. The basic population of 1919—"B actual population"—was, as has been noted on page 51, 56,253,200, whereas the census population of 1920 was 55,963,053. It is apparent now why the writer considers a knowledge of the history of the census essential for a proper understanding of the values and limitations of the various figures of Japanese population.

CHAPTER V

REGIONAL AND OCCUPATIONAL DISTRIBUTION OF POPULATION

§ 1. Introductory: Population Growth since the Early Meiji Period

A. *Present Population of the Japanese Empire*

The return of the latest census, as of October 1, 1935, reported the population in Japan proper as 69,254,148.[1] The 1930 figure was 64,450,005. The latter is about 71 per cent of the total population of the Japanese Empire in the same year, 90,396,043, and about 70 per cent of the gross total population of all territories under Japanese jurisdiction, including leased and mandatory territories. The gross total population under Japanese jurisdiction in 1930 was 91,793,680. These 1930 figures with other related figures are shown in Table X.

This table shows that excepting Kwantung Leased Territory and the South Manchuria Railway Zone, which consists mainly of urbanized districts in Manchuria, Japan proper is the most densely populated of the geographical divisions

[1] The final return of the entire population of the Japanese Empire in 1935 is not yet available ; but the preliminary figures are given below:

Division.	Population.	No. of Males per 100 Females.
Japan proper	69,251,265	100·6
Chosen	22,898,695	103·8
Taiwan	5,212,719	104·2
Karafuto	331,949	127·8
Total	97,694,628	101·6
Kwantung Leased Territory and South Manchuria Ry. Zone . .	1,656,763	150·4
South Sea Mandatory . . .	102,238	126·6
Grand total	99,453,629	102·3

57

TABLE X

AREA AND CENSUS POPULATION OF THE JAPANESE EMPIRE, AS OF
OCTOBER 1, 1930 [1]

Division.	Area (Sq. Km.).	Population.	Density (per Sq. Km.).	No. of Males per 100 Females.
Japan proper	382,309	64,450,005	169	101·0
Chosen	220,741	21,058,305	95	104·6
Taiwan	35,974	4,592,537	128	105·1
Karafuto	36,090	295,196	8	133·1
Total	675,113	90,396,043	134	102·1
Kwantung Leased Territory and South Manchuria Railway Zone . . .	3,753	1,38,011	355	155·9
South Sea Mandatory. .	2,149	69,626	32	119·7
Grand Total . . .	681,015	91,793,680	135	102·7

shown in the table. At the same time, however, it is
noticeable that the ratio of males per 100 females is lowest
in Japan proper.

As to the nationality elements of the population as well
as those of Japan's colonies, the census of 1930 gives the
following figures :

TABLE XI

NATIVITY CLASSIFICATION OF THE JAPANESE POPULATION, 1930 [2]

Japanese	63,972,025*
Natives of Chosen	419,009
Natives of Taiwan	4,611
Natives of Karafuto	22
Natives of South Sea Mandatory . .	18
Chinese	39,440
Russians	3,587
Americans	3,640
Englishmen	3,144
Germans	1,228
Frenchmen	694
Others	2,587
Total	64,450,005

* Includes 15,803 Ainu in Hokkaido.

It should be noted that among the non-Japanese groups
cited in the above table, the Chosenese residents in Japan

[1] *Tokei Nenkan,* cited, No. 51, 1932, pp. 8, 18.   [2] *Ibid.,* No. 54, 1935, p. 45.

proper increased more than tenfold during the course of the decade, 1920–30.[1] Nevertheless, it is obvious that foreign and colonial elements, with the exception of the Chosenese, are relatively small in Japan.

B. *Population Statistics since 1872*

The estimated population of Japan proper in 1872, when the first enumeration of the domicile population was conducted, and at five-year intervals from 1875 to 1920 and the returns of the five censuses taken since 1920 will be cited from Table IX, together with other related figures. Table XIII supplements Table XII by giving the annual rates of population growth and the population-index covering the corresponding period.

TABLE XII

GENERAL TREND OF POPULATION IN JAPAN PROPER, 1872–1935 [2]

Year.	Population (Unit 1,000).	Index Number.	Average Annual Increase (Unit 1,000).	Rate of Average Annual Increase (per 1,000).
" Estimated Actual Population " as of January 1*				
1872† . .	34,806	100·0	—	—
1875 . .	35,316	101·5	180·9‡	5·1‡
1880 . .	36,649	105·3	266·6	7·4
1885 . .	38,313	110·1	332·8	7·9
1890 . .	39,902	114·6	317·8	8·2
1895 . .	41,557	119·4	331·0	8·2
1900 . .	43,847	126·0	458·0	10·8
1905 . .	46,620	133·9	554·6	12·3
1910 . .	49,184	141·3	512·8	10·8
1915 . .	52,752	151·6	713·6	14·1
1920 . .	55,473	159·4	544·2	10·1
Census Returns as of October 1				
1920 . .	55,963	160·8	653·3§	11·8§
1925 . .	59,737	171·6	754·8	13·1
1930 . .	64,450	185·2	942·6	15·3
1935 . .	69,254	199·0	960·8	14·4

* For the definition of the " estimated actual population " see p. 52.
† March 8, 1872.
‡ Adjusted annual increase of 2·82 years from March 8, 1872, to January 1, 1875.
§ Adjusted annual increase of 0·75 year from January 1 to October 1.

[1] See *infra*, p. 207.
[2] *Population du Japon depuis 1872*, cited, pp. 4–7 ; *The Tokyo Nichi Nichi*, cited, April 28, 1936.

TABLE XIII

RATE OF ANNUAL INCREASE OF TOTAL POPULATION AND INDEX
NUMBER OF TOTAL POPULATION, 1872–1935
(Supplementing Table XII)

Year.	Rate of Increase (per 1,000).	Index No. of Total Population.	Year.	Rate of Increase (per 1,000).	Index No. of Total Population.
1872	—	100·0	1900	11·7	126·0
1873	4·8	100·5	1901	13·6	127·4
1874	4·6	101·0	1902	12·9	129·2
1875	6·8	101·5	1903	10·5	130·9
1876	8·9	102·2	1904	10·5	132·5
1877	8·2	103·1	1905	9·0	133·9
1878	8·2	103·9	1906	8·0	135·1
1879	5·1	104·8	1907	11·6	136·2
1880	8·6	105·3	1908	12·3	137·8
1881	7·9	106·2	1909	13·0	139·5
1882	8·3	107·0	1910	13·6	141·3
1883	10·5	107·9	1911	14·6	143·2
1884	9·2	109·1	1912	14·4	145·3
1885	5·9	110·1	1913	14·3	147·4
1886	4·2	110·7	1914	13·7	149·5
1887	8·4	111·2	1915	14·1	151·6
1888	11·4	112·1	1916	11·9	153·7
1889	10·9	113·4	1917	11·2	155·5
1890	8·7	114·6	1918	5·4	157·3
1891	6·4	115·6	1919	8·0	158·1
1892	8·7	116·4	1920	11·3	159·4
1893	6·9	117·4	1925	13·1	171·6
1894	10·1	118·2		(1921–5)	
1895	10·5	119·4	1930	15·3	185·2
1896	9·7	120·6		(1926–30)	
1897	11·5	121·8	1935	14·4	199·0
1898	12·1	123·2		(1931–5)	
1899	10·2	124·7			

Figures in the above table and more detailed statistics
available indicate that Japan's population during the sixty-
three years, from March 8, 1872, to October 1, 1935, grew
from 34,806,000 to 69,254,148, the percentage of increase
being 99·0. Of this total increase, the first thirty-one years
contributed 32 per cent and the second half from 1904 to
1935 contributed 67 per cent.

The average rate of annual increase was as low as 5·1
per thousand for the four-year period 1872–5. It rose

gradually and reached 10·8 in 1896–1900. Since then it has never dropped below this mark except in the period 1916–20, in which the epidemic years of 1918–19 are included. Because of the radically low rates of growth of 5·4 in 1918 and 8·0 in 1919, the five-year average declined to 10·1. The only other serious disturbances in the rate of increase during this post-Sino-Japanese War period were in 1905 and 1906, when the rate dropped from 10·5 in 1904 to 9·0 and 8·0 respectively. This drop was undoubtedly due to the Russo-Japanese War in 1905 and the " Hinoe-uma," or the fire and horse combination of zodiacal and calendarical cycles, in 1906. This combination of signs, which occurs once in sixty years, is popularly regarded as conducive to bad luck to females born in the years governed by it ; therefore, parents, fearful for the future of their female infants, especially as to their later marital relations, postpone the registration of their births.[1]

C. *Statistical Comparison with Other Countries*

With regard to the population of Japan in comparison with that of other nations, as has been noted before, Japan was comparatively densely populated even in the early periods.[2] However, owing to the rapid increase in population which was characteristic of the West throughout the nineteenth century, particularly at the time of the Meiji Reformation in the early 'seventies, the Japanese position dropped to seventh in the world.[3] Following that came a period of slow growth up to the time of the Sino-Japanese War, and by 1890 it was once more greater than that of France. The fact that the Japanese population has continued to grow rapidly in the twentieth century when the growth of Western populations has begun to decline, is proved by the census reports or estimates made within the last five years ; these show Japan's population to be fifth in the world, surpassed only by the populations of China, India, Russia, and the United States. The population of the

[1] *Population du Japon depuis 1872*, cited, p. 8.
[2] *Supra*, pp. 5, 8.
[3] Cf. Honjo, E., *Jinko Oyobi Jinko Mondai*, cited, p. 197.

Japanese Empire, with its colonies, likewise ranks fifth among world colonial empires, ranking after that of China, the British Empire, Russia, and the United States.[1]

In order to compare the pre- and post-Reformation trends of Japanese population with the trends of other selected nations, the numbers of the population, numbers of increase, and rates of increase of the seven nations previously mentioned [2] are tabulated in two half-century periods of 1820–70 and 1870–1920 as follows :

TABLE XIV

POPULATION GROWTH OF JAPAN AND OF SOME SPECIFIED WESTERN NATIONS, 1820–70, 1870–1920 [3]

(Unit One Million)

	Population Number.			Increase of Population.			
				1820–70.		1870–1920.	
	1820.	1870.	1920.	Number.	Percentage.	Number.	Percentage.
Russia . . .	46·0	76·5	132·1	30·5	66·3	55·6	72·7
France . . .	30·9	36·1	38·8†	5·2	16·8	2·7	7·5
Japan . . .	30·0	34·3	55·5	4·3	14·3	21·2	61·8
Germany . .	27·0	41·1	59·2*	14·1	52·2	18·1	44·0
Italy . . .	19·1	26·8	38·7†	7·7	40·3	11·9	44·4
England and Wales . .	12·0	22·7	37·9†	10·7	89·2	15·2	67·0
U.S.A. . . .	9·0	39·8	105 7	30·8	342·2	65·9	165·6

* 1919 ;   † 1921 ;   Territorial changes are not adjusted.

The above table shows an increase of 61·8 per cent in the population of Japan during the latter half of the century as compared to 14·3 per cent in the first half.   The Japanese ratio of increase for the period from 1870–1920 ranks fourth among the seven nations cited in the table, falling behind the United States, Russia, England and Wales.   It should be noted here that while the population increased with such rapidity, the area of Japan proper remained definitely fixed. Therefore, the density index rose with the population index.

[1] *Tokei Nenkan*, cited, No. 51, 1932, p. 426.   [2] See *supra*, p. 8.
[3] For population of 1820 and 1870 see *supra*, p. 9.   For 1920, *Tokei Nenkan*, cited, No. 51, 1932, p. 412.

Given the population index of 185·2 per cent and the density of 169 per square kilometre in 1930, we can compute the density in 1872, arriving at the figure 91. This figure is higher than the density of France in 1930 (83) and is almost identical with Hungary (93) in the same year. As may be observed, the present density of Japan ranks among the highest in the world and is comparable only to that of a few nations in North-Western Europe. When compared to the individual states in the United States in 1930, Japan's population density is about one-half of that of Massachusetts (328) and approximates that of New York (164).

At this juncture, the area and population of a selected group of nations will be tabulated.

TABLE XV

AREA, POPULATION, AND DENSITY OF POPULATION OF SPECIFIED COUNTRIES, ESTIMATED AS OF DECEMBER 31, 1930 [1]

Country.	Area (1,000 Sq. Km.).	Population (000's omitted).	Density per Sq. Km.
Asia :			
China proper	5,059	411,770	80
India	4,675	352,370	75
Japan proper	382	64,450	169
Dutch East India . . .	1,900	61,000	32
Manchuria *	1,193	34,105	29
French Indo-China . . .	737	23,440	32
Philippine Islands . . .	296	12,335	42
Europe :			
European Russia proper .	5,999	127,050	21
Germany	469	64,484	137
United Kingdom	244	45,987	188
France	551	41,800	76
Italy	310	41,100	133
Belgium	30	8,092	270
The Netherlands	34	7,921	233
Other Continents :			
U.S.A.	7,839	123,630	16·0
Brazil	8,325	41,079	4·8
Argentina	2,793	11,447	4·1
Canada	9,557	10,290	1·1
South Africa	1,222	8,075	6·6
Australia	7,704	6,501	0·6
New Zealand	268	1,505	0·6

* November, 1932. Cf. *Kokusei Zukai*, 1933, p. 417.

[1] *Statistical Year-Book of League of Nations*, cited, 1931-2, Table 2.

Japan is mountainous and the percentage of arable land was estimated in 1930 at only 15·4. This ratio is lower than that of many of the other densely populated nations. The percentages of Switzerland and the Irish Free State are 12·1 and 22·0 respectively, Belgium's arable land amounts to 40·4 per cent and that of Italy is 44·6 per cent. The density of population per square hectare tilled land in Japan was computed in 1930 as 11·0, a figure which is higher than that of the Netherlands (8·7) and Switzerland (8·2), and far in excess of that of Italy, which is 3·0.[1]

In the foregoing pages, the recent general trend of the Japanese population has been taken up. The economic and social significance of this trend, however, can be estimated only after such factors as urban-rural and industrial and occupational distributions are studied in detail, together with the demographic factors of marriage, birth, and death. These points will be considered in subsequent sections of the present and the following chapter.

§ 2. REGIONAL DISTRIBUTION OF THE POPULATION

A. *Changes in the Regional Distribution*

Before entering upon a study of the regional distribution of the population in Japan, it must be noted that Japan proper is divided into eleven regions. Of these eleven regions, four—Hokkaido, Shikoku, Kyushu and Okinawa —are composed of isolated islands or groups of islands. The Honshu or Hondo occupies the remaining seven regions, which are, counting from north to south, Tohoku, Kwanto, Hokuroku, Tosan, Tokai, Kinki, and Chugoku. These eleven regions are divided geographically into one district (Hokkaido) and forty-six prefectures, as follows :

Hokkaido : Hokkaido district 1
Tohoku : Aomori, Iwate, Miyagi, Akita, Yamagata, Fukushima 6
Kwanto : Ibaragi, Tochigi, Gumma, Saitama, Chiba, Tokyo, Kanagawa 7

---

[1] For land, *Kochi Kakucho Kairyo Jigyo Yoran* (Annual Report on Land Reclamation and Improvement Works), Bureau of Agriculture, Department of Agriculture and Forestry, Japan, 1932, p. 86. For population, *Tokei Nenkan*, cited, No. 51, 1932, p. 426. Dates of the land and population statistics are 1930, except the population of Italy, whihc is 1931.

Hokuroku : Niigata, Toyama, Ishikawa, Fukui . . . 4
Tosan : Yamanashi, Nagano, Gifu 3
Tokai : Shizuoka, Aichi, Miye 3
Kinki : Shiga, Kyoto, Osaka, Hyogo, Nara, Wakayama . 6
Chugoku : Tottori, Shimane, Okayama, Hiroshima, Yamaguchi 5
Shikoku : Tokushima, Kagawa, Ehime, Kochi . . . 4
Kyushu : Oita, Fukuoka, Saga, Nagasaki, Kumamoto, Miya-
zaki, Kagoshima 7
Okinawa : Okinawa 1

Existing statistics regarding the geographical distribution of the population prior to 1920 are very unsatisfactory.[1]
According to the statistics available, the population of
every region except Hokuroku has increased steadily since
the early Meiji Era. However, in spite of the consistent
population gains in the ten regions, the ratios of the regional
distribution of the population have fluctuated widely.
This is evidenced by the figures in the following table, which
compare the five-year average percentage of the total population of Japan in each of the eleven regions for 1881-5 with
that of 1927-31.

TABLE XVI
REGIONAL DISTRIBUTION OF POPULATION IN 1881-5 AND 1927-31 [2]

Region.	1881-85.	1927-31.	Increase or Decrease (-).
Eastern Japan—			
Hokkaido	0·5	4·3	3·8
Tohoku .	10·6	10·2	− 0·4
Kwanto .	16·3	21·1	4·8
Hokuroku	9·8	6·4	− 3·4
Tosan .	6·2	5·5	− 0·7
Tokai .	8·7	8·6	− 0·1
Total	52·1	56·2	4·1
Western Japan—			
Kinki .	13·8	15·2	1·4
Chugoku	11·4	8·4	− 3·0
Shikoku	7·2	5·2	− 2·0
Kyushu .	14·5	14·1	− 0·4
Okinawa	1·0	1·0	0·0
Total	47·9	43·8	− 4·1

This comparison shows clearly that during the last half-
century, four regions—Tohoku, Tokai, Kyushu, and Okinawa—barely maintained their *status quo* in relation to the

[1] *Supra*, p. 49.
[2] Taniguchi, Yoshihiko, " Division between Rice Producers and Consumers," *Keizai Ronso*, 32 : 4, April, 1931, p. 688.

entire population of Japan. Four other regions lost their relative positions during this period ; snowy Hokuroku facing the Japan Sea, mountain-locked Tosan in Eastern Japan, Chugoku which is located at the western end of Hondo, and Shikoku, an island, situated south of Chugoku across the Inland Sea.

This decline in eight regions was balanced by the heavy population gains in three regions : Hokkaido, Kwanto and Kinki. Hokkaido is an exceptional instance of internal colonization in Japan. Kwanto and Kinki embrace the nation's largest industrial cities ; Tokyo and Yokohama belonging to the former and Osaka, Kyoto, and Kobe to the latter. Thus it can be seen that the regional re-distribution of population is an aspect of the greater movement of industrialization and urbanization.

B. *Comparison of Concentration of Population by Prefectures*

According to the preliminary report of the census of 1930, 63,540,830, or 99·2 per cent of the nation's population, were born in Japan proper. Let us classify this part of the population according to the place of birth, comparing the ratio with that of 1920. Table XVII classifies this group in the population according to the place of birth and compares the ratio of 1930 with that of 1920.

TABLE XVII
CLASSIFICATION OF NATIVE JAPANESE ACCORDING TO PLACE OF BIRTH, 1920–30 [1]

Nativity.	Number 1930.	Percentage of Total.	
		1920.	1930.
Born in the same town . . .	39,962,700	63·7	62·9
Born in other towns within the same prefecture	13,189,850	21·5	20·8
Born in other prefectures . .	10,390,280	14·9	16·4

[1] *Showa Gonen Kokusei Chosa Kekka no Gaikan* (General Preliminary Report of the Census of 1930), Bureau of Statistics, Japan, Dec., 1932, p. 13.

The population composition of Tokyo and Osaka tends toward a high degree of mobility ; 50·5 per cent of Tokyo's population in 1930 were migrants from other prefectures, while 44·9 per cent of Osaka's population were migrants. Other districts (Hokkaido) and prefectures which have high percentages of inhabitants of this class are Hokkaido, 34·2 ; Kyoto, 31·1 ; Hyogo, 23·7 ; in the Kinki Regions ; Kanagawa in Kwanto, 31·1 ; and Fukuoka, an important mining centre in Kyushu, 21·6. Only twelve prefectures contain populations of which less than 6 per cent were born in other prefectures. Among them Akita, 2·8 per cent, and Yamagata, 2·0 per cent, in the Tohoku Region, Fukui in Hokuroku, 2·6 per cent, and Okinawa, 1·1 per cent, are lowest.[1]

Of the Japanese natives who, by 1930, had emigrated to other prefectures, the ratios ranged from 28·6 per cent to 53 per cent. These ratios of dispersion are in sharp contrast to the ratios of concentration or the percentage of immigrant population by prefectures, which has been considered in some detail above. In the ratio of concentration only seven prefectures were above the average and forty prefectures below. In contrast to this, the ratio of dispersion of all prefectures of Japan (forty-six prefectures and one district) were divided evenly ; twenty-four were above and twenty-three were below the average.

In this inter-prefecture movement of the population, nine prefectures gained 5,332,300 at the expense of the other thirty-eight. These nine prefectures include not only the six prefectures in which the " Six largest cities " of the nation are situated, but also include the mining centres of Fukuoka, Hokkaido, and Miyazaki, the latter a prefecture in Kyushu regarded as an internal colony second only to Hokkaido in importance. The net gain due to immigration in these prefectures is as follows : [2]

Tokyo	2,280,790	Kyoto	248,520
Osaka	1,149,870	Hyogo	153,860
Hokkaido	829,450	Aichi	75,980
Fukuoka	316,350	Miyazaki	22,970
Kanagawa	252,510		

---

[1] *Ibid.*, p. 14. [2] *Ibid.*, p. 16.

The net losses of the thirty-eight other prefectures range downward rather evenly from the 389,920 of Niigata to 8,750 of Nagasaki. However, it should be noticed that sixteen out of the nineteen prefectures which lost more than 150,000 are : all three prefectures of the Tosan Region, six out of eight prefectures in Hokuroku and Shikoku, four out of the six prefectures of Tohoku, and three out of the seven prefectures of Kwanto. All of these regions except Shikoku and Kwanto are remote agricultural regions in the northeast. Shikoku is a mountainous island in Western Japan and Kwanto is the region in which the industrial centres of Tokyo and Yokohama are located.

The above study points out a single unmistakable fact, viz. that the population of Japan is being re-distributed more and more unevenly, due to the heavy concentration in the great industrial centres. The movement of internal colonization to Hokkaido and, less extensively, to the Miyazaki prefecture, counterbalances to some extent this tendency of concentration.

§ 3. URBAN-RURAL DISTRIBUTION

A. *Local Administrative Units of Japan*

The present local administrative units of Japan were created by the Municipal, Town, and Village Organization Act of 1889. By that act the original rural unit of the *mura* lost its legal entity and the present *mura* or village was formed, embracing several original *mura*. Since the promulgation of the Act of 1889 there have been official efforts to make the new *mura* the true social as well as the administrative unit of Japan. For example, in 1909 old community properties were unified under the ownership of the new *mura*. Geographical and social barriers, however, prevent the new *mura* from being a unit in anything but in an administrative sense.[1]

This explains why we take 10,000 population as the

[1] Cf. *Nihon Nominshi* (The History of Japanese Peasants), Tokyo, Nihon Gakujitsu Fukyukai, 1925, p. 334 ; Nagaya, T., " Development of Cities and Urbanization of the Population," *Toshi Mondai*, Vol. II, 1926, p. 34.

demarcation point between the urban and rural communities, in contrast to the norm set by the International Statistical Institute in 1887, which classified localities of 2,000 people and over as urban communities. Some writers, e.g. Mr. Toshio Nagaya and Dr. Hiroshi Nasu, prefer a 5,000 norm for Japan. However, this cannot be regarded as an adequate standard.[1]

The Bureau of Statistics classifies communities in eleven types, dependent on their population and ranging from 500 to 100,000. However, only five terms are used by the Bureau ; they are as follows :

Village . . . . . under 10,000
Local town . . . . 10,000 to 19,999
Small city . . . . 20,000 to 49,999
Medium city . . . . 50,000 to 99,999
Large city . . . . 100,000 and over

There is a crude and popular classification of " city " and " non-city " communities. Cities in this classification indicate the large communities of about 30,000 or over which are organized according to the City Organization Regulation.[2] In 1925 there were 101 cities thus organized, compared to 139 communities of population over 30,000.[3]

B. *Trend toward Urbanization*

There are certain economic and social causes of concentration of population. Compared to this natural growth, the organization of cities in conformity with the City Organization Regulation is more arbitrary. Hence,

[1] e.g. Yugi, Tokyo Prefecture, the home of the writer, was reported as having a population of 5,247 on October 1, 1930. Yugi is, however, far from qualifying as an urban community, as it is but the union of eleven old *mura*. Among them Nakayama, where the writer was born, is composed of about 42 households and 200 inhabitants, all of whom live at the bottom of a lonely valley. Hence the inhabitants of Nakayama are, in fact, rural dwellers. The same is true of the other ten old *mura* in Yugi. For the population on October 1, 1930, see Bureau of Statistics, Japan, *Showa Gonen Kokusei Chosa Hokoku* (Report of the Census of 1930), Vol. V, *Population by City, Town, and Village*, p. 52.

[2] There is no definite population limit to admit a community to classification as a city. However, the general norm of minimum city population is about 30,000. Cf. *Hyakka Daijiten* (The Great Encyclopædia), Tokyo, Heibonsha, 1932, Vol. II, p. 485, " Cities, Towns, and Villages."

[3] *Tokei Nenkan*, cited, No. 51, 1932, pp. 38, 39.

although the city and non-city classification is sometimes convenient for detailed reports on economic and social affairs published by cities, it is not as satisfactory for a scientific study of the population as the classification of communities under the order of population units. Following are the statistics of local units at five-year intervals from 1893 to 1918 and from 1920 to 1925 :

TABLE XVIII

LOCAL ORGANIZATIONS CLASSIFIED ACCORDING TO SIZE OF COM-MUNITY, 1893–1925 [1]

I Year.	II 9,999 and Under.	III 10,000– 19,999.	IV 20,000– 49,999.	V 50,000– 99,999.	VI Over 100,000.	VII Total III–VI.	VIII Grand Total.
1893	14,946	144	52	12	6	214	15,160
1898	13,794	153	60	12	8	233	14,027
1903	13,038	186	64	16	9	275	13,313
1908	12,084	268	76	19	10	373	12,457
1913	11,887	335	97	26	11	469	12,356
1918	11,705	378	132	32	14	556	12,261
1920	11,687	374	136	31	16	557	12,244
1925	11,410	392	145	51	21	609	12,019

This table shows that the number of all local organizations decreased from 15,160 in 1893 to 12,019 in 1925, or 3,141 in 33 years. During the same period rural units decreased from 14,946 to 11,410 and urban units increased from 214 to 609. In percentage rural communities still occupied, in 1925, about 95 per cent of the whole. Yet it is significant that the percentage of urban units increased from 1·4 in 1893 to 5·1 in 1925. The decline in the number of rural units is due partially to the development of rural communities into the urban class, but more largely to their unification and reorganization as well as their annexation, by cities.[2]

The above statistical survey of local units has a value *per se*. But the figures in such statistics are sometimes

---

[1] *1920–30 Seiji Keizai Nenkan*, cited, p. 260 ; *Tokei Nenkan*, cited, No. 51, 1932, p. 38.
[2] Cf. Takano, I., *Honpo Jinko no Genzai Oyobi Shorai*, cited, p. 174.

deceptive, for the same weight is given in the table to a village of 500 inhabitants as to a community of one million. The true significance of urbanization is to be sought in statistics of population concentration rather than in statistics giving the number of communities. The percentage of the total population resident in each of the five types of communities in the several census years since 1893 is as follows :

TABLE XIX

Distribution of Population by Size of Community, 1893–1925 [1]

I Year.	II 9,999 and Under.	III 10,000– 19,999.	IV 20,000– 49,999.	V 50,000– 99,999.	VI 100,000 and Over.	VII Total III–VI.	VIII Grand Total.
1893	84·03	—	9·99*	—	5·98	15·97	100·00
1898	82·29	4·46	3·85	1·70	7·70	17·71	100·00
1903	79·30	5·11	4·16	2·22	9·21	20·70	100·00
1908	75·07	6·93	4·68	2·61	10·71	24·93	100·00
1913	72·39	8·16	5·32	3·36	10·77	27·61	100·00
1918	68·08	8·72	6·72	3·93	12·55	31·92	100·00
1920	67·77	9·07	7·33	3·76	12·07	32·23	100·00
1925	63·41	8·75	7·44	5·77	14·63	36·59	100·00

* III–V.

The statistics in the above table reveal that in 1893, a year before the Sino-Japanese War, the rural population comprised 84·03 per cent of the total population. The urban population included 15·97 per cent, of which 5·98 per cent lived in cities of over 100,000. By 1925 the percentage of the rural population had dropped to 63·41 and the urban population had increased to 36·59. Further, 40 per cent of the urban population were inhabitants of great cities of over 100,000.

Assuming that rapid urbanization is a recent development, it will be interesting now to see the relative growth of the urban and rural populations in the light of the increase in the total population of Japan. The following table

[1] *1920–30 Seiji Keizai Nenkan*, cited, p. 261 ; *Tokei Nenkan*, cited, 1932, p. 38.

illustrates the vigour of the tendency toward urbanization.
The year 1893 has been taken as the base.

TABLE XX

INCREASE OF URBAN AND RURAL POPULATION, 1893–1925 [1]

From 1893 to:	Dura-tion (Yrs.).	Population Increase by Community Classes.				
		I 9,999 and Under.	II 10,000– 99,999.	III 100,000 and Over.	IV Total II–III.	V Grand Total.
1898	5	2,015,665	343,463	983,117	1,326,580	3,342,245
1903	10	3,149,513	1,377,656	1,954,771	3,332,427	6,481,940
1908	15	3,499,763	3,159,885	3,022,042	6,181,927	9,681,690
1913	20	4,563,166	5,084,397	3,422,911	8,507,308	13,070,474
1918	25	4,201,211	7,047,624	4,777,646	11,825,270	16,026,481
1920	27	2,582,789	7,080,663	4,238,805	11,319,468	13,902,257
1925	32	2,539,374	8,910,208	6,226,444	15,136,652	17,676,026

The above statistics reveal the highly interesting fact
that while the total population of Japan increased to the
extent of almost 17·7 millions during the period from 1893
to 1925, the rural districts absorbed only slightly more than
2·5 millions or 14 per cent of this increase, in contrast to
the urban communities which absorbed the remaining
15 millions, or 86 per cent. Moreover, the greater portion
of the rural gain was made during the first five years from
1893 to 1898. Eliminating this first five-year period when
rural absorption was still dominant, rural districts received,
out of the total increase of 14 millions from 1898 to 1925,
only 524,000, or 3·65 per cent. During the period from 1913
to 1918, years in which identical methods of estimating the
population were applied, the rural districts lost in population to the extent of 362,000; during the inter-censual
period, from 1920 to 1925, the rural population suffered a
further loss of 43,000.

Statistics showing the relative urban-rural shares in
the total population increase from 1898 to 1925 and from
1920 to 1925 are shown in Table XXI.

[1] *1920–30 Seiji Keizai Nenkan*, cited, p. 261 ; *Tokei Nenkan*, cited,
No. 51, 1932, p. 38. Notice the discrepancy between the figures of 1918
and 1920. This is due to the change in the census method which resulted
in the substantial elimination of false figures since 1920. Cf. *supra*, p. 56
et passim.

TABLE XXI

INCREASE OF URBAN AND RURAL POPULATION DURING TWO
PERIODS : 1898–1925 AND 1920–30

Periods.	Community Groups.				Grand Total.
	9,999 and Under.	10,000–99,999.	100,000 and Over.	Total Over 10,000.	
1898–1925	523,709	8,566,745	5,243,327	13,810,072	14,323,781
1920–1930	−43,415	1,829,545	1,987,639	3,817,184	3,773,769

Mark − indicates decline of the number.

It has been intimated that the classification of the population into urban and rural communities is somewhat arbitrary. For observation of city life as an organic whole, the suburbs must be included. To this end the population trend in twenty-four industrial centres, including great cities, mining districts and manufacturing centres, may be compared with that of all Japan.

TABLE XXII

POPULATION INCREASE IN INDUSTRIAL CENTRES AND OTHER AREAS,
1920–5 [1]

Area.	Increase 1920–5.	Percentage of Increase.
Twenty-four Industrial Centres .	676,259	8·5
Their suburbs	1,093,322	55·8
Total	1,764,581	17·8
All other areas	2,009,070	4·3
All Japan	3,773,651	6·7

Table XXII shows that during the period of 1920–5, while all Japan gained 6·7 per cent in population, twenty-four industrial centres gained 17·8 per cent. Within city or town limits these industrial centres show a saturation of population, and the five-year increase was only 8·5 per cent. In marked contrast to this figure is the 55·8 per cent gain in the population of the suburbs. This fact graphically demonstrates Japan's share in the modern phenomenon

[1] Inoma, K., " Urbanization of Population," *The Tokyo Asahi*, June 17, 1927, p. 7.

of city progress. Undoubtedly the change in the character of the city—from a consumption centre, as the cities of pre-industrial revolution days had been, to a production centre—is the motivating factor in this development. Two of Japan's " Six largest cities," Kobe and Yokohama, rose in the course of a few decades from solitary fishing hamlets to their present dominant positions. Other great cities like Sapporo, Otaru and Yahata experienced a similar rapid development.

It is not to be assumed that the causal factor in the rapid growth of cities in Japan is the greater natural increase in urban districts. On the contrary, the rates of natural increase in 1925 were 16 per 1,000 in rural and 12 per 1,000 in urban districts.[1] Here lies the explanation for the close relationship between the regional movements and the urbanization of population. It was stated in the preceding section that the regional movements of the population are merely a phase of the great movement of industrialization and urbanization.

C. *Demographic Effects of Urbanization*

Urbanization is important not only in so far as it reflects the economic conditions of a nation, but is also most significant in reflecting the trend of population. From the relative growth of urban and rural populations, in spite of their comparative ratios of natural increase, it may be inferred that in urban districts the middle aged groups are larger than in rural districts. The following statistics (Table XXIII) of the age distribution in cities and non-cities[2] coincide with this common inference.

As is evident from these figures, the ratio of the middle-aged groups, from 15 to 39 years, in urban districts far exceeds that for rural districts ; on the other hand, in the ratios of the groups under 14 and over 45 years of age, non-city areas dominate over city areas.

Low death rates in urban districts may be said to be a

[1] Hashimoto, D., and Nagai, S., Editors, *Konnichi no Noson Mondai* (Present-Day Rural Problems), Tokyo, Sanyusha, 1932, p. 17.
[2] *Supra*, p. 69.

TABLE XXIII

DISTRIBUTIONS OF FIVE-YEAR AGE PERIODS IN CITY AND NON-CITY
DISTRICTS, 1925 [1]
(Per 1,000 Population)

Age Period.	City.	Non-City.	Age Period.	City.	Non-City.
0–4 . .	120	142	45–49 . .	48	52
5–9 . .	92	122	50–54 . .	36	42
10–14 . .	104	115	55–59 . .	27	35
15–19 . .	130	90	60–64 . .	19	28
20–24 . .	114	77	65–69 . .	15	24
25–29 . .	91	69	70–74 . .	10	17
30–34 . .	71	60	75–79 . .	5	10
35–39 . .	62	57	80–84 . .	2	4
40–44 . .	54	54	Over 85 .	0	1

result of the above-mentioned age composition. However,
low demographic rates in urban communities are not
restricted to the death rate; in cities the rates are low in
marriage, divorce, and birth as well. As may be seen by
comparing the figures given below for cities of over 100,000
population in 1930, with the corresponding figures for all
Japan in the same year. The table follows:

TABLE XXIV

RATES OF MARRIAGE, DIVORCE, BIRTH, AND DEATH, AND RATE
OF NATURAL INCREASE, OF GREAT CITIES AND JAPAN
PROPER, 1930 [2]
(Per 1,000 Population)

Area.	Marriage Rate.	Divorce Rate.	Birth Rate.	Death Rate.	Rate of Natural Increase.
Great cities . .	6·41	0·77	25·92	15·81	10·11
Japan proper . .	7·86	0·80	32·35	18·17	14·18

Such statistical ratios emphasize the fact that city life
intensifies the action of those influences which tend to
decrease the number of marriages, births, etc. The rural-
urban relationship is comparable, in some measure, to the
relationship between Japan and the Occident. Urbanization is significant not only as a reflection of the existing
economic conditions, but because the growing cities in turn

[1] Hashimoto, D., and Nagai, S., Editors, *op. cit.*, p. 15.
[2] *Jinko Dotai Tokei Kijutsuhen*, cited, 1930, pp. 13, 22, 31, 85.

react on the social development of the nation. " The big city is doing things to us the outcome of which we cannot yet fully see." [1]

Japan, with 40 per cent of her people in urban areas, cannot neglect the problem of concentration in any consideration of the economic and social factors which are so closely bound up with the character of the population.

§ 4.   OCCUPATIONAL DISTRIBUTION

A. *Statistical Data of Occupations*

Our study of the regional and urban-rural movements of the population, with which we dealt at some length in the two previous sections, is of no significance unless we supplement our data with a study of the occupational distribution of the population.

Materials for this important part of the study of population movements are very scarce in Japan. The *Zenkoku Kenbun Kosekihyo*, or " Tables of Census Register " of the Home Department, contain occupational classifications of the population for five-year periods beginning with 1872. Adequate occupational classification, however, began only with the census of 1920.

The crudeness of the occupational statistics of the period of 1872–6 is an established fact.[2] Nevertheless, these statistics are of unique value because they afford us the only material of this kind on a national scale, of the early Meiji period.   They have, therefore, been used widely as reference for the computation and construction of statistics of the occupational distribution since the Meiji Reformation.

According to the original report on March 8, 1872, the number of gainfully employed workers was 19,176,219 or 56 per cent of the total domicile population. During the succeeding four years the number increased gradually, the index number rising from 100, as of March 8, 1872, to 105 on January 1, 1876.   During this same period, however,

[1] Thompson, W. S., *Population Problems*, New York, McGraw-Hill, 1930, p. 333.

[2] *Kokusei Zukai*, cited, 1931, p. 73 ; *1920–30 Seiji Keizai Nenkan*, cited, p. 276 ; Nakagawa, T., " Trend of Agricultural, Industrial, and Commercial Population in Japan," *Keizai Kenkyu*, 4 : 4, Oct., 1927, p. 70.

the index of those employed in fisheries increased to 765.
Despite the figures, such a great change in one occupation
is improbable, and suggests an error of some sort, or a change
in the registration system. More detailed data as to occupational shifts during this period follow on page 78.

Since the census report of 1920, elaborate statistics are
available concerning the numbers and occupations of those
gainfully employed, and of those who subsist on unearned
income, and the dependents of both groups. Thus the
entire population can be classified according to the source
of income. The statistics of the major divisions are shown
on page 79.

The result of the census of 1930 shows that 29,619,640,
or 46·2 per cent, were gainfully employed,[1] and the remaining
34,830,365, or 53·8 per cent, were dependent on the first
group ; those who subsist on unearned income were included
in this second group. These gainfully employed people,
when classified into general divisions of occupation, reveal
the following facts :

TABLE XXVII

OCCUPATIONAL DISTRIBUTION OF GAINFULLY EMPLOYED
WORKERS, 1930 [2]

Occupation.	Gainfully Employed Workers.		Males per 100 Females.
	Number.	Percentage of Total.	
Agriculture	14,140,107	47·7	121·04
Aquatic industries	546,624	1·9	1,100·16
Mining	251,220	0·9	512·05
Manufacturing	5,699,581	19·3	298·45
Commerce	4,478,098	15·1	205·84
Transportation	1,107,574	3·7	1,302·37
Official and professional services	2,044,151	6·9	480·15
Household employment . .	781,319	2·6	12·08
Miscellaneous.	570,966	1·9	590·40
Total	29,619,640	100·0	179·71

The above figures are all we have concerning the distri-

[1] It must be noted that the occupation indicates the social status and
the " gainfully occupied " group in the census report necessarily includes
some who are unemployed. For unemployment statistics see *infra*,
p. 230 ff.

[2] *Tokei Nenkan*, cited, No. 54, 1935, p. 32.

TABLE XXV

OCCUPATIONAL DISTRIBUTION OF GAINFULLY EMPLOYED WORKERS, 1872–6 [1]

Occupation.	1872.			1873.		1874.		1875.		1876.	
	Population.	Per cent.	Ind. No.	Population.	Ind. No.	Population.	Ind. No.	Population.	Ind. No.	Population.	Ind. No.
Agriculture .	14,787,441	77·1	100	15,320,367	104	15,262,887	103	15,122,237	102	15,656,621	106
Manufacturing. .	718,727	3·7	100	688,964	96	708,095	99	723,583	101	748,596	104
Commerce .	1,328,832	6·9	100	1,289,070	97	1,301,678	98	1,304,340	98	1,357,956	102
Fisheries .	3,558	—*	100	3,558	100	15,308	430	26,640	749	27,206	765
Official and professional services .	130,186	0·7	100	119,866	92	118,042	91	160,109	123	161,943	124
Others .	2,207,475	11·5	100	2,223,993	101	2,202,668	100	2,252,036	102	2,323,671	105
Total .	19,176,219	100·0	100	19,645,818	102	19,608,678	102	19,588,945	102	20,275,993	105

Dates : January 1 except in 1872, when the date was March 8.

* Less than 0·1 per cent.

[1] *Ishin Igo Teikoku Tokei Zairyo Isan* (Collected Statistical Materials of Japan since the Reformation), Bureau of Statistics, Japan, Series II, pp. 1–55.

TABLE XXVI

OCCUPATIONAL DIVISIONS OF JAPANESE POPULATION, 1920[1]

Occupation.	Gainfully Employed Workers.					Dependents.			
	Male.	Female.	Total.	Per cent of Total Workers.	Per cent of Total Population.	Male.	Female.	Total.	Per cent of Total Population.
Agriculture	7,749,988	6,378,372	14,128,360	50·43	25·25	5,434,951	7,410,571	12,845,522	22·95
Fisheries	517,065	41,249	558,314	1·99	1·00	332,253	552,035	884,288	1·58
Mining	327,918	96,546	424,464	1·52	0·76	187,025	318,641	505,666	0·90
Manufacturing	3,716,354	1,583,894	5,300,248	18·92	9·47	1,825,647	3,505,051	5,330,698	9·53
Commerce	2,158,399	1,029,603	3,188,002	11·38	5·70	1,352,020	2,601,573	3,953,593	7·06
Transportation	975,221	62,017	1,037,238	3·70	1·85	519,076	975,850	1,494,926	2·67
Official and professional service	1,134,025	307,807	1,441,832	5·15	2·58	570,078	1,103,528	1,673,606	2·99
Household emp.	70,849	584,348	655,197	2·34	1·17	6,209	13,251	19,460	0·04
Others	337,088	190,363	527,451	1·89	0·94	203,101	352,751	555,852	0·99
Those who depend on unearned income	387,865	364,066	751,931	2·68	1·34	239,053	447,352	686,405	1·23
Total	17,374,772	10,638,265	28,013,037	100·00	50·06	10,669,413	17,280,603	27,950,016	49·94

[1] *Tokei Nenkan*, cited, No. 51, 1932, pp. 28–35. Domestic servants who live in the home of their employer were categorically treated in the original census report differently from the general group of gainfully employed workers. In this table these domestic servants were considered as ordinary " household employment," which originally indicated only servants living out.

bution of occupations on a national scale. Using these figures, supplemented by some other data the scope of which was more limited in areas surveyed and occupations studied, several attempts have been made to construct statistics of occupational distribution from the beginning of the Meiji period to 1919.[1] However, none of these attempts can be favourably compared as to material and scope with the census returns of 1920 and 1930 which are given above.

B. *Trend of Occupational Distribution within the Population*

In the following table the ratios of the occupational groups previously enumerated against all gainful workers, excluding those who depend on unearned incomes, are compared. The registration figures of 1872, the validity of which have been questioned, are added for the sake of reference.

TABLE XXVIII

OCCUPATIONAL DISTRIBUTION OF GAINFULLY EMPLOYED WORKERS
IN 1872, 1920 AND 1930
(Percentages)

Occupation.	1872.	1920.	1930.
Agriculture	77·1	51·8	47·7
Aquatic industries	— *	2·1	1·9
Mining	—	1·6	0·9
Manufacturing	3·7	19·4	19·3
Commerce	6·9	11·7	15·1
Transportation	—	3·8	3·7
Official and professional services .	0·7	5·3	6·9
Household employment . . .	—	2·4	2·6
Miscellaneous.	11·5	1·9	1·9
Total	100·0	100·0	100·0
Ratio of gainfully employed workers per 100 inhabitants	56·0	48·7	46·2

* Less than 0·1 per cent.

[1] Cf. Nakagawa, T., "Trends of Agricultural, Manufacturing, and Commercial Population in Japan," *Keizai Kenkyu*, 4 : 4, Oct., 1927, pp. 68–84 ; "Estimates of the Agricultural, Industrial, and Commercial Population in Japan," *Tokei Shushi*, No. 556 ; *Ishin igo Teikoku Tokei Zairyo Isan*, cited, Series II ; *1920–30 Seiji Keizai Nenkan*, cited, p. 275 ff. ; Hijikata, Seibi, "The Problem of Unemployment viewed in the Light of the Trend of Occupational Population," *Social Reform*, No. 106, pp. 76–87.

The above table shows that the ratio of the agricultural population declined from 77·1 per cent in 1872 to 47·7 per cent in 1930. The marked decrease in this group, which constituted the greater part of the entire population in the early Meiji Period, has been compensated by gains in the fields of official and professional services, manufacturing and commerce. In other words, the decline of agriculture as an occupation was offset by the rise of the cultural, industrial and commercial occupations.

During the period between the census of 1920 and that of 1930 the percentage of gainfully employed workers to the total population dropped from 48·7 (or 50·06 if those who subsist on unearned income are included) to 46·2. One factor (the acceleration of the diminution in the importance of agriculture as an occupation) appears to stand out most conspicuously among the causal elements. However, it is quite significant that the occupational importance of mining and manufacturing also declined during this period. Especially in the case of mining, a decrease is noticeable not only in the ratio figures, but also in the actual numbers of people employed in this field.

Such losses in the agricultural, industrial and mining occupations were balanced by the gains in commercial and in official and professional service fields, in which the increases were 1,290,096 and 602,319 respectively. Together these gains embraced 80·5 per cent of the total increase of gainfully engaged workers for the ten-year period studied. In this increase of the commercial class, employers and proprietor-workers in commercial enterprises increased about 500,000 ; this figure approaches that of the increase in the number of employees in the same field, which includes the family labour force other than that of the head of the family, and which reached the number of about 700,000. According to the report of the census of 1930, there were 1,242,486 proprietor-worker merchants without employees. This figure represents 27·7 per cent of the total population engaged in commerce.

A universal tendency accompanying modern technical progress is the release of an increasingly greater proportion

G

of the population from primary extractive industries such as agriculture and mining.[1]   It is noticeable, however, that in Japan even manufacturing shares the same tendency and shows that it has approached the saturation point in so far as absorbing additional numbers of the employable population is concerned.[2]   At the same time it must also be noted that the increasing numbers of small traders, petty officials and professional groups are exposed to a chronic state of semi-unemployment.   That the petty trader class especially is exposed to the dangers of un-employment is attested to by the fact that small merchants recognize the menace to them which is inherent in the rapid development of department stores and producers' and consumers' co-operatives.   The rapid and continued increase in the official and professional services signifies both an increased specialization of occupation and a rising cultural standard of the nation.

C. *Comparison with Other Countries*

The above occupational make-up of the Japanese population will now be compared with that of some other countries.   Such comparison will throw a further light on the present status of the Japanese population structure and on the possible future course that it may follow.   With this in view, the occupational statistics of eight countries including Japan are compiled in a comparable form.   In doing this, care was taken to select countries of possible variance in economic development, with the census years as close to that of Japan as possible.

The most important indices in the study of the occupational distribution, as regards the population trend as well as the trend of general national economy, are those of agriculture and manufacturing.   Although the international comparison of the occupational distribution must not be taken literally, we may, however, at this point make the

[1] W. S. Thompson anticipates that fifty years hence even three-fourths to four-fifths of all people may live in urban communities.   Thompson, W. S., *Population Problems*, cited, p. 319.
[2] For the actual progress of industry, see *infra*, pp. 213–5.

TABLE XXIX

Occupational Distributions of Gainfully Employed Workers of Specified Countries at Recent Comparable Census Years [1]

(Unit 1,000)

Country.	Year.	Total Pop.	Dependents.	Gain'ly Employed.	Agri. and Aquatic.	Mfg. and Mining.	Commerce and Trans.	Official and Prof.	Domestic.	Others.
Japan	1930	64,450	34,830	29,620	14,687	5,951	4,478	2,044	781	571
United Kingdom*	1931	44,796	23,741	21,055	1,398	7,942	5,223	2,800	1,554	2,136
U.S.A.	1930	122,775	73,945	48,830	10,722	15,095	9,924	4,110	8,978	
Germany	1933	65,219	32,922	32,297	9,344	13,051	5,931	2,701	1,270	—
France	1931	41,835	20,222	21,613	7,704	7,280	3,764	1,971	893	—
Italy	"	41,177	23,914	17,263	8,169	5,225	2,218	1,112	540	—
Canada	"	10,377	6,449	3,928	1,224	737	867	519	143	439
India	"	349,759	200,845	148,814	99,810	15,698	10,482	4,147	10,893	7,779
Percentages.										
Japan	1930	100·0	54·0	46·0	49·6	20·2	18·8	6·9	2·6	1·9
United Kingdom*	1931	100·0	53·0	47·0	6·6	37·7	24·8	13·3	7·4	10·1
U.S.A.	1930	100·0	60·2	39·8	22·0	30·9	20·4	8·4	18·4	
Germany	1933	100·0	50·5	49·5	28·9	40·4	18·4	8·4	3·9	—
France	1931	100·0	48·3	51·7	35·6	33·6	17·4	9·1	4·1	—
Italy	"	100·0	58·1	41·9	47·3	30·3	12·8	6·4	3·1	—
Canada	"	100·0	62·2	37·8	30·9	18·8	22·1	13·2	3·6	11·2
India	"	100·0	57·5	42·5	67·1	10·5	7·1	2·8	7·3	5·2

* Exclusive of Northern Ireland.

[1] *Statistical Yearbook of League of Nations*, cited, 1934–5; *Tokei Nenkan*, cited, No. 54, 1935, pp. 441–2.

following observation : combining agriculture and the aquatic industries, the ratio of gainfully employed workers in these occupations in Japan was 49·6 per 100 in 1930. This figure is higher than that of any other country in the table except India (67·1), although the Italian figure (47·3) is not far below Japan's. Compared with the above ratio of Japan, that of United Kingdom is as low as 6·6.

It is only a natural concomitance with the above situation that in the case of manufacturing combined with mining the Japanese ratio, 20·2, is lower than that of all other countries in the table except India (10·5) and Canada (18·8). However, in commerce and transportation Japan ranks the fourth, coming after United Kingdom, Canada, and the United States. This relatively high ratio of Japan in these fields is perhaps the result of the predominance of small retailers, a point which has already been discussed.

The final consideration in our study of the occupational distribution of the population is that of the ratio of gainfully employed workers to total population. As shown by the figure in the previous table, all countries fall within the range of 37·8 per cent of Canada and 51·7 per cent of France, and it is difficult to find any definite tendency according to country. Therefore, in view of the variance in the ratio of age group under fifteen, the majority of whom are likely to remain unengaged,[1] an attempt is made in

TABLE XXX

RATIO OF ALL GAINFULLY EMPLOYED WORKERS PER 100 POPULATION AGED 15 AND OVER IN JAPAN AND OTHER SPECIFIED COUNTRIES [2]

Country.	Year.	Male.	Female.	Total.
Japan . . .	1930	92·85	51·92	72·47
India . . .	1931	93·58	46·56	70·81
France . . .	1926	91·84	47·66	69·61
United Kingdom* .	1931	92·47	34·85	61·98
Italy . . .	,,	95·54	25·98	59·51
U.S.A. . .	1930	86·78	25·10	56·51
Canada . .	1931	87·77	19·71	55·36

* Exclusive of Northern Ireland.

---

[1] E.g. the rate of occupied children per 100 children of the age of fourteen and under was 3·32 in Japan in 1930.
[2] *Statistical Year-Book of League of Nations*, cited, 1934–5; *Tokei Nenkan*, cited, No. 54, 1935, pp. 441–2.

Table XXX to show the ratio of all occupied groups irrespective of age against the group aged fifteen or more. In this table Germany is excluded because the age classification of her population report does not fit our requirement in this particular case.

In the above table Japan now ranks at the head of the entire group. This change comes from the elimination of the distorting influence of relatively large proportion in the bracket of those under fifteen years of age. The table shows also the fact that the high percentage in Japan is the result of the high percentage for the females. The question whether this is a mere concomitant phenomenon of the low *per capita* income of the population or whether this is caused merely by differences in census criteria for determining women's occupational status will be left to the search of the readers.

SUMMARY OF CHAPTER V

Up to the beginning of the nineteenth century, Japan, when compared with the major European nations, was a densely populated country. With the industrialization of the West, which took place in the early nineteenth century, the population of Western nations increased rapidly, while the Japanese population remained static. However, coincident with the fast progress in the national economy since the Reformation of 1868, Japan's population has increased 99 per cent in the past 63 years—from the fifth year of Meiji (1872) up to 1935. Of this increase of 99 per cent or 35 millions, the first 31 years contributed only 31 per cent, and the later 31 years, from the time of the Russo-Japanese War, contributed 68 per cent. Japan, now embracing 69 million people, faces the critical problem of finding a place for herself among the nations of the world.

An attempt has been made to study the regional, urban-rural, and occupational distribution of the population. The occupational distribution of the population lends significance to the geographical distribution. The undercurrent of these movements is a dual factor—industrialization and urbanization. These, more than anything else, direct the future trends of the nation's population.

The census of 1930 revealed several important facts concerning the movement toward urbanization. In that census it was revealed that thirty-eight prefectures experienced a net population loss of 5·3 millions, which, however, was balanced by a net gain of equal amount in nine prefectures. Further, out of the total increase of the population during the years between 1898 and 1925, which amounted to 14·3 millions, 13·8 millions, or 96 per cent, were absorbed into urban districts. Since 1920, the rural population has been actually decreasing.

This trend in geographical re-distribution of population is reflected in the statistics of occupational distribution. About a half century ago nearly 80 per cent of Japan's occupational population was engaged almost exclusively in agriculture and aquatic industries. To-day nearly 40 per cent of the nation's gainfully employed workers are engaged in mining, manufacturing, commerce and transportation. However, owing to technical improvements in such major industries as manufacturing, an increased productivity does not necessarily imply a corresponding increased capacity for population absorption in these urban industries. Hence urbanization as a process carries with it, beside industrialization, the creation and concentration of a class of petty traders and petty professional workers.

CHAPTER VI

DEMOGRAPHIC ANALYSIS OF THE RECENT TREND OF THE JAPANESE POPULATION

§ 1. SEX AND AGE DISTRIBUTIONS

A. *Sex Distribution*

SINCE the practice of infanticide is not likely to be prevalent in countries equipped with a comprehensive system of census or registration, there is no marked disparity in the statistically recorded sex ratio, i.e. the ratio of males per 100 females. In general, everywhere in the world, except in most of the north-western European nations, the male population exceeds the female population. In these European countries, the sex ratios are considerably lower than elsewhere. The ratio was 91·31 in England and Wales in 1921 and 93·74 in Germany in 1925. In these countries the effect of the Great War on the sex ratio is quite evident. The fact that non-belligerent nations in Europe showed the same tendency should, however, be noted here. Switzerland's ratio was 92·85 in 1920 and that of Norway was 93·67. This would suggest that the low ratios in North-Western Europe may be attributed to other factors as well, namely, the heavy drain caused by the emigration of males, and the high level of economic security enjoyed by European women, which prolongs their life-span.

The sex ratio in Japan was 102·95 in 1872, and this figure was maintained until 1896, when it dropped to 101. In 1908 it again reached 102. The census of 1920 recorded the ratio at 102·10, that of 1925 at 102·30, and the 1930 census showed a drop to 101·03.[1] Contrasting these ratios with those of European countries, alarmists score Japan for the low social position of its women on the ground that the

---

[1] *Tokei Zensho*, cited, p. 9.

excess of males is due to the high toll of female life resulting from the abuse of womanhood.

A conclusive study of the causes of the above high sex ratio, however, will reveal that the male births constantly exceed the female births anywhere from 2 to 8, and about 4 per 100, on an average per year.[1] In addition, the emigration movement, which usually means a heavier drain of men than of women, is almost negligible in Japan compared with that of European nations.

In cities, in the narrow sense, i.e. communities of over 30,000 population which are under municipal organization,[2] the ratio of males per 100 females was 108·7 in 1920, and in the vast non-city districts the ratio was less than par : 98·7. Small cities are like non-city districts in that the female population is greater than the male population. But the sex ratio in cities of over 50,000 population is so high that it not only makes up for the inferior ratio of males in the areas of all non-city districts and small cities, but brings the sex ratio of the whole nation to a high figure, i.e. 102·10 in 1920. Sex ratios in 1920 by population classes of communities in Japan are cited again in the following simplified table : [3]

TABLE XXXI

SEX RATIO OF POPULATION BY SIZE OF COMMUNITY, 1920

Size of Community.		Males per 100 Females.
Japan		102·1
Non-city districts		98·7
Cities		108·7
Cities under 30,000		91
30,000– 49,999		99
50,000– 99,999		105
100,000– 999,999		109
1,000,000 and over		117

The above table illustrates the differential distribution of the male and female population in rural districts and in cities according to size.

The municipal census of Tokyo in 1920 revealed the

[1] *Tokei Zensho*, cited, p. 13.   [2] *Supra*, p. 69.
[3] Nagaya, T., " Development of Cities and Urbanization of the Population," *Toshi Mondai*, Vol. II, 1926, p. 48.

following sex ratios according to the kind of household. " Secondary households " includes such living quarters as barracks, ships, dormitories, hospitals, poor houses and prisons.[1]

Common households .	.	.	.	.	111·98
Secondary households	.	:	.	.	344·04
Average for Tokyo .	.	.	.	.	116·88

It is noticeable that the sex ratio in common households, 111·98, exceeds the average ratio of all cities (108·7), as well as that of large cities of between 100,000 and 1,000,000 population, which is 109. However, the high ratio of 117 for all Tokyo, like the ratio for all cities of over one million population, is, to some degree at least, based on the extraordinarily high ratio of male population in secondary households.[2]

In a summary of the foregoing study, it may be said in brief that the excess of male population is concentrated in the large cities. We may note in this connection that Mr. Toshio Nagaya rather facetiously observed this situation by saying that the high sex ratio in Japan is due to the great number of soldiers, students and city labourers.

B. *Age Distribution*

Two tables on the next page list the age distribution in two forms ; the first divides the population into five-year age classes ; the second shows the age distribution by classifying the population into three age groups, i.e. minors, middle-aged and aged. Both tabulations deal with the period from 1884 to 1930.

These tables present a fair view of the trend of the age distribution of the Japanese population. The outstanding fact which the two tables reveal is the steady increase of younger groups in recent decades at the expense of older groups. The age class under fourteen, which occupied 316·2 per 1,000 in 1884, moved forward to 365·8 in 1930. During the same period the middle-age and old-

[1] *Ibid.*, p. 49.   [2] *Ibid.*, p. 50.

TABLE XXXII

DISTRIBUTION OF POPULATION BY FIVE-YEAR AGE PERIODS,
1884–1930 [1]

(Per 1,000 Population)

Age Period.	1884.	1893.	1903.	1913.	1920.	1925.	1930.
Under 5 . .	112·5	117·5	128·1	133·4	133·3	138·3	139·8
5–9 . . .	110·8	107·2	109·4	110·9	122·5	115·9	120·5
10–14 . . .	92·9	106·7	97·3	105·1	109·0	112·7	105·5
15–19 . . .	91·5	100·1	91·6	92·4	96·8	98·5	101·5
20–24 . . .	75·8	79·2	90·1	80·1	82·4	84·7	85·8
25–29 . . .	81·4	78·1	82·9	74·4	70·1	73·5	75·0
30–34 . . .	76·5	62·0	64·8	71·7	64·5	62·2	65·4
35–39 . . .	69·5	67·2	63·4	66·1	60·9	57·7	55·6
40–44 . . .	59·6	61·7	49·5	51·4	58·0	53·9	51·0
45–49 . . .	48·5	54·7	53·1	49·7	47·5	51·1	47·3
50–54 . . .	47·7	44·9	47·5	37·9	39·9	41·0	43·9
55–59 . . .	42·1	33·9	40·1	39·0	32·9	33·3	34·4
60–64 . . .	33·9	31·9	30·5	32·4	29·6	26·3	26·7
65–69 . . .	24·8	24·7	20·3	24·6	23·5	21·7	19·5
70–74 . . .	17·2	16·4	16·0	15·7	16·0	15·4	14·4
75–79 . . .	10·1	8·6	9·4	8·0	8·6	8·8	8·6
Over 80 . .	5·2	6·6	6·0	7·2	4·5	4·8	5·1

TABLE XXXIII

DISTRIBUTION OF THREE FUNCTIONAL AGE GROUPS, 1884–1930 [2]

(Per 1,000 Population)

Year	Under 15.	15–59.	60 and Over.
1884 . . .	316·2	592·6	91·0
1888 . . .	337·3	574·6	88·0
1893 . . .	331·0	581·8	87·1
1897 . . .	328·3	589·5	82·1
1902 . . .	334·8	583·0	82·2
1908 . . .	342·2	572·6	85·2
1913 . . .	349·4	562·7	87·9
1918 . . .	351·0	560·7	88·3
1920 . . .	364·8	553·0	82·2
1925 . . .	367·0	556·2	76·8
1930 . . .	365·8	559·3	74·9

[1] For 1884–93, *Tokei Nenkan*, cited, No. 27, 1908, pp. 36–7. For 1903–13, *ibid.*, No. 43, 1924, pp. 22–3. For 1920–30, *Showa Gonen Kokusei Chosa Kekka no Gaikan*, cited, Table 4.

[2] Honjo, E., *Jinko Oyobi Jinko Mondai*, cited, p. 200 ; *Tokei Nenkan*, cited, No. 43, 1924, p. 22 ; *Showa Gonen Kokusei Chosa Kekka no Gaikan*, cited, Table 4.

age classes dropped in ratios from 592·6 and 91·0 to 559·3 and 74·9 per 1,000 respectively. The inference that this tendency is alive and growing and is likely to be further accentuated in the immediate future may be drawn from the unprecedentedly high ratio of the infant class (four years of age and under). The ratio in 1930 was 139·8 per 1,000 as compared to 112·5 in 1884.

In the table below, the age distribution in Japan is compared to that of several other nations in the census year nearest to 1925.

TABLE XXXIV

DISTRIBUTION OF POPULATION BY FIVE-YEAR AGE PERIODS IN JAPAN AND OTHER SPECIFIED COUNTRIES [1]

(Per 1,000 Population)

Age Period.	Japan.	U.S.A.	Italy.	Germany.	England and Wales.	France.
Under 5 . . .	13·8	10·9	9·3	9·4	8·8	6·2
5–9	11·6	10·8	10·7	6·4	9·3	7·7
10–14 . . .	11·3	10·1	11·0	10·0	9·7	8·8
15–19 . . .	9·9	8·9	9·9	10·5	9·3	8·9
20–29 . . .	15·8	17·4	16·1	18·4	16·1	15·0
30–39 . . .	12·0	15·0	12·9	14·2	14·6	14·3
40–49 . . .	10·5	11·5	10·6	12·4	13·2	13·8
50–59 . . .	7·4	7·9	8·7	9·6	9·5	11·4
60 and Over .	7·7	7·6	10·9	9·2	9·4	14·0

Dates : U.S.A., 1920 ; Italy, England and Wales, France, 1921 ; Japan, Germany, 1925.

Were these comparative ratios of age distribution plotted in diagrams, one would see pyramidal shapes representing the age compositions of the populations of the United States and Japan. Of the two nations, the pyramid of the United States would show a gentler slope indicating imminent shrinkage of the base in the near future. The Japanese diagrams would have a heavier foundation, and, due to the shrinkage in the middle-age and old-age groups, the slope would be steeper.

[1] *Statistical Year-Book of League of Nations*, cited, 1932–3, Table 3.

Diagrams of the German and Italian population would show pyramidal shapes at the upper part but the bases would be weak and irregular. Compared with other countries, the German population in particular shows the effect of the Great War upon the numbers in its child-classes and in the group of middle-aged males. The diagrams would show somewhat of a shrinkage of minors from 10 to 15 years of age and an extraordinarily large shrinkage of the 5–9 year age group. The 0–4 group would show a gain but a little less than the 10–25 classes.

The diagram of England and Wales would show the maximum width at the age of 10–20 and narrow down near the base. In the case of France, the maximum width is the 15–20 group, and because of the large ratio of older groups the decline of the lower parts is more prominent. If the shape of the diagram of England and Wales could be said to resemble a dome, that of France might be spoken of as resembling a boat.

Inasmuch as the age classes, e.g. minors, middle-aged, and old-aged, do not have uniform proportional bearing upon the factors of occupation, marriage, divorce, birth and death, and since the distribution of these age classes shifts from year to year and from country to country, historical comparisons of crude demographic ratios of different countries, as, for example, the birth rate per 1,000 population, are sometimes meaningless. Hence the necessity for the computation of standardized ratios which are called adjusted, refined, or specific ratios. The above study in the sex and age distribution of the Japanese population is a preliminary step toward an intensive survey of the demographic trends of the nation.

§ 2. MARRIAGE AND DIVORCE

A. *Marriage Statistics in Japan*

Before entering upon a statistical survey of marriage, it must be noted that in Japan there are a considerable number of couples who are informally married. Many such informal

unions are entered into with the customary social or religious
ceremony of marriage, but they are informal unions because
they are not registered.   Under the vigilant unified family
registration system of Japan, the cancellation of the woman's
registration under her maiden name and her adoption into
her husband's family involve certain legal complications.
If the man is adopted into his wife's house a similar process
must be followed in his case.   The *ex post facto* nature of
marriage registration in Japan also contributes to a delay
in registrations.

Registration is a necessary requirement for the legal
validity of a marriage in Japan.   Recently, however, the
official attitude has tended to become more lenient.   Such
a modified view was adopted by the census authorities, and
since the first census of 1920 the reports on marital conditions cover not only the legal, but also the informal
marriages.

The comprehensive ratios of marital relations, as recorded
for 1925, are presented by five-year age groups in Table
XXXV.   As this table depicts, the ratio of married persons
to the total population in each of the five-year age groups
rises rapidly for men at the age period of 25–29 and for
women at 20–24.   The highest point of the specific marriage
ratio is reached among men at the age of 35–39 (92 per cent)
and among women at the age of 30–34 (90 per cent).   After
the prime of life is past the ratio of married persons drops,
gradually for men and rather sharply for women.   At the
age of 75–79, over 50 per cent of men are still married, while
the ratio for women falls below 50 per cent at the age limit
of 60–64.   Inasmuch as the table reveals that the reduction
in the number of married persons is mainly due to the death
of the partner, we may regard the smaller ratio of married
persons among aged women as a reflection of the younger
age of wives and the greater longevity of women as compared
with the opposite sex.[1]

[1] See age of marriage and the expectancy of life of men and women,
infra, pp. 97–9; 116, footnote.

TABLE XXXV
MARITAL CONDITIONS, BY AGE AND SEX GROUPS, 1925 [1]
(Per 1,000 of Specific Groups)

Age Period.	Unmarried.	Married.	Separated by Death.	Divorced.
I. *Male*				
Under 14 . . .	1,000·0	0	0	0
15–19	982·2	16·6	·1	1·1
20–24	724·5	260·3	2·3	12·9
25–29	249·5	716·9	9·2	24·4
30–34	71·4	889·7	15·9	23·0
35–39	34·3	920·4	24·2	21·1
40–44	22·6	917·1	38·9	21·4
45–49	19·3	899·3	59·4	22·0
50–54	15·0	875·4	86·7	22·9
55–59	12·4	839·4	125·5	22·7
60–64	10·1	789·3	178·0	22·6
65–69	9·3	712·2	257·0	21·5
70–74	8·3	618·8	353·7	19·3
75–79	7·5	506·6	469·7	16·3
80 and Over . .	6·5	364·2	616·8	12·6
II. *Female*				
Under 14 . . .	999·7	0·3	0	0
15–19	859·2	132·4	·8	7·6
20–24	295·6	670·7	6·5	27·2
25–29	78·1	876·2	16·8	29·0
30–34	35·4	903·9	34·3	26·4
35–39	22·9	889·3	62·3	25·5
40–44	18·9	849·2	104·9	27·0
45–49	17·9	789·6	163·7	28·8
50–54	14·3	711·1	246·0	28·5
55–59	11·2	597·8	364·5	26·5
60–64	8·7	483·9	484·6	22·8
65–69	7·3	352·0	621·8	18·9
70–74	6·0	231·2	747·1	15·7
75–79	5·7	132·5	849·5	12·3
80 and Over . .	4·8	53·6	932·3	9·2

B. *Informal Marriages and Illegitimate Births*

The preceding data includes both registered and informal marriages. All of the marriage statistics which follow were, however, derived from records of registered unions and have

[1] *Showa Gonen Kokusei Chosa Kekka no Gaikan*, cited, Table 3.

nothing to do with informal marriages. It is desirable, therefore, to separate the figures given above so as to show as accurately as possible the number of marriages which were legal and the number which were informal. In connection with this issue, it will be convenient to make a few remarks on the closely related subject of illegitimate births.

The computation of informal unions was made by the Bureau of Statistics by means of a comparison of the respective numbers of the legally married population in 1918 and the entire married population as reported by the census of 1925. It was estimated by this means that in 1925 there were 2,173,026 men and 2,039,644 women whose unions were informal.[1] These figures correspond to 18·3 per cent of the total number of married men and 16·9 per cent of the total number of married women, including those informally married.

The fact that many informal unions became legal ones before a child was born may be inferred from the report that in 1925 92·7 per cent of all births were legitimate, and only 7·3 per cent illegitimate. The ratio of illegitimate births has recently begun what appears to be a gradual decline. In the first decade of the twentieth century the ratio reached more than 10 per cent. After that it fell to 8 per cent by 1922, and by 1930 it had dropped to 6·44 per cent.[2] Yet even this is a very high rate compared to other nations. The Sanitary Bureau attributes this high ratio of illegitimate births to the quasi-official institution of informal marriages.[3] Nevertheless, the reduction of illegitimate births has considerable bearing on racial as well as social hygiene. The ratio of still-births among illegitimate children is very high ; in 1926 the rate of still-births per 100 live births among

---

[1] *Fubo no Nenrei to Shussei tono Kankei* (Relationship between the Age of Parents and Birth of Children), Bureau of Statistics, Japan, 1927, p. 46. The large discrepancy in the number of men and women informally married is perhaps due to the incompleteness of census enumeration of this factor.

[2] *Tokei Zensho*, cited, p. 13 ; *Jinko Dotai Tokei Kijutsuhen*, cited, 1930, p. 34.

[3] *Annual Report of the Sanitary Bureau*, Sanitary Bureau, Home Department, Japan, 1930, p. 91.

illegitimate children was 14·3 as compared to the 4·6 which prevailed among legitimate births.[1]

C. *Trend of Marriage Rates*

Marriage is generally held to be the most stable factor among the ever-changing features of vital statistics in advanced nations in recent decades. Since 1886 the annual marriage rates in Japan have not shifted far from the mark of 8 or 9 per 1,000 inhabitants. The quinquennial averages from 1886 to 1930 always remained at the mark of 8 per 1,000 except for 1896–1900, when it rose to 9·1.

The actual number of marriages gradually rose from 315,000 in 1886 to half a million in 1918. At this point the increase was arrested, except for some minor fluctuations, until 1920, when the number jumped to 546,000. Since the population increased during this period of 1918–30 by nearly 8 millions, the annual rate of marriage declined from 9·0 to 7·9 for the corresponding years. This is, however, not conclusive evidence of a real decline.

As has been pointed out in previous pages,[2] the age composition of the population underwent a great change during the period under consideration, in favour of the group below marriageable age. Consequently, the rate of married persons per 1,000 general population may not be used as a guide in our study of the trend of marriage. Therefore, the writer has attempted to determine the trend of marriages in specific age groups. Because of the lack of uniform reports on the ages of married persons in the period to be considered, it is necessary to arrive at our results by relating the number of marriages among inhabitants of all ages to the population aged 15–34. It is true that the ratio so derived is not a true specific for the age group of 15–34. However, inasmuch as the great majority of marriages occur between the ages of 15 and 34,[3] this device may serve as a better

[1] *Annual Report of the Sanitary Bureau*, Sanitary Bureau, Home Department, Japan, 1930, p. 91.
[2] See *supra*, pp. 89–91.
[3] In 1930 this age group contributed 85·95 per cent of the marriages among men and 93·67 per cent of marriages among women.

approach to the examination of the marriage trend than the marriage rate per 1,000 gross population. The rate thus calculated, when contrasted to the ordinary marriage rate at about five-year intervals since 1898, reveals the following interesting facts :

TABLE XXXVI

NUMBER OF MARRIAGES, RATE OF MARRIAGE PER 1,000 POPULATION AND RATE OF MARRIAGE OF ALL AGES PER 1,000 POPULATION, AGED 15–34, 1898–1935 [1]

Year.	Number of Marriages.	Rate per 1,000 Population.	Population aged 15–34.	Rate of all Marriages per 1,000 Population aged 15–34.
1898	471,298	10·8	14,600,999	32
1903	370,961	8·0	15,390,001	24
1908	461,254	9·4	16,240,243	28
1913	431,287	8·2	16,999,040	25
1918	500,580	9·0	17,975,983	28
1920	546,207	9·8	17,561,766	31
1925	521,438	8·7	19,055,362	27
1930	506,674	7·9	21,120,409	24
1935	556,730	8·0	—	—

Both of the above rates show fluctuations at the same time, but the fluctuations of the second rate are wider and its course is more difficult to determine. However, it is evident from the three successive censuses of 1920, 1925, and 1930, that the rate of marriage in this age group declined from 31 to 27 and finally to 24. Inasmuch as the figures in these census years are generally regarded as reliable, this decline in the marriage rate cannot be ignored.

D. *Age of Marriages*

The following figures, giving in five-year periods the average age at which first marriages take place for both sexes, throw

[1] *Tokei Nenkan*, cited, No. 43, 1924, pp. 22–3 ; *Showa Gonen Kokusei Chosa Kekka no Gaikan*, cited, Table 2 ; *Annual Report of the Sanitary Bureau*, cited, 1930, pp. 86–7 ; *The Tokyo Asahi*, Oct. 6, 1933.

much light on the complex movements of the marriage trend.

TABLE XXXVII
Average Age of First Marriage by Sexes, 1908–30 [1]

Period.	Male.		Female.		Excess of Age of Males.
	Age.	Index.	Age.	Index.	
1908–10 . . .	26·88	100·0	22·92	100·0	3·96
1911–15 . . .	27·06	100·7	22·97	100·2	4·09
1916–20 . . .	27·29	101·5	23·16	101·0	4·13
1921–25 . . .	27·06	100·7	23·05	100·7	4·01
1926–30 . . .	27·25	101·4	23·13	100·9	4·12

The above table indicates that during the periods covered the average age of persons entering first marriages rose to a peak for both sexes during the years 1916–20. It dropped somewhat in the next five-year period, but more recently the tendency has been towards the mark set in 1916–20.

The following table reveals the distribution of specified groups of age of marriage per 1,000 first marriages.

TABLE XXXVIII
Distribution of Specified Groups of Age of Marriage, 1909–30 [2]
(Per 1,000 First Marriages)

Period.	Under 20.	20–24.	25–29.	30–39.	40–49.	50 and Over.
		I. *Male*				
1909–13 . . .	56·9	359·0	366·9	182·6	27·2	7·4
1914–18 . . .	47·7	352·9	375·5	182·2	32·3	9·4
1919–23 . . .	43·4	358·0	383·5	172·0	32·7	10·4
1924–28 . . .	30·1	356·0	417·5	159·6	26·8	10·0
1929–30 . . .	23·6	326·3	450·3	164·0	25·4	10·4
		II. *Female*				
1909–13 . . .	307·0	448·7	155·9	74·8	11·2	2·4
1914–18 . . .	299·2	455·0	149·5	77·6	15·4	3·3
1919–23 . . .	280·6	486·9	142·9	68·5	17·1	4·0
1924–28 . . .	262·6	511·8	146·0	59·9	15·1	4·6
1929–30 . . .	231·5	544·3	146·2	58·8	14·1	5·1

[1] *Jinko Dotai Tokei Kijutsuhen*, cited, 1930, p. 6.　　[2] *Ibid.*, p. 7.

This table shows us that during the interval between the 1909–13 period and the 1929–30 period the ratio of distribution of groups of age of marriage per 1,000 first marriages rose sharply for males at 25–29, and slightly for those over 50. It is noteworthy, however, that the ratio declined not only among younger groups but also among groups of ages between 30 and 49. This same tendency holds true for females, except that the greatest number of first marriages takes place in the 20–24 age group. It is the writer's opinion that the concentration of first marriages in these two age groups, i.e. 25–29 for the male and 20–24 for the female, is one of the stabilizing factors in family life. Particularly notable is its influence on divorce, which we are now in a position to consider.

E. *Divorces*

Japan has in the past been reputed to have a high rate of divorce. In 1883, when the first divorce statistics were obtained, there were 127,162 divorces, the rate per 1,000 inhabitants being 3·39. In 1898 the annual number of divorces had dropped below 100,000, and by 1909 it reached the 50,000 level. It has remained constant at that point ever since, despite the fact that the population has increased in the intervening years. Hence the rate of divorces per 1,000 population has steadily declined and in 1920 it reached the European standard—which is below 1·0.

The number of divorces will be cited together with the rate of divorces per 1,000 population and the rate per 100 marriages which have taken place in the same calendar year at five-year intervals since 1883. The estimated rates in the United States as recorded in the *World Almanac* are also cited for comparison.

The rapid decline in both the actual number and the rate of divorce in Japan since the beginning of this century is too obvious for extensive comment. In Japan the will of the husband is still the dominant factor in family relationships. Thus the divorces through " mutual agreement " between the parties involved (such divorces in 1930 represented 99·3

TABLE XXXIX

NUMBER OF DIVORCES IN JAPAN, RATE OF DIVORCE PER 1,000
POPULATION AND PER 100 MARRIAGES IN JAPAN AND THE
UNITED STATES, 1883–1935 [1]

Year.	Number of Divorces, Japan.	Rate per 1,000 Population.		Rate per 100 Marriages.	
		Japan.	U.S.A.	Japan.	U.S.A.
1883 . .	127,162	3·39	—	26·5	—
1885 . .	113,565	2·97	—	22·9	—
1890 . .	109,088	2·69	0·53	33·5	5·9
1895 . .	110,838	2·62	0·58	30·3	6·5
1900 . .	63,828	1·42	0·73	18·4	7·9
1905 . .	60,061	1·26	0·82	17·1	8·2
1910 . .	59,432	1·17	0·90	13·5	8·8
1915 . .	59,942	1·10	1·05	13·5	10·4
1920 . .	55,511	0·99	1·60	10·2	13·4
1925 . .	51,687	0·87	1·52	9·9	14·8
1930 . .	51,259	0·80	1·58	10·1	16·9
1935 . .	48,528	0·70	—	8·7	—

per cent of the total) often represent nothing more than an
unwilling consent wrung from the wife by her husband. In
view of this fact, the rapid decline in divorce is an exceed-
ingly encouraging sign.

F. *Relationship of Marriage to Fertility*

Marriage remains the customary channel for childbirth.
Yet since the last quarter of the last century, it has become
an established fact in the Western world that there is no
longer a direct correlation between the marriage rate and
the birth rate. As a typical case illustrating the discrepancy
between the rates, the marriage and birth rates of England
and Wales, and as a more moderate example, those of

[1] *Tokei Zensho*, cited, p. 12 ; *Annual Report of the Sanitary Bureau*,
cited, 1930, pp. 86–7 ; *Jinko Dotai Tokei Kijutsuhen*, cited, 1930, p. 17 ;
The Tokyo Asahi, Oct. 6, 1933 ; *World Almanac*, New York, World-
Telegram Co., 1934, p. 246.

Germany, will be cited below in five-year averages at twenty-year intervals beginning with 1886.

TABLE XL

MARRIAGE AND BIRTH RATES OF ENGLAND AND WALES AND
GERMANY, 1886–90, 1906–10, 1926–30 [1]

Rates per 1,000
Population.

		1886–90.	1906–10.	1926–30.
I. *England and Wales*				
Marriage rate .	.	7·9	8·0	7·6
Birth rate .	.	31·4	26·1	16·8
II. *Germany*				
Marriage rate .	.	7·4	7·6	8·7
Birth rate .	.	36·5	31·6	18·4

In both cases the marriage rates maintained an almost constant level throughout the forty years, yet the birth rate in that period declined to almost one-half. In Germany the decline of the birth rate was slower but after the Great War it fell considerably. These rates are crude rates. However, the increasing discrepancy between both sets of figures is too great to be attributed to the increasingly changing age distribution in both nations. The causal factor in this discrepancy must be found in an artificial element intervening between the natural marital relationship and physiological child-bearing.

The corresponding rates in Japan were as follows :

TABLE XLI

MARRIAGE AND BIRTH RATES OF JAPAN, 1886–90, 1906–10, 1926–30 [2]

Rates per 1,000
Population.

		1886–90.	1906–10.	1926–30.
Marriage rate .	.	6·8	7·4	8·7
Birth rate .	.	26·9	30·4	34·9

Pending a detailed study of those forces which inhibit child-bearing in Japan, which will be considered in Chapter XI, at this point it may be stated that in Japan the factors controlling the rate of births vary greatly from those of the Occident. It is because of this very condition that the recent trend in the advancement of the age of marriage is worthy of serious attention.

[1] *Annual Report of the Sanitary Bureau*, cited, 1930, pp. 88, 93.
[2] *Ibid.*, pp. 4, 5, 11, 14.

The Bureau of Statistics of Japan, in its investigation in 1927, which was based upon the census data of 1925, has made a unique contribution to the study of the relationship between the ages of parents and the frequency of child-bearing. From that study we know that in 1925, one-quarter of the legitimate children born were fathered by men aged 26·9 years and under, one-half by men 31·7 years and under, and three-quarters by men 38·6 years and under. Further, viewed from the angle of maternity, one-quarter of the legitimate children born were mothered by women aged 22·8 years and under, one-half by those aged 27·1 years and under, and three-quarters by those aged 33·6 and under. Illegitimate births, as compared to legitimate births, were extended over both younger and older age groups for both fathers and mothers. The Bureau of Statistics, in this same study, went through much painstaking labour to compute the specific fertility rates of married persons of both sexes. Since the ages of fathers of illegitimate children are officially unknown, the Bureau computed the specific fertility rate of married men and women for legitimate births, and the rate of formally unmarried women for illegitimate births. The statistics of the latter rate will be omitted from our analysis here.

As has been noted before,[1] the census enumeration of the married population includes informal marriages. The Bureau of Statistics applies, therefore, the ratio of formally married persons at each age of the population in 1918 to the corresponding age population in 1925. By dividing this estimate of the formally married population in 1925 by the legitimate births at each age of parents, the following rates of fertility per 1,000 specific married population were deduced.

The table opposite indicates that at the age of 15 the fertility rate is 463 per 1,000 married women. For females between the ages of 17 and 21 it is more than 500, the peak being 545 at the age of 19. After 19 the rate declines rather rapidly, closing with zero at 50. For men the fertility is 363 at the age of 17 and the peak comes at 23, when the rate

[1] See *supra*, p. 93.

TABLE XLII
Specific Fertility of Married Men and Women [1]
(Per 1,000 of Specific Groups)

Age.	Per 1,000 Married Men.	Per 1,000 Married Women.	Age.	Per 1,000 Married Men.	Per 1,000 Married Women.
15	—	462·573	45	130·480	15·513
16	—	492·608	46	110·856	9·778
17	363·035	543·235	47	90·823	7·104
18	407·731	507·194	48	77·830	4·673
19	470·056	545,237	49	58,960	1·568
20	461·953	544·603	50	49·126	—
21	493·262	515·208	51	39·734	—
22	498·981	462·767	52	31·393	—
23	536·227	433·649	53	24·738	—
24	491·303	395·664	54	20·995	—
25	467·643	371·668/	55	17·534	—
26	457·524	363·705	56	13·959	—
27	420·382	342·822	57	9·579	—
28	401·338	330·809	58	8·460	—
29	393·791	320·208	59	7·063	—
30	368·043	303·639	60	5·032	—
31	350·483	289·044	61	4·303	—
32	341·776	284·244	62	3·325	—
33	315·019	260·034	63	2·475	—
34	315·144	262·648	64	2·384	—
35	303·809	250·947	65	1·554	—
36	285·742	228·741	66	1·520	—
37	264·871	211·218	67	1·341	—
38	256·867	195·062	68	1·042	—
39	247·127	149·158	69	1·174	—
40	230·502	119·222			
41	210·228	92·553			
42	191·909	65·741			
43	173·424	42·456			
44	151·057	26·379			

is 536. Compared with that of women, men's fertility declines more slowly as their age advances, and extends for a longer period ; at 30 years the rate is 368, at 40 it is 231, above 47 years the rate declines to less than 100, and in the group above 57 years of age it is less than 10.

To arrive at the rate of fecundity (power of child-bearing), as opposed to that of fertility (actual number of child-births),

[1] *Fubo no Nenrei to Shussei tono Kankei*, cited, p. 49.

the number of births previously reported by each couple must be adjusted. This, due to the present incomplete state of statistical material, is quite definitely impossible.[1]

When we consider the above table on fertility in respect to our study of the marriage rates, we find that the average age of men, 27·25, and that of women, 23·13, are more than four years beyond the corresponding ages for the peaks of fertility. From the previous table we can calculate the probable decline in fertility due to a year's delay in marriage during the course of five years following the peak of fertility, i.e. between the age of 19 and 24 among females, and of 23 and 28 among males, as follows:

TABLE XLIII

PROBABLE DECLINE OF FERTILITY DUE TO DELAY OF ONE YEAR IN MARRIAGE PER 1,000 MARRIED MEN AND WOMEN AT SPECIFIED AGES

Delay of One Year at Age	Decline in Fertility per 1,000 Men.	Delay of One Year at Age	Decline in Fertility per 1,000 Women.
23	44·924	19	0·634
24	23·660	20	29·395
25	10·119	21	52·441
26	37·142	22	29·118
27	19·044	23	37·985

The above table graphically illustrates the point previously made: the recent advance in the age of both men and women entering first marriages conduces to an appreciable decline in the fertility rates. Hence this advance in the marriage-age, in view of its significance in the fertility rate, must be considered as a potent force in the study of the vital trends of the nation.

To sum up, the existence of the quasi-official institution of informal marriage complicates the compilation of the marriage statistics of Japan. The relatively high rate of illegitimacy is also partially due to this social but non-legal institution of informal marriage. Nevertheless, the rate of still-births compared to that of live-births is high

[1] The census authorities of Japan planned to collect elaborate statistical data on the fertility of men and women, incorporating this material into the census of October 1, 1935. Due to financial considerations, however, this plan may be postponed. See *supra*, p. 51.

among illegitimate births ; hence the recent reduction of illegitimacy greatly contributes to the decrease in the nation's rate of still-births.

The rate of marriage in Japan has steadily declined in recent years. At the same time the age of marriage has tended toward a concentration at the age period of 25–29 for men and at 20–24 for women. The steady decline in the divorce rate in recent years may possibly be considered as a concomitant of this concentration.

In its relationship to the stability of society as expressed in the institution of the family, the decrease in divorces may be regarded as a force counterbalancing the effects of the declining rate of marriage. However, the prime of fertility, which was computed as occurring at the age of 23 for men and at 19 for women, is followed by a sharp decrease in fertility. The advancement in the age of marriage, therefore, portends further change in the birth rate of the nation.

§ 3. FERTILITY

A. *Trend of Crude Birth Rates*

As in the case of the death rate, the birth rate was low in Japan at the beginning of the Meiji Period. Table LV (pp. 124–6) shows that in 1872 the birth rate was 17·1 per 1,000. The average for 1872–5 was 22·8. Expressed in quinquennial averages, the birth rate has risen gradually ever since.

The rates are far lower than those of North-western Europe,[1] which exceeded 32·0 in every five-year average between 1861 and 1880. After the latter date, the European rates began to drop. The declining birth rate in North-western Europe and the rising rate in Japan crossed each other at about the end of the last century, a period which marked Japan's entry in the field of industrial activity. Since then the two sets of birth rates have never met. The north-

[1] N.W. Europe : Present territory of Belgium, Denmark, Gt. Britain and N. Ireland, Ireland, Finland, France, Germany, Saar Territory, Holland, Luxemburg, Sweden, and Switzerland. Kuczynski, R. R., *The Balance of Births and Deaths*, New York, Macmillan, 1928–31, Vol. I, p. 9.

western European rate was but 55 per cent of Japan's in 1926.

The two trends mentioned above are compared in the following table:

TABLE XLIV

BIRTH RATES OF JAPAN AND NORTH-WESTERN EUROPE, 1871–1926 [1]
(Per 1,000 Population)

Year.	Japan.	N.W. Europe.
1871–75	22·8 (1872–5)	32·7
1876–80	25·0	32·8
1881–85	26·0	31·4
1886–90	28·5	30·2
1891–95	28·6	29·7
1896–1900 . . .	31·0	29·4
1901–05	31·8	28·4
1906–10	32·7	26·6
1911–15	33·5	24·2 (1911–4)
1916–20	33·0	17·0 (1915–9)
1920–21	35·7	23·8
1922–23	34·6	21·0
1924–25	34·4	19·9
1926	34·8	19·2

For the definition of North-Western Europe see footnote, page 105.

The upward trend of the Japanese rate continued steadily, reaching the peak five-year average of 34·6 in the 1921–5 period. The high point of the annual birth rate was 36·2 in 1920. Since then the tendency has been toward a decline. The quinquennial average for 1931–5 was 31·7. It must be noted that the Japanese peak of the five-year birth rate average, i.e. 34·6 (1921–5), was close to the five-year average in Germany for 1901–5, which was 34·3; and the peak of the annual rate in Japan, 36·2 in 1920, was lower than the birth rate of Austria in 1902, 37·0. It may be added that the birth rate of many Eastern European countries is still as high as Japan's. For example, as late as 1926, the rate in Bulgaria was 37·3. [2]

The actual number of births per year since 1920 has ranged from 1·9 to 2·1 millions. The slow increase in the

---

[1] *Ibid.*, p. 9; *Tokei Zensho*, cited, p. 12.
[2] *Jinko Dotai Tokei Kijutsuhen*, cited, 1930, p. 115; *Annual Report of the Sanitary Bureau*, cited, 1930, p. 93.

number of births, accompanied by the marked increase in the total population, due to the rapid decline in the number of deaths, was followed by a tendency toward a declining birth rate—a point which was considered in previous pages. The actual number of births since 1920 and the rates of these births per 1,000 population are cited below. These figures are taken from Table LV (pp. 124–6) :

TABLE XLV

Number of Births and Birth Rate, 1920–35 [1]
(Per 1,000 Population)

Year.	Number of Births.	Birth Rate (per 1,000).
1920	2,025,564	36·2
1921	1,990,876	35·1
1922	1,969,314	34·2
1923	2,043,297	34·9
1924	1,998,520	33·8
1925	2,086,091	34·9
Average * . . .	2,017,620	34·6
1926	2,104,405	34·8
1927	2,060,737	33·6
1928	2,135,852	34·4
1929	2,077,026	33·0
1930	2,085,101	32·4
Average . . .	2,092,624	33·6
1931	2,102,784	32·1
1932	2,182,743	32·9
1933	2,121,125	31·6
1934	2,043,807	30·0
1935	2,190,681	31·6
Average . . .	2,128,228	31·7

* Average for 1921–5.

Whether this relative decline in the birth rate will continue, or whether some other tendency will manifest itself in the near future, cannot be determined by studying the crude birth rates alone ; we must carefully examine the qualitative aspects of population statistics, i.e. the age and sex distributions, in order to arrive at well-founded conclusions.

[1] *Ibid.*, p. 92 ; *The Tokyo Nichinichi*, June 19, 1934.

B. *Trend of Refined Birth Rates*

The pivotal point in the study of population trends is
that of the relationship of deaths to births.   There is, however, a definite limit to the extent to which the death rate
of a nation may be changed, for every man dies sometime
or other, and the effect on the ultimate population trend is
at most secondary.   This is especially true of the reduction
of the number of deaths among age classes which have
passed the reproduction period.   The decline of deaths
among these classes cannot counteract or counterpoise the
decline in births.   Herein lies the significance of the study
of births for the estimate of the future trend of population.

The first step in determining the real trend of births is the
computation of the ratio of women of child-bearing age.
It has been noted in Section 1 that the ratio of the middle-
aged group has declined in Japan during recent years.[1]
The ratio of women between the ages of 15 and 49 is 47 per
100.   Professor Crocker compared these statistics of Japan
with those of three other nations in the census year nearest
to 1925, and his figures demonstrated that the Japanese ratio
ranks lowest.[2]   The ratio nearest to that of Japan is that
of France, which is 52 per 100.   In view of the high crude
birth rate of Japan, this low ratio of women of child-bearing
age obviously indicates a very high rate of births per female
of the specified age period.   The annual number of births
of Japan per woman aged 15 to 49 is 0·15 compared to
0·12 of England and Wales, the nearest figure.

According to Professor Crocker, there is one other element
in population statistics which must be given attention
in any consideration of the population trend.   It is the
ratio of female children aged 1 to 14 to all females.   In
this ratio Japan again leads all the European countries
enumerated.

These three ratios as compiled by Crocker are tabulated
as follows :

[1] *Supra*, pp. 89–92.
[2] Crocker, W. R., *The Japanese Population Problem*, London, G. Allen
& Unwin Co., 1931, p. 90.

TABLE XLVI

RATIO OF FEMALES AGED 14–49 PER 100 FEMALES, ANNUAL NUMBER
OF BIRTHS PER FEMALE AGED 15–49, AND RATIO OF FEMALES
UNDER 15 PER 100 FEMALES, OF JAPAN AND OTHER SPECIFIED
NATIONS [1]

Country.	Ratio of Females aged 14–49 per 100, All Females.	Annual Births per Female aged 15–49.	Ratio of Females aged 1–14 per 100, All Females.
Japan . . .	47	·15	36
Italy	—	—	30
Germany . .	55	·07	26
England and Wales	54	·12	—
France . .	52	·07	21

The above statistics reveal the significant factor behind the recently demonstrated declining trend of the birth rate. At present the Japanese rate appears unreasonably low because, in spite of the high reproductivity of each woman, the ratio of women of child-bearing ages is low. However, the high proportion of future mothers will increase the birth rate in the near future to such a degree as to nullify the effects of any birth control movements. This is the keynote of Crocker's work on the Japanese population problem, which is subtitled *The Coming Crisis*.

In the foregoing study, the present position of Japan's population in relation to the figures of other nations has been roughly estimated. The historical aspect of the Japanese trend remains to be studied in the light of a similarly refined technique.

Professor Crocker computed the refined birth rate per married woman aged 15–44 since 1898. He overlooked, however, the fact which has been noted in Section 2 of this chapter,[2] viz. that the list of married women prior to 1920 excluded those informally married, whereas the census reports since 1920 have included this group. With this disparity in view, Dr. Teijiro Ueda of Tokyo Commercial College computed the annual birth rates per females aged 15–44. Compared to crude rates they are as follows :

[1] *Ibid.*, pp. 80–92.   [2] See *supra*, pp. 92–6.

TABLE XLVII
Birth Rate per 1,000 Population and Annual Rate of Births per Females aged 15–44, 1898–1930 [1]

Year.	Birth Rate per 1,000 Population.	Annual Births per Females aged 15–44.
1898	. . . . . 31·3	·141
1903	. . . . . 32·0	·146
1908	. . . . . 33·7	·154
1913	. . . . . 33·2	·153
1918	. . . . . 32·2	·146
1920	. . . . . 36·2	·169
1925	. . . . . 34·9	·165
1930	. . . . . 32·4	·157

The above fertility table for women aged 15–44 shows that there are two peaks, one in 1908 and the other in 1920. Since 1920, in which year the highest point was reached, the fertility has been steadily declining. These figures reveal a very high correlation between the fertility rate and the crude birth rate, but this may perhaps be regarded as only a coincidence. It is to the refined birth rate that we must refer, and upon that we must base our study if we are to find the basic underlying current of the population trend.

C. *Application of Kuczynski Methods of Computation of Net-Fertility*

Devices such as these refined birth rates are important achievements in the field of vital statistics. These methods, however, neglect a qualitative analysis of the group of women of child-bearing ages ; that is, they disregard the age distribution within the group. Logically, chronological comparisons of all specific birth rates should be made. As a matter of fact, however, this process involves the calculation of thirty-five specific birth rates, between the ages of 15 and 49, in every year, and a comparison of such numerous rates makes the whole picture vague.

At this point, we must turn to Robert R. Kuczynski,[2]

[1] Ueda, T., " An Estimate of Future Population of Japan," *Social Reform*, No. 152, May, 1933, p. 15, or ——, Editor, *Nihon Jinko Mondai Kenkyu* (Studies of Japanese Population Problem), Tokyo, Kyochokai, 1933, p. 20.

[2] Kuczynski, R. R., *op. cit.*, p. 21 ; ——, *Fertility and Reproduction*, New York, Falcon, 1932, p. 7.

who, as early as 1907, recognized this problem and proposed a remedial method of statistical analysis. By adding all the thirty-five specific birth rates of one year, Kuczynski arrived at what he terms " the total fertility rate." This total rate denotes exactly the number of children to be born to a given number of women of child-bearing age ; it further assumes that the fertility of these women remains unchanged and that none of them dies before passing the child-bearing age.

Applying this total fertility rate to the female births only, Kuczynski obtained a rate which he called the gross reproduction rate. The method of the calculation is indicated by the formula :

$$\frac{\text{Total fertility rate} \times \text{Female births}}{\text{Total number of births}} = \text{Gross reproduction rate.}$$

From the material obtained by the Bureau of Statistics concerning the " Relationship Between the Age of Parents and the Birth of Children," which has been cited extensively in § 2 of this chapter,[1] Mr. Takeo Soda, of the Kyochokai, or the Association for Harmonious Co-operation, calculated the gross reproduction rate of Japan in 1925. This Japanese rate will be compared to the European rates for the year 1926, calculated by Kuczynski as follows :

TABLE XLVIII

BIRTH RATE PER 1,000 POPULATION AND GROSS REPRODUCTION RATE OF JAPAN AND OTHER SPECIFIED NATIONS, 1926 [2]

Country.	Birth Rate (per 1,000).	Gross Reproduction Rate.
Japan (1925)	34·9	2·39
Finland	21·7	1·43
Denmark	20·5	1·27
Norway	19·7	1·33
Germany	19·5	1·07
France	18·8	1·15
England and Wales	17·8	1·05
Sweden	18·9	1·11

The gross reproduction rate of Japan, 2·39, signifies that 100 women give birth (live) to 239 female children,

[1] *Supra*, p. 102 ff.
[2] Soda, T., " Estimate of Population Growth," Series I, *Social Reform*, No. 150, March, 1933, p. 34, or Ueda, T., Editor, *op. cit.*, p. 84.

assuming none of the 100 women dies between the ages of
15 and 50.

Next, instead of assuming that none of the 100 women
dies during their child-bearing ages, Kuczynski adjusted his
figures to mortality rates.   By applying these rates for female
births only he derived what he calls the " net reproduction
rate." [1]   Necessary data for this calculation are the number
of women in each of the child-bearing ages, specific female
births, and finally, a life table for females.   Mr. Soda calculated such a net reproduction rate of Japan for 1925.   He
based his calculations upon the materials derived from the
" Relationship Between the Age of Parents and the Birth of
Children," which has been mentioned already, and the fourth
life table of the Bureau of Statistics, which is based upon the
mortality statistics between 1921 and 1925.   By this method
Mr. Soda found the net reproduction rate to be 1·495.
This Japanese rate will be compared with those of European
nations classified in two groups, north-western and south-
western.   The figures of European Nations follow :

TABLE XLIX

NET REPRODUCTION RATE OF NORTH-WESTERN AND SOUTH-EASTERN
EUROPEAN NATIONS [2]

N.W. Europe.	Year.	Rate.	S.E. Europe.	Year.	Rate.
Finland . .	1921–5	1·146	Russia . .	1928	1·70
Sweden . .	1921–2	1·137	Ukraine .	1929	1·40
Denmark .	1926	1·097	Italy . .	1921–2	1·40
England and			Poland . .	1927	1·30
Wales . .	1921	1·087	Bulgaria .	1929	1·30
France . .	1922–5	0·937	E. Czecho-		
Germany .	1925	0·937	slovakia .	1929	1·30
Latvia . .	1929	0·900	Hungary .	1930	1·20
Estonia . .	1929	0·650	Austria . .	1928	0·80

The net reproduction rate " 1 " indicates that the popula-
tion is merely maintaining its *status quo*.   France, Germany,
Latvia, Austria and Estonia do not reproduce themselves.
To illustrate this condition, the case of Austria will be

---

[1] Kuczynski, R. R., *Balance of Births and Deaths*, cited, pp. 42–4.
[2] *Ibid.*, cited, Vol. I, pp. 50–1 ; Vol. II, 1931, p. 64.

examined briefly. One thousand women born in Austria in 1926, when adjusted to the prevailing fertility and mortality rates of women, will produce only 800 females before they pass the child-bearing age. Hence Austria is not reproducing herself.

In this respect Japan's condition presents a considerable contrast to the situation existent in many north-western European countries. In fact, Japan is practically in the same position as many south-eastern European nations. Her net reproduction rate, being 1·495, signifies an increase of approximately 50 per cent for a generation. Hence, if we assume that a generation corresponds to a period of thirty years, the population of Japan will be 96,378,537 in 1960.

The above-mentioned Kuczynski methods are undoubtedly some of the most important contributions made in the field of vital statistics. Nevertheless, these methods are based on many assumptions which may not necessarily satisfy a more searching analysis. The net reproduction rate assumes not only a static population based on a life table and an even age distribution, but also presupposes a fertility rate for new-born females equal to that of their mothers.

This last assumption is decidedly a questionable one ; to render it tenable, all the economic and social factors in the population trend would, necessarily, be ineffectual and devoid of significance. This is contrary to factual data and to general opinion among students of population problems. Consequently other estimates of fertility and the future trend of the population will be considered later, in § 5 of this chapter.

§ 4. Mortality

A. *General Trend of Death Rates*

Resolved into their simplest terms, all population problems can be stated in terms of birth and death. We are now in a position to examine these very important factors. Table LV of the appendix at the end of this section shows that the death rate in 1872 was 12·2 per 1,000 and the average for the following five years, 1876–80, was 17·9. These

I

rates were far lower than those of any European country at that time. However, although the European trend had already begun to decline at that period, the Japanese death rate took an upward direction, so that by 1890 the five-year average rate had increased to 20.

The annual average death rate in five-year periods was maintained at this level of 20 until 1911–15, the only exception being the period of 1891–5, when it rose to 21·1. The average rate increased rapidly to 23·6 in the 1916–20 period, due, undoubtedly, to the world-wide epidemic of influenza in 1918, in which year the death rate rose to 26·8—a record never before or since reached in Japan. Another high annual rate, 25·4 in 1920, is misleading in that it was partially due to the more precise computations of the census inaugurated in that year, which eliminated certain erroneous figures from the basic population.[1] Although the 1916–20 period marks the peak of the death rate of Japan thus far, the next five-year period, 1921–5, showed a considerable decline—21·9. The rate further declined during the two quinquennial periods of 1926–30 and 1931–5, when it was reported as 19·4 and 17·9 respectively. The latest annual rate available, that of 1935, was 16·8, the lowest point attained since 1881.

The actual number of deaths in each year since 1920 is cited below, together with the rates per 1,000 population.

TABLE L

NUMBER AND RATE OF DEATHS PER 1,000 POPULATION, 1920–35 [2]

Year.					Number of Deaths.	Death Rate (per 1,000).
1920 .	.	.	.	.	1,422,096	25·4
1921 .	.	.	.	.	1,288,570	22·7
1922 .	.	.	.	.	1,286,941	22·3
1923 .	.	.	.	.	1,332,485	22·8
1924 .	.	.	.	.	1,254,946	21·2
1925 .	.	.	.	.	1,210,706	20·3
Average *		.	.	.	1,274,730	21·9

* Average for 1921–5.

[1] See *supra*, p. 56.
[2] *The Tokyo Nichinichi*, July 19, 1934 ; *Annual Report of the Sanitary Bureau*, cited, 1930, p. 100.

TABLE L (*continued*)

NUMBER AND RATE OF DEATHS PER 1,000 POPULATION, 1920–35

Year.					Number of Deaths.	Death Rate (per 1,000).
1926	.	.	.	.	1,160,734	19·2
1927	.	.	.	.	1,214,323	19·8
1928	.	.	.	.	1,236,711	19·9
1929	.	.	.	.	1,261,228	20·0
1930	.	.	.	.	1,170,867	18·2
Average	.	.	.	.	1,208,773	19·4
1931	.	.	.	.	1,240,891	19·0
1932	.	.	.	.	1,174,875	17·7
1933	.	.	.	.	1,193,916	17·8
1934	.	.	.	.	1,234,583	18·1
1935	.	.	.	.	1,162,058	16·8
Average	.	.	.	.	1,201,265	17·9

In recapitulation, several pertinent points concerning the death rate in Japan may now be made : the death rate was unusually low in the early Meiji Period ; within three quinquennial periods, or by 1886, the rate had risen to 20 per 1,000 population and continued at this level until 1915 ; during the Great War and in the post-War period the annual death rate reached the peak ; since then the general trend has been downward.[1]

Although, owing to divergent age distribution from nation to nation, international comparisons of crude death rates are sometimes without value, we must conclude that the recent Japanese average death rate of about 20 is extra-ordinarily high. Even the lowest record of recent decades, the 16·8 point reached in 1935, is nearly double the death rate of The Netherlands in 1930, which was reported as 9·1, and ranks with the rates of Spain and Portugal, which were 17·3 and 18·8 respectively in 1930.

It must be noted, however, that the peak annual death rate of Japan, 26·8 in 1918, and the peak quinquennial average rate, 23·6 in 1916–20, are rather low compared to the high rates once prevalent among certain other nations which now have low rates. As late as 1886–90, the five-year averages of Austria, Italy, Germany and The Netherlands

[1] For footnote, see next page.

were 28·9, 27·2, 24·4 and 20·5 respectively. At the same
period, the death rates in Hungary and Spain were as high
as 32·1 and 30·9 respectively.

[1] A confirmation of this tendency will be observed in the following
table, which cites the average age at the time of death during the period
from 1886 to 1929. (See *ibid.*, pp. 97–9.)

AVERAGE AGE OF DEATH OF MALE AND FEMALE, 1886–1929

Year.	Male.	Female.	Year.	Male.	Female.
1886 . .	36·13	38·91	1910 . .	30·99	31·36
1890 . .	36·39	37·17	1915 . .	31·14	31·44
1895 . .	34·77	35·67	1920 . .	31·09	30·97
1900 . .	33·84	34·93	1925 . .	32·15	32·29
1905 . .	33·56	34·62	1929 . .	32·57	33·27

The latest official figure on life expectancy in Japan was based on the
mortality statistics for the period 1921–5, and, when compared to earlier
figures, reveals a considerable decline. However, it is possible that
statistics based on more recent data would indicate some improvement.
The following figures depict the expectancy of life at birth, at 20 years
of age, at 40, and at 60 in designated periods. (See *ibid.*, 1932, p. 107 ;
Tokei Zensho, cited, pp. 23–4.)

EXPECTANCY OF LIFE OF MALE AND FEMALE AT SPECIFIED AGES,
1891–1925

Age.	1891–8.		1899–1903.		1908–13.		1921–5.	
	Male.	Female.	Male.	Female.	Male.	Female.	Male.	Female.
At birth . .	42·8	44·3	43·97	44·85	44·25	44·73	42·06	43·20
At 20 . . .	39·8	40·8	40·34	41·06	41·06	41·67	39·10	40·38
At 40 . . .	25·7	27·8	26·03	28·19	26·62	29·03	25·13	28·09
At 60 . . .	12·8	14·2	12·76	14·32	13·28	14·99	11·67	14·12

In this table the figures for the latest periods are considerably lower than those for similar age
groups in most north-western European nations. The figures for Germany, and France are cited
below, together with those of Japan at comparable periods. (Cf. *Annual Report of the Sanitary
Bureau*, cited, 1932, p. 108.)

EXPECTANCY OF LIFE OF MALE AND FEMALE IN GERMANY, FRANCE, AND
JAPAN AT SPECIFIED AGES

Country.	At Birth.		At 20.		At 40.		At 60.	
	Male.	Female.	Male.	Female.	Male.	Female.	Male.	Female.
Germany . .	55·97	58·82	46·70	46·09	30·05	31·37	14·60	15·51
France . .	52·18	55·87	42·93	46·16	27·82	30·82	13·84	15·63
Japan . . .	42·06	43·20	39·10	40·38	25·13	28·09	11·67	14·12

Dates : Germany, 1921–26 ; France, 1920–25 ; Japan, 1921–25.

B. *Specific and Adjusted Death Rates*

It is a universal fact that the mortality among infants and small children is high. The high ratio of this group in total population of Japan [1] partially explains the high crude death rate of the nation. Therefore, in order to compare the mortality rates of Japan with those of different nations and arrive at tenable conclusions, it is expedient to compute the death rates of specific age groups. By applying these specific death rates to a standard age distribution it is possible to eliminate the variations in the general death rates due to mere differences in age composition. The standardized death rates thus arrived at are referred to as adjusted death rates. For the standardization of age distribution for this purpose the age composition of England and Wales in 1901, the so-called " standard million," is generally adopted. The specific and adjusted death rates for Japan in 1925 have been calculated by the author as follows :

TABLE LI

SPECIFIC AND ADJUSTED DEATH RATES IN 1925 [2]

Age Period.	Population.	No. of Deaths.	Specific Death Rate.	" Standard Million."	Adjusted Death Rate.
Under 5 . .	8,264,583	461,400	55·8	114,262	6·38
5–9 . . .	6,924,432	31,963	4·6	107,209	0·49
10–14 . .	6,735,030	24,214	3·6	102,735	0·37
15–19 . .	5,885,277	50,244	8·5	99,796	0·85
20–24 . .	5,060,527	50,002	9·9	95,946	0·95
25–34 . .	8,109,558	69,252	8·5	161,579	1·37
35–44 . .	6,671,142	66,710	10·0	122,849	1·23
45–54 . .	5,506,052	81,723	14·8	89,222	1·32
55–64 . .	3,559,158	106,905	30·0	59,741	1·79
Over 65 . .	3,021,063	268,293	88·8	46,661	4·14
Total . .	59,736,822	1,210,706	—	1,000,000	18·89

[1] *Infra*, p. 123, footnote.
[2] For the detailed population and death figures, see *Annual Report of the Sanitary Bureau*, cited, 1930, Table 4.

The adjusted rate is 18·89 compared to the crude rate of 20·27. This illustrates that the age distribution exerts considerable influence, making the crude death rate of Japan appear unreasonably high. However, Japan's adjusted death rate in 1925 (18·89) was higher than that of England and Wales in 1901 (17·1), on which the " standard million " was based. The adjusted death rate of the 1920 registration area of the United States was 11·46 in 1925 compared to the crude rate of 11·90.[1]

The specific death rate of the above table has been reconstructed to conform to the system of age division used in the United States. The comparative specific death rates of the registration area of the United States [2] and Japan in 1925 are cited below:

TABLE LII
SPECIFIC DEATH RATES OF JAPAN AND THE UNITED STATES, 1925

Age Period.	Japan.	U.S.A.
Less than 1 . . . — .	154·6	75·3
4 and under	30·7	6·3
1–4	55·8	19·7
5–9	4·6	2·1
10–14	3·6	1·8
15–19	8·5	3·3
20–24	9·9	4·3
25–34	8·5	4·8
35–44	10·0	7·3
45–54	14·8	12·4
55–64	30·0	25·2
65 74	66·0	57·6
Over 75	162·5	141·1

These figures negate the premise of some Japanese sanitary experts who contend that the nation's death rates are high because of the proportionately high ratio of infant groups, whose death rates are high in any case.[3] The above table reveals that the death rates among the Japanese are high at every specific age period. The mortality of infants is double that of the United States. But still more striking

[1] *U.S. Mortality Statistics*, Bureau of the Census, U.S. Department of Commerce, 1927, Part II, p. 16.
[2] *Ibid.*, 1926, Part II, p. 26.
[3] *Annual Report of the Sanitary Bureau*, cited, 1928, p. 93.

are the persistently high death rates, more than two-fold those of the United States, throughout the youngest groups up to thirty-four. This is especially to be noted in the case of the age group of 15–19, where the Japanese rate is 2·6 times that of the United States. The causes of such a high toll of young lives will be looked into later.[1]

C. *Causes of Death*

The total deaths during the year 1930 were classified as to causes in their general divisions as follows :

TABLE LIII

GENERAL CLASSIFICATION OF CAUSES OF DEATH, 1930 [2]

Cause of Death.	Number of Deaths.	Percentage of Total.
Disease	1,053,747	90·00
Senility	76,591	6·54
External cause . . .	26,571	2·27
Suicide	13,942	1·19
Execution. . . .	16	—*
Total . . .	1,170,867	100·00

* Less than 0·01 per cent.

The above general classification of the causes of deaths shows that senility accounts for only 6·54 per cent of the total.

It is understood that many actual cases of deaths from senility are being classified technically as deaths from disease. Therefore, the above tabulation cannot be taken literally. Nevertheless, it is also certain that a large proportion of deaths are caused by diseases and that these diseases can be controlled to a great extent by promoting better sanitation and general welfare. This fact will be seen from the following list of major diseases with over 5,000 casualties. The total number of deaths from these diseases corresponds to 80·9 per cent of all deaths.

[1] See *infra*, pp. 120–1.
[2] *Jinko Dotai Tokei Kijutsuhen*, cited, 1930, p. 56.

TABLE LIV
Diseases Resulting in More Than 5,000 Deaths, 1930 [1]

Diarrhœa and enteritis	142,583
Cerebral hæmorrhage and softening of the brain	104,735
Pneumonia and bronchial pneumonia	101,046
Pulmonary tuberculosis	86,082
Nephritis	63,435
Malformation and congenital debility	62,103
Meningitis	47,532
Cancer	43,536
Organic disease of the heart	37,486
Disease of the stomach	22,917
Tuberculosis of the intestines and peritoneum	22,302
Peritonitis (non-puerperal)	20,207
Pleurisy	16,581
Beri-beri	15,419
Acute bronchitis	14,344
Chronic bronchitis	13,586
Typhoid fever	8,350
Whooping cough	7,437
Syphilis	6,016
Measles	5,965
Tuberculosis of the meninges and central nervous system	5,847
Influenza	5,207
Total	852,716

Among the controllable diseases, the most notable one is tuberculosis. Its infectious nature, especially among young people, and the slow stages of its prolonged development, leading to ultimate collapse, call for serious attention not only from the standpoint of national demography, but more especially from the point of view of social and economic well being. In 1930 pulmonary tuberculosis took a toll of 86,000 lives, or 7·35 per cent of all deaths, and 8·25 per cent of the total deaths due to disease.

In the same year this disease, together with other types of tuberculosis, resulted in 114,231 deaths. When we exclude the groups under 15 and over 60 years of age the toll of tuberculosis reached 30·07 per cent of all deaths. In other words, in 1930 one-third of all deaths of persons of economically productive age were caused by a controllable disease of tuberculosis. Furthermore, within this age group percentages exceed 40 among some of the younger groups. The specific ratios of five-year age periods from 15–19 to 55–59 follows:

[1] *Jinko Dotai Tokei Kijutsuhen*, cited 1930, p. 57.

Age Period.	Percentage of Tuberculosis Deaths among all Deaths.	Age Period.	Percentage of Tuberculosis Deaths among all Deaths.
15–19	. . . . 40·59	40–44	. . . . 16·62
20–24	. . . . 46·05	45–49	. . . . 12·13
25–29	. . . . 40·08	50–54	. . . . 8·75
30–34	. . . . 30·30	55–59	. . . . 5·93
35–39	. . . . 21·32		

The foregoing observations incidentally confirm the essential validity of the report made in 1915 by the late Yasunori Nikaido, Director of the Bureau of Statistics, then an expert of the Sanitary Bureau. The report concludes with the statement that the increasing death rate of Japan is due to the high mortality among infant and middle-aged groups, and that the high mortality of the latter group is due to the prevalence of tuberculosis.[1]

D. *Condition of the Public Health*

The incidence of tuberculosis in Japan, and the mortality directly attributable to this disease, reflect the general backwardness that characterizes the nation's health situation. At the present time, there are but 5 beds in tuberculosis hospitals and sanatoria per 100 deaths from that disease. That this is a lamentably inadequate figure is obvious ; it becomes strikingly apparent when compared to those of other countries, such as Denmark and Canada, which have more than 100, Germany, which has 84, the United States, which has 83, and England, which has 61.[2] There is no comfort derived from the fact that other, and often more virulent, diseases are treated in Japan with much the same degree of indifference as is tuberculosis.

The Sanitary Bureau of the Home Department conducted a very elaborate survey of sanitary conditions and health problems of the rural population of Japan. Each village studied was observed individually and the survey, which covered 134 villages, extended over a period of ten years, ending with the year 1928. The investigation of the morbidity rate, conducted as a part of this survey, included 68 villages with a population of 138,462 men and women

[1] Nikaido, Y., " Statistical Observation of the Births and Deaths in Japan," *Tokei Shushi*, No. 413, July, 1915.
[2] *Kokusei Zukai*, cited, 1933, p. 402.

for whom complete medical examinations were effected. The investigation revealed that there were 214,137 cases of disease listed for these persons, thereby making an average of 1·55 cases for each one. Only 10 per cent of the rural population examined were found free from disease.[1]

The survey also lists the diseases most common to rural Japan. Those with which more than 3 per cent of persons examined were afflicted are as follows : parasitism, 73 per cent ; trachoma, 15 per cent ; diseases of the eyes and ears (other than trachoma), 6 per cent ; and diseases of the respiratory organs (of which the highest frequency is tuberculosis), 3·9 per cent. With regard to the high morbidity of parasitism, 10·5 per cent of the entire population examined were afflicted with three kinds of parasitism, 32·1 per cent by two, and 34·8 per cent by one. This prevalence of parasitism in rural Japan is without parallel elsewhere in advanced nations.[2]

The incidence of leprosy places Japan among the " three great leprosy countries " of the world,[3] the other two being China and India. The number of patients in Japan at present may number more than 20,000.[4] Of these only about 5,000 are segregated in leprosia. It is of interest to note that in 1932 three of the fifteen public and privately endowed leprosy institutions were maintained by foreigners.[5]

So much for the adverse conditions. The recent tendency is toward an effort to improve sanitary conditions in conformity with the decline of the general death rate. Deaths from tuberculosis, which rose from 72,000 in 1898 to the

[1] *Noson Hoken Eisei Jicchi Chosa Seiseki* (Result of Investigation of Hygienic Condition of Rural Japan), Sanitary Bureau, Home Department, Japan, 1929, pp. 1–21. Originally about 200,000 persons of 134 villages were investigated. However, part of the records were lost by the fire due to the great earthquake of Tokyo in 1923. This study is one of the most comprehensive sanitary surveys ever undertaken in any nation.
[2] *Ibid.*, pp. 1–21.
[3] *Asahi Nenkan*, Osaka, Osaka Asahi Shimbunsha, 1935, p. 361.
[4] According to the enumeration made by the police force on March 31, 1928, the leprosy patients numbered 16,261. Due to the fact that the police included in their figures only those whose illness was obvious to the non-professional, this total is an underestimate. Cf. *Nagashima Kaitaku* (Development of the Nagashima Government Leprosia), Nagashima Aiseien, Publisher : Tokyo, Nagasaki Shoten, 1932, p. 40.
[5] *Annual Report of the Sanitary Bureau*, cited, 1932, Table 74.

peak record of 140,747 in 1918, have gradually decreased to 86,000 in 1930, as has been shown. Ratios per 100,000 population were 155, 253, and 197 in 1899, 1918 and 1929 respectively.[1]

The infant mortality rate (deaths of infants under one year of age per 1,000 births in the same calendar year), which rose from 95 per 1,000 infants under one year of age in 1886 to the peak of 189 in 1918, has declined almost every year since then. The rate was 124 in 1930. Three recent quinquennial averages were 174 for 1916–20, 159 for 1921–5, and 137 for 1926–30.[2] The general death rate in 1932, which was 17·72, the lowest rate since 1881, was reported as due to the absence of epidemics, to the prevalence of mild seasons, and to the improvement in infant care. With so high a birth rate, there is little hope for a further marked improvement of this favourable trend of recent years. Nevertheless, the fact that of all causes of death infant mortality is most sensitive to changes in the social environment, leads us to believe that the prospect of improved control of the general mortality in Japan lies largely in this field.[3]

[1] *Tokei Zensho*, cited, pp. 16–20 ; *Annual Report of the Sanitary Bureau*, cited, 1930, p. 105.

[2] *Ibid.*, 1931, p. 111.

[3] Some pertinent factors related to the sanitary conditions prevalent in Japan will be compared to those of several European nations. Among a selected group of nations the rate of deaths per 100,000 population from all kinds of tuberculosis, and, among this, the rate of deaths from pulmonary tuberculosis, and, in addition to these, the infant mortality rates, may be compared as follows (*Annual Report of the Sanitary Bureau*, cited, 1931, pp. 113, 117).

RATE OF DEATH FROM ALL TUBERCULOSIS, PULMONARY TUBERCULOSIS, AND INFANT MORTALITY RATE OF JAPAN AND OTHER SELECTED NATIONS, 1930

Country.	All Tuberculosis (per 100,000).	Pulmonary Tuberculosis (per 100,000).	Infant Mortality (per 1,000 Births).
Finland	250	216	78
Japan	168	134	124
France	167*	142*	78
Spain.	127	103	117
Italy	122*	90*	125*
Ireland	128	95	68
Switzerland . . .	125	98	51

* 1929.

In brief, the death rate of Japan reached its peak in 1918. Since then the rate has tended to decline, but it is still high compared with many nations in the West. A comparative study of the specific death rates reveals the fact that this high death rate of Japan is not due solely to the difference in age composition. Surveys of sanitary conditions reveal many situations requiring serious attention. Fortunately, the recent tendency is toward a rapid improvement of these conditions. An analysis of the major causes of death indicates the tendency toward a gradual decline, in conformity with the movement of the general death rate. However, in view of the increasing number of births, it may be concluded that there is definitely a limit to the fall of the death rate.

Appendix to § 4

TABLE LV

Birth Rate, Death Rate, and Rate of Natural Increase of Japan, 1872–1935 [1]

Year.	Birth Rate.	Death Rate.	Natural Increase Rate.
1872	17·1	12·2	4·9
1873	24·1	19·6	4·5
1874	24·6	20·5	4·1
1875	25·3	19·1	6·2
Average	22·8	17·9	4·9
1876	26·1	17·7	8·4
1877	25·5	17·8	7·7
1878	24·5	16·9	7·6
1879	24·4	20·1	4·3
1880	24·3	16·6	7·7
Average	25·0	17·8	7·2
1881	25·6	18·7	6·9
1882	24·9	18·1	6·8
1883	26·8	18·1	8·7
1884	25·8	18·6	7·2
1885	26·9	23·2	3·7
Average	26·0	19·3	6·7

[1] *Tokei Zensho*, cited, p. 12 ; *Annual Report of the Sanitary Bureau*, cited, 1930, pp. 99–100.

TABLE LV (*continued*)

Year.			Birth Rate.	Death Rate.	Natural Increase Rate.
1886	.	.	27·3	24·4	2·9
1887	.	.	27·1	19·3	7·8
1888	.	.	29·6	19·0	10·6
1889	.	.	30·2	20·2	10·0
1890	.	.	28·3	20·4	7·9
Average	.	.	28·5	20·7	7·8
1891	.	.	26·7	21·0	5·7
1892	.	.	29·4	21·6	7·8
1893	.	.	28·5	22·7	5·8
1894	.	.	28·9	20·1	8·8
1895	.	.	29·5	20·2	9·3
Average	.	.	28·6	21·1	7·5
1896	.	.	30·0	21·4	8·6
1897	.	.	30·9	20·3	10·6
1898	.	.	31·3	20·4	10·9
1899	.	.	31·3	21·1	10·2
1900	.	.	31·7	20·3	11·4
Average	.	.	31·0	20·7	10·3
1901	.	.	33·1	20·4	12·7
1902	.	.	32·9	20·9	12·0
1903	.	.	32·0	20·0	12·0
1904	.	.	30·5	20·3	10·2
1905	.	.	30·4	21·1	9·3
Average	.	.	31·8	20·5	11·3
1906	.	.	28·8	19·8	9·0
1907	.	.	32·9	20·7	12·2
1908	.	.	33·7	20·9	12·8
1909	.	.	33·9	21·9	12·0
1910	.	.	33·9	21·1	12·8
Average	.	.	32·7	20·9	11·8
1911	.	.	34·1	20·4	13·7
1912	.	.	33·3	19·9	13·4
1913	.	.	33·2	19·4	13·8
1914	.	.	33·7	20·5	13·2
1915	.	.	33·1	20·1	13·0
Average	.	.	33·5	20·1	13·4
1916	.	.	32·7	21·5	11·2
1917	.	.	32·3	21·4	10·9
1918	.	.	32·2	26·8	5·4
1919	.	.	31·6	22·8	8·8
1920	.	.	36·2	25·4	10·8
Average	.	.	33·0	23·6	9·4

TABLE LV (*continued*)

Year.			Birth Rate.	Death Rate.	Natural Increase Rate.
1921	.	.	35·1	22·7	12·4
1922	.	.	34·2	22·3	11·9
1923	.	.	34·9	22·8	12·1
1924	.	.	33·8	21·2	12·6
1925	.	.	34·9	20·3	14·6
Average		.	32·6	21·9	10·7
1926	.	.	34·8	19·2	15·6
1927	.	.	33·6	19·8	13·8
1928	.	.	34·4	19·9	14·5
1929	.	.	33·0	20·0	13·0
1930	.	.	32·4	18·2	14·2
Average		.	33·6	19·4	14·2
1931	.	.	32·2	19·0	13·2
1932	.	.	32·9	17·7	15·2
1933	.	.	31·6	17·8	13·8
1934	.	.	30·0	18·1	11·9
1935	.	.	31·6	16·8	14·8
Average		.	31·7	17·9	13·8

§ 5. ESTIMATE OF FUTURE GENERAL AND WORKING POPULATION

It has been observed that the trend of population is sensitive to prevailing economic and social conditions. Therefore, its future trend in the long run is as difficult to estimate as the economic and social background itself, and is, of course, above and beyond the field of simple numerical calculation. However, the trend of the immediate future, say a generation of thirty years, can be calculated with a certain degree of exactitude. It is with this population of the immediate future that an economic and social study of the population is most vitally concerned.

A. *Estimates by Various Writers*

The simplest and most generally applicable method of estimating the future population is the direct application of the present rate of increase. Sir George Knibbs, celebrated Australian statistician, applied the 1906–11 rate of average annual increase in Japan, which was 10·8 per 1,000 and showed that the Japanese population doubles every 64·2 years.[1] Apparently Sir George neglected to consider the age distribution. Therefore, although his estimate thus far nearly coincides with the actual growth, viz. that the population of Japan increased 99 per cent, in the 64 years from 1872 to 1935,[2] the scientific basis of this calculation is weak.

Another British writer, H. L. Wilkinson, extending the application of this method, paints an imaginary picture of the future Japanese population. He estimates that by A.D. 2000 Japan will have a population of over 120 million if she continues to increase at the annual rate of 10 per 1,000. Further, at the rate of 13·3, Japan, according to Wilkinson, will at the same date have a population of 170 million.[3]

A similar estimate of the future population uses as a base the 1909–13 average rate of annual increase, which was 14·17 per thousand. The figures follow : [4]

1917	56,032,000
1927	64,501,000
1937	74,246,000
1947	85,464,000
1957	98,376,000
1967	113,239,000
2017	228,839,000

The Bureau of Statistics in 1927 submitted an estimate of the future population to the Population and Food Commission which used this report as reference material. The Bureau's computation was based on the general trend of the fifty-three years from 1872 to 1925, adjusted to the cyclical fluctuations found in the thirty-seven years between 1888 and 1925. The figures are cited below :

[1] Knibbs, G. H., *The Shadow of the World Future*, London, Benn, 1928, p. 47.
[2] *Supra*, p. 60.
[3] Wilkinson, H. L., *The World's Population Problems and a White Australia*, London, King, 1930, p. 198.
[4] *Kome Jukyu no Genzai Oyobi Shorai* (Present and Future of the Supply and Demand for Rice), Department of Agriculture and Forestry, Japan, p. 3.

TABLE LVI

POPULATION OF JAPAN FROM 1926 TO 1959 AS ESTIMATED BY THE
BUREAU OF STATISTICS [1]

(By Five-Year Intervals)

Year.	Estimated Population.	Average Annual Increase.	Population Index.	
			1872 = 100.	1926 = 100.
1926	59,975,000	321,000	172	100
1930	63,257,000	753,000	182	105
1935	66,833,000	781,000	192	111
1940	71,681,000	1,033,000	206	120
1945	76,144,000	798,000	219	127
1950	80,768,000	1,083,000	232	135
1955	86,563,000	1,092,000	249	144
1959	90,347,000	910,000	260	151

This estimate is closer to reality than others which
have applied only a single rate of increase. Yet it presupposes that the population trend in the past will be
repeated in the future—a supposition which may be unwarranted.

In addition to this computation which assumes a
repetition of the population trend, another estimate was
made in which the calculations were based upon the
assumption that in nations of parallel economic and social
development there exist similar trends in population growths.
Former Director Yasumaro Shimojo of the Bureau of
Statistics has estimated the trend of the Japanese population
in the immediate future. In his calculations he used two
bases : the parallel movement of birth and death rates, and
the vital trends of different nations. He found that the
Japanese trend retraced the path of the German population
trend, lagging behind the latter by a few decades. According to the calculations of Dr. Shimojo, the German rate of

---

[1] *Jinko Mondai ni Kansuru Chosa Komoku Oyobi Kore ni Taisuru
Hosaku no Sankoan* (References to the Subjects and Methods of Investigation into the Population Problem), the Population and Food Commission, Japan, 1927.

increase will reach zero in 1947, which will be duplicated in Japan in 1970, at which date the population of Japan will be 85,542,100. Following is a chart illustrating Shimojo's estimated rates of increase and the numbers of the population by five-year periods :

TABLE LVII

POPULATION OF JAPAN FROM 1926 TO 1970 AS ESTIMATED BY
DR. SHIMOJO [1]

(By Five-Year Intervals)

Year.	Average Annual Rate of Natural Increase (per 1,000).	Estimated Population.
1926	15·593	—
1930	14·173	64,095,200
1935	12·398	68,527,400
1940	10·623	72,626,700
1945	8·848	76,298,600
1950	7·073	79,454,000
1955	5·298	82,014,100
1960	3·523	83,912,700
1965	1·748	85,099,500
1970	0·027	85,542,100

A somewhat more complex method of estimating trends of population is the logistic curve of Professor Raymond Pearl. It is based upon the assumption that the rate of population increase is not definite and is, moreover, a function constant in the population. The late Dr. Inagaki of Tokyo Imperial University, following the technique of Dr. Pearl, produced certain function constants which he believed were applicable to the Japanese trend. Applying these function constants, Dr. Inagaki maintained that the population will reach 100 millions in 2201, and that when it reaches 104 millions the rate of increase will become zero.[2] Although Dr. Inagaki's calculations are widely quoted in Japan without criticism, the errors in his formulae and calculations are too serious to warrant further attention.

[1] Shimojo, Y., *Shakai Seisaku no Riron to Shisetsu* (The Theory and Practice of Social Policy), Tokyo, 1931, Kakuron, Chap. I.
[2] Inagaki, " A New Theory of Population," *Tokei Jiho*, No. 16, 1926.

K

B. *Estimates by Dr. Ueda and Mr. Soda*

None of the methods discussed above gives any cognizance to the qualitative aspect of the population figures ; they deal only with the lump total of the general population, which, it must be pointed out, is composed of elements divergent as to age and sex. The first estimates that recognized the qualitative aspects of the population structure were made simultaneously by Mr. Takeo Soda of the Kyochokai and Dr. Teijiro Ueda of Tokyo Commercial College. Dr. Ueda calculated the survival rates of each five-year class by comparing the 10–14 age group of 1930 with the 5–9 age group of 1925, and so on through the age scale. Applying these survival rates of 1925–30 to the present population, Dr. Ueda calculated the population at five-year intervals up to 1950. Of course the group of age 4 and under of 1935, the 5–9 group of 1940, the 10–14 group of 1945, and the 15–19 group of 1950 had not as yet been born when he made his calculation. These gaps were filled by Dr. Ueda with the assumed number of births, 2·1 millions for each year between 1931 and 1950.

This assumption of a fixed number of births may be justified to a certain extent from the writer's study in § 3.[1] In view of the increase of the total population, this constancy of the annual number of births is a simplified method of adjusting the declining birth rate, and has been widely applied by such authorities as Cannan and Bowley. However, in the light of the present tendency in Japan, the definite determination of the survival rate among infant classes is especially problematical.[2] Therefore, Dr. Ueda attempted to correct the survival table by presupposing that the increase in the survival rate which occurred between the two periods of 1920–5 and 1925–30 will be repeated just once more. Ueda's revised calculations credited the groups between 19 and under with an increase of 1,209,000 in 1950 over the number given in the following tables. The survival rate of the five-year age periods and the computed future population are as follows :

[1] *Supra*, pp. 106–7.
[2] Cf. *supra*, p. 123.

TABLE LVIII
RATE OF SURVIVAL PER PERSON IN PERIOD 1925–30 [1]
(By Five-Year Age Groups)

Age Period.	Survival Rate.	Age Period.	Survival Rate.
5–9	·936647	45–49 . . .	·963288
10–14	·970052	50–54 . . .	·938441
15–19	·931348	55–59 . . .	·935724
20–24	·926410	60–64 . . .	·850163
25–29	·952938	65–69 . . .	·806693
30–34	·931379	70–74 . . .	·686094
35–39	·953123	75–79 . . .	·588568
40–44	·980533	Over 80 . . .	·671110

TABLE LIX
POPULATION OF JAPAN FROM 1930 TO 1950 AS ESTIMATED BY DR. UEDA, BY FIVE-YEAR AGE GROUPS AND BY FIVE-YEAR INTERVALS [2]
(Unit 1,000)

Age Period.	1930.	1935.	1940.	1945.	1950.
Under 15 . . .	9,044	9,077	9,077	9,077	9,077
5–9	7,741	8,471	8,501	8,501	8,501
10–14	6,717	7,509	8,217	8,246	8,246
14 and under .	23,502	25,057	25,795	25,824	25,824
15–19	6,272	6,255	6,993	7,653	7,679
20–24	5,452	5,811	5,795	6,478	7,090
25–29	4,822	5,195	5,537	5,522	6,174
30–34	4,091	4,491	4,839	5,159	5,143
35–39	3,541	3,900	4,280	4,612	4,915
40–44	3,382	3,472	3,824	4,197	4,522
45–49	3,103	3,258	3,345	3,683	4,043
50–54	2,867	2,912	3,057	3,139	3,457
55–59	2,293	2,682	2,725	2,860	2,937
15–59	35,827	37,980	40,399	43,306	45,963
60–64	1,692	1,949	2,280	2,316	2,432
65–69	1,265	1,365	1,572	1,839	1,869
70–74	888	868	936	1,079	1,262
75–79	541	522	510	551	635
Over 80 . . .	351	363	350	342	370
Total Population	4,737	5,068	5,652	6,130	6,568
Grand Total. .	64,066	68,105	71,846	75,260	78,355
Increase in five years . .		4,039	3,740	3,415	3,094
Five-year rate of increase .		6·30%	5·49%	4·75%	4·11%
Annual rate of increase. .		1·26%	1·10%	0·95%	0·82%

[1] Ueda, T., Editor, *op. cit.*, pp. 9–10.   [2] *Ibid.*, pp. 22–3.

From the above two tables we learn that upon the assumption of 2·1 million annual births and the specific survival rate of 1925–30 applied to the total population, the population will increase every five years after 1930 by 4,040,000, 3,743,000, 3,417,000 and 3,097,000, up to 1950. The total populations calculated are 68,106,000 in 1935, 71,846,000 in 1940, 75,261,000 in 1945, and 78,355,000 in 1950.

In this connection, the work of Mr. Soda is also deserving of attention, for, although he probably derived the fundamental idea from Kuczynski's fertility statistics, his findings are both elaborate and unique. He applied the specific birth rates of 1925 by five-year age classes of mothers to specified groups of women. By this means he obtained an estimate of the number of births up to 1945, at which date the final group whose actual number is known in 1930 enters the child-bearing age. Mr. Soda obtained an estimate of the 1945 child-bearing groups by applying these new elements and the existing population to the fourth life table which was constructed by the Bureau of Statistics on the basis of the mortality rates of 1921–5. By repeating the computation of births and its application to the life table, he obtained estimates of the population up to 1960. Specific birth rates in 1925, the estimated numbers of births, and the estimated trend of the population are depicted in the following tables. These figures are based on Mr. Soda's calculations.

TABLE LX

ANNUAL NUMBER OF BIRTHS PER 1,000 WOMEN IN SPECIFIED FIVE-YEAR AGE PERIODS [1]

Age Period.	Annual Number of Births per 1,000 Women.	Age Period.	Annual Number of Births per 1,000 Women.
15–19	41·17	35–39	172·58
20–24	218·08	40–44	71·61
25–29	248·31	45–49	9·49
30–34	218·58		

[1] Soda, T., " Calculation of the Estimated Increase of Population," *Social Reform*, No. 152, May, 1933, pp. 38–9, or Ueda, T., Editor, *op. cit.*, pp. 99–104.

TABLE LXI
Annual Number of Births and Gross Population in 1925–60 as Estimated by Mr. T. Soda [1]
(Unit 1,000)

Year.	No. of Births.	Gross Population.	Annual Increase.
1925 .	—	59,736	—
1926 .	—	60,418	682·2
1927 .	—	61,048	629·7
1928 .	—	61,743	695·2
1929 .	—	62,368	625·0
1930 .	—	62,997	628·8
1931 .	2,237·5	63,757	760·0
1932 .	2,258·1	64,507	750·0
1933 .	2,299·2	65,276	769·0
1934 .	2,339·8	66,064	788·0
1935 .	2,379·9	66,860	796·2
1936 .	2,419·7	67,683	823·1
1937 .	2,454·7	68,521	837·4
1938 .	2,485·2	69,368	846·8
1939 .	2,513·6	70,223	855·1
1940 .	2,560·1	71,123	900·3
1941 .	2,596·1	71,997	873·6
1942 .	2,630·8	72,903	906·4
1943 .	2,661·6	73,819	915·8
1944 .	2,690·8	74,743	924·3
1945 .	2,721·0	75,667	933·6
1946 .	2,751·5	76,628	961·0
1947 .	2,774·4	77,572	944·5
1948 .	2,817·0	78,638	1,066·0
1949 .	2,821·7	79,487	849·1
1950 .	2,840·9	80,437	950·4
1951 .	2,870·1	81,397	959·7
1952 .	2,894·9	82,362	964·7
1953 .	2,922·4	83,331	969·1
1954 .	2,951·6	84,308	977·5
1955 .	2,980·3	85,292	984·2
1956 .	3,013·5	86,287	994·9
1957 .	3,047·2	87,291	1,003·3
1958 .	3,066·6	88,292	1,001·8
1959 .	3,106·9	89,312	1,019·9
1960 .	3,151·0	90,351	1,038·7

According to the above table calculated by Mr. Soda, the number of births will gradually increase from 2,237,500 in 1931 to 3,151,000 in 1960. The total population will reach 70 millions in 1939, 80 millions in 1950, and 90 millions in 1960.

There are two assumptions in the above calculations of Mr. Soda : the constancy of the specific birth rate of 1925 and

[1] Ueda, T., Editor, *op. cit.*, pp. 100–4.

the constancy of the mortality rate of 1921-5, on which the fourth life table of the Bureau of Statistics is based. The value of Mr. Soda's estimates extends only so far as these assumptions are justified. Nevertheless, in view of the fact that the fundamental fallacy in previous estimates of the future population was the disregard of the qualitative elements in the population composition, Soda's calculations, by taking cognizance of the age and sex distribution, shed considerable light on a hitherto unexplored angle of the problem. Dr. Ueda's assumption of the constancy of the number of births leaves somewhat untouched a point vital to a clear-cut analysis of the trend of the age distribution of mothers and their fertility.

C. *Résumé of Estimates*

At this juncture it may be expedient to reiterate certain points discussed in the last section. It will be recalled that Soda, guided by Kuczynski, placed the net reproduction rate of Japan at 1·495. Using this as a base, Soda estimated that the population one generation after 1930 will be 96,379,000. If we assume that a generation corresponds to a period of thirty years, the number will be attained in 1960.

Soda's estimates are compared, below, with those of other students of the problem.

TABLE LXII

COMPARISON OF JAPAN'S POPULATION IN 1950-60 AS ESTIMATED BY VARIOUS METHODS

Year.	Soda's Estimates.	Other Estimates.	
1950	80,437,000	Dr. Ueda	78,355,000
1957	87,291,000	By a crude increase rate 14·17	98,376,000
1958	88,292,000	Dr. Inagaki's logistic curve	80,000,000
1959	89,312,000	Bureau of Statistics	90,347,000
1960	90,351,000	Dr. Shimojo	83,912,700
1960	90,351,000	Net reproduction rate 1·495	96,379,000

According to the study of Dr. Ueda, if the number of births remains fixed at 2·1 millions a year, the population

of Japan will become stationary when it reaches 94 millions.[1]
All estimates of the future population involve some degree
of prophecy. However, one conclusion reasonably certain
is that the growth of the Japanese population will continue
for at least a generation. Social conditions may in the
meantime change greatly and thereby affect the basis of
Soda's estimate—the specific birth rate. Whatever this
may be, the next generation is bound to bring the Japanese
population to 80 or 90 millions. Herein lies the pivotal
point of Crocker's thesis. He maintains that the Japanese
population problem, " the coming crisis," is primarily and
fundamentally the problem of making an adequate dis-
position of the additional 20 millions who, in spite of all
promises of declining fertility, are certain to come.[2]

D. *Outlook for the Working Population*

Supporting so large a general population presents, of
course, a serious problem, but it resolves itself down to the
economic resources of the nation and involves the question
of subsistence in the Malthusian sense. There is, however,
another aspect to the Japanese population problem, and this
aspect is of vital importance in that it is of an accentuating
nature. It is the changing age distribution in favour of the
middle-aged group. This is likely, through unemployment
and other problems, to intensify the pressure of the population on the economic and social resources of the country.

It has been noted that in 1920 48·7 per cent and in 1930
46·2 per cent of the total population of Japan were classified
as employed in gainful occupations.[3] Applying these ratios
to the estimated increase of the population in the immediate
future, we may infer that about 450,000 must annually be
placed within the nation's occupational positions. Of the
estimated future population destined, statistically speaking
at least, to have an occupation of one kind or another,
particular attention must be given to the middle-aged.
The changing age composition of the population in favour
of this group compared to the older one and the shift in

---

[1] *Ibid.*, p. 25.   [2] Crocker, W. R., *op. cit.*, pp. 92, 204 ff.
[3] *Supra*, pp. 80–1.

the social attitude, which increasingly discourages the employment of the older groups as well as of the minors, makes this necessary.

Mr. Soda estimated the age distribution of the future population according to its functional units, viz. 14 and under, 15–59, and 60–99 at five-year intervals. The figures follow :

TABLE LXIII

DISTRIBUTION OF THREE FUNCTIONAL AGE CLASSES IN 1925–60 AS ESTIMATED BY MR. SODA

(Unit 1,000)

Year.	Age Group 0–14.	Percentage Distribution.	Age Group 15–59.	Percentage Distribution.	Age Group 60–99.	Percentage Distribution.
1925	21,924	36·70	33,223	55·62	4,589	7·68
1930	22,301	35·40	35,964	57·06	4,731	7·51
1935	23,471	35·10	38,374	57·40	5,014	7·50
1940	24,769	34·83	40,838	57·42	5,515	7·75
1945	26,794	35·41	43,012	56·84	5,870	7·75
1950	28,562	35·51	45,738	56·86	6,136	7·63
1955	30,121	35·32	48,834	57·26	6,336	7·42
1960	31,624	35·00	51,998	57·55	6,728	7·45

Of the figures by Mr. Soda, those involving the 15–59 age group will be compared with Dr. Ueda's data which has already been noted. Annual average increases have been added by the writer. The figures are as follows :

TABLE LXIV

POPULATION OF MIDDLE-AGED GROUP IN 1925–60, AS ESTIMATED BY DR. UEDA AND MR. T. SODA

(Unit 1,000)

Year.	Soda's Estimate.			Ueda's Estimate.		
	Population aged 15–59.	Five-Year Increase.	Average Annual Increase.	Population aged 15–59.	Five-Year Increase.	Average Annual Increase.
1925	33,223	—	—	33,223	—	—
1930	35,964	2,741	548·2	35,827	2,704	540·8
1935	38,374	2,410	484·0	37,980	2,053	410·6
1940	40,838	2,464	492·8	40,399	2,419	483·8
1945	43,012	2,174	434·8	43,306	2,907	581·4
1950	45,738	2,726	545·2	45,963	2,657	531·4
1955	48,834	3,096	619·2	—	—	—
1960	51,998	3,164	632·8	—	—	—

The ratio of the 15–59 group to the total population was 55·30 per cent in 1920 and 55·62 per cent in 1925.[1] The percentage in 1960 will be 57·55, according to Soda's calculations. The estimates of Dr. Ueda and Mr. Soda coincide almost exactly with regard to the middle group in the future. Both estimates show an annual increase of about a half-million up to 1950, and Soda's estimates run to over 600,000 by 1960.

According to the census of 1930, 73·09 per cent of the 15–59 age group was gainfully employed.[2] This figure, when compared to that of Western nations, is rather high.[3] Nevertheless, indications do not point to an appreciable change in this specific ratio in the near future. This would indicate that between now and 1950 at least 400,000 people will seek positions annually in Japan's economic system. Furthermore, between 1950 and 1960 the annual increment in the working population will swell to 450,000. Unless the present economic system is radically changed, this demand for a place in the economic structure is reasonable and normal, and it must be complied with if the nation's social stability and progress is to be insured. The ability to absorb these great numbers is the real test of Japan's social system and economic resources. Herein lies the crucial problem of the Japanese population.

SUMMARY OF CHAPTER VI

A study of the age and sex distribution has revealed much interesting and significant material concerning the movements of population. Inasmuch as none of the age and sex groups has a uniform proportional bearing upon occupation, marriage, divorce, and birth and death, trends of these factors of population must be closely examined. The high ratio of males per female is noticeable, but one feature of great significance is the high ratio of minor age groups. For consideration of the future trends of the Japanese population this fact must be kept in mind.

The quasi-official institution of informal marriage in

---

[1] *Supra*, p. 90.   [2] *Tokei Nenkan*, cited, No. 54, 1935, p. 33.
[3] *Supra*, pp. 83–5.

Japan complicates marriage statistics of the nation. It has been found that in Japan the marriage rate, which is regarded as one of the most stable elements in demography, is declining. With the fast shift in fertility at the age of prime, as well as the social importance of family life, this decline in marriage is often regarded with concern by students of population and by sociologists. The steady decline in both the illegitimacy and divorce rate has been noted as a promising aspect of Japanese demography.

Beginning at an unusually low level, the Japanese birth rate has gradually risen since the Reformation. At about the beginning of this century Japan's rising birth rate crossed the declining rate of North-Western Europe. Since then its increase has been phenomenal. The death rate has risen steadily, thereby following the path of the birth rate. Evidence shows that since the post-Great War period the trend of the refined birth and death rates has been downward.

At no time have Japan's birth and death rates reached the peak of those of Western nations, although those of the nations of the West are now, in fact, lower than those of Japan. The recent decline of the death rate has been more rapid than that of the birth rate. This disparity in births and deaths is the causal factor in the present high rate of natural increase. Japan's natural increase in 1932 was over one million, one of the largest figures in the world. In view of the high birth rate in recent years and the consequent high proportion of potential mothers, the trend of the crude birth rate in the near future will not necessarily coincide with the trend of the refined birth rate.

Estimates of the future population involve a refined technique in the adjustment of the age and sex distribution and in the determination of the fertility and mortality rates of the national population. The many complex calculations made by experts have produced one salient point of reasonable certainty, viz. that by 1960 the Japanese population will be between eighty and ninety million people. This means that within thirty years the nation's total population will inevitably be increased by twenty millions. In a crude sense, the crux of the Japanese population problem is the adequate disposal of this vast increment. The present stagnation in the economic structure, especially in agriculture, accentuates the gravity of the situation, which is further augmented by the impending increase of the proportion of the Japanese population within the working age groups ; in actual figures these groups are gaining about half a million annually. The absorption of this added labour force into productive channels is the real test of Japan's social and economic system—a test which the nation cannot attempt to evade.

CHAPTER VII

RURAL ECONOMIC SITUATION AND POPULATION TREND

It has been already noted that the present growth of the Japanese population is dependent on, and a concomitant with, the growth and development of cities.[1] Nevertheless, the fundamental aspects of the Japanese population problem cannot be fully understood without a detailed study of the rural population in the light of rural economy.

The population density of Japan in 1872, the fifth year of Meiji, was higher than the present density of France and was equal to that of present-day Hungary.[2] In view of the fact that about 80 per cent of the population was engaged in agriculture,[3] it may be deduced that such a large population capacity was possible only under a system of extremely small farms of the type which prevailed in Japan at that time. The historic and economic background of this peculiar agricultural system will be briefly considered.

A. Conditioning Factors in the Small-Farming System

Historically, the smallness of the farm in Japan is a characteristic feature of Oriental culture. Oriental people are accustomed to subsist on cereals and to wear cotton and silk, making relatively little use of animal products, such as meat, wool or fur. Between the middle of the seventh century and that of the ninth century the periodic redistribution of acreage [4] amounted, in modern measure, to

[1] *Supra*, pp. 71-4.   [2] *Supra*, p. 63.   [3] See *supra*, p. 78.
[4] *Supra*, p. 3, footnote.

about 0·24 cho (1 cho equals approximately 1 hectare or 2·45 acres) per male and 0·16 per female over six years of age.[1] This corresponds to approximately 1·2 cho for the average present-day rural family [2] and is almost equal to the present average acreage.

Small farms survived during the Tokugawa Era by reason of the strengthening of the primogenitive system and the government's prohibitions on the permanent disposal of lands.[3] Furthermore, the rulers were antagonistic to powerful esquires and enacted measures calculated to inhibit their rise. According to the late Dr. Takimoto, a noted student of economic history of the Tokugawa Era, a holding of 0·5 cho was regarded as a good average-sized farm.[4] This fact must be borne in mind in considering that the soil of Japan under the seclusionist policy of the pre-Meiji Period supported 30 million people.

In addition to these basic historic elements, there exist certain factors which have encouraged the survival of the system of extremely small farms, or which at least have retarded the rapid readjustment of land distribution to modern conditions. One factor which is closely related to the historical background of the Japanese system of agriculture and which retards the readjustment in tillage is the fact that in an old agricultural country like Japan, the highly prized holdings of a farmer are scattered throughout a village. This dispersion of property helps to perpetuate the system of small farms.

However, the fundamental factors in the persistence of the small farming system are the peculiar topographic nature of Japan and the concentration on rice cultivation in the paddy fields. Neither one of the two factors alone explains

---

[1] Uchida, G., *op. cit.*, Vol. I, pp. 17–18 ; *Taguchi-Ukichi Zenshu*, cited, Vol. III, p. 452, " Population."

[2] The average size of a family in the study made in 1929 by the Bureau of Agriculture was males over 8 years 3·557 and females over 8 years 3·762. Should the land be distributed according to the ancient rule, the holding of one family would be 1·154 cho. Cf. *Noka Keizai Chosa* (Investigation of the Rural Household Economy), Bureau of Agriculture, Department of Agriculture and Forestry, Japan, 1929, p. 12.

[3] See *supra*, p. 14.

[4] Takimoto, S., *Nihon Keizaishi* (Economic History of Japan), N.D., p. 72.

the situation ; it is the combination of both that helped stabilize the small-farm system. The validity of these contentions is substantiated by the fact that in California rice is cultivated by machinery in large fields, and that in many hilly countries of Europe the farmsteads are not as small as those in Japan. The average size of one field in Japan is estimated at 0·06 cho.[1]

B. FARM STATISTICS

In the post-Reformation era, particularly after 1910, detailed statistics on farms were compiled by the Bureau of Agriculture of the Department of Agriculture and Forestry.[2] Acreage per farm and other related figures are cited below at five-year intervals since 1910.

TABLE LXV

NUMBER OF FARMS, TOTAL AND PER FARM ACREAGE, 1910–30 [3]
(Denomination Cho)

Year.	Cultivated Land.	Per cent of Land Area.	No. of Farms (Households).	Acreage per Farm.		
				Upland Fields.	Paddy Fields.	Total.
1910	5,715,405	14·7	5,497,919	·529	·510	1·039
1915	5,922,118	15·2	5,535,008	·537	·533	1·070
1920	6,147,790	15·7	5,573,097	·546	·557	1·103
1925	6,067,015	15·8	5,548,599	·559	·534	1·093
1930	5,915,709	15·4	5,599,670	·572	·484	1·056

The above table shows that during the period covered, the total cultivated land remained practically stationary at approximately 5·9–6·1 million cho, while the number of farms also remained stationary at 5·5 millions and the average acreage of one farm remained at about 1·05 cho.

[1] *Social Reform*, No. 108, p. 90.

[2] In 1925 the Department of Agriculture and Commerce was supplanted by two distinct departments, namely, the Department of Agriculture and Forestry and the Department of Commerce and Industry.

[3] *Honpo Nogyo Yoran* (Agricultural Abstract of Japan), Bureau of Agriculture, Department of Agriculture and Forestry, Japan, 1931, pp. 1–2, 7–8.

The recorded maximum average acreage per farm was 1·113 cho in 1922. However, even these low figures do not represent the true situation in Japan, for they include Hokkaido, which was opened in the Meiji Period and is a somewhat different unit within Japan proper.

In Hokkaido the average size of the farms is 4·55 cho. Furthermore, 80 per cent of all the farms of Japan with an acreage of more than 5 cho are located in Hokkaido. In fact, the average size of farms in Japan proper, if Hokkaido is excluded, falls as low as 0·99 cho. Within Japan proper, excluding Hokkaido, the farms grow gradually smaller than this low average as one proceeds southward into the older and warmer regions. The average is about 1·5 cho in North-Western Japan, 1 cho in Kwanto, and between 0·7 and 0·8 cho in Kinki and regions farther south. These figures, however, include farms which are operated as a subsidiary business ; about 30 per cent of all farms in Japan are conducted on this basis. Excluding this group of farms the average acreage for specialized farms is estimated at considerably less than 1·5 cho.

Recent tendencies in Japan's farm acreage are further analysed in the following table, which classifies the farms into six groups and gives their ratios compared to the total number.

TABLE LXVI

DISTRIBUTION OF FARMS OF SPECIFIED ACREAGES, 1910–30 [1]
(Percentages)

Year.	Under 0·5 Cho.	0·5–1·0 Cho.	1·0–2·0 Cho.	2·0–3·0 Cho.	3·0–5·0 Cho.	Over 5·0 Cho.
1910 . .	37·5	33·0	19·3	6·0	2·9	1·3
1915 . .	36·5	33·4	20·0	6·1	2·7	1·3
1920 . .	35·6	33·2	20·5	6·2	2·8	1·7
1925 . .	35·2	33·8	21·4	6·8	2·5	1·4
1930 . .	34·6	34·2	21·9	5·7	2·3	1·3

This condensed table indicates that the comparatively large farms of from 2 to 3 and 3 to 5 cho, and the extremely

[1] *Honpo Nogyo Yoran*, cited, 1931, p. 34.

small farms under 0·5 cho, are gradually diminishing in number. Moreover, the decline in these two groups is balanced by an increase in the ratio of farms whose acreage ranges between 0·5 and 2·0 cho. The ratio of large farms, of more than 5 cho, is likely to remain unchanged, unless their numbers increase. From the standpoint of farm acreage, it may, in general, be said that Japanese agriculture is tending toward two extremes : a basic family occupation and a relatively large capitalistic enterprise.

In this connection it may be pertinent to compare the present acreage of Japanese farms with those of other nations. In the following table farms in Japan are compared with those of other nations in respect to size.

TABLE LXVII

AVERAGE SIZE OF FARMS IN JAPAN AND OTHER SPECIFIED COUNTRIES [1]

Country.	Date of Investigation.	Average Acreage (Cho).
Denmark	1919	16·1
Great Britain	1926	9·0
Germany	1925	4·3
Ireland	1913	3·0
China	N.D.	1·2
Japanese Empire	1929	1·29
Karafuto	1929	2·77
Taiwan	1926	1·99
Chosen	1929	1·65
Japan proper	1929	1·06

As is indicated in the above table, Japan resembles other Oriental regions, some of which are now included in the Japanese Empire. The size of her farms is less than one-half of that of Ireland, whose farms are generally regarded as extremely small according to Western standards. In view of these statistical figures, the operation of Japanese agriculture may appear peculiar to Western people, particularly to those of the New World.[2]

---

[1] Hashimoto, D., and Nagai, S., Editors, *op. cit.*, p. 104.
[2] An American author with considerable romantic fervour, observed the following (Beard, M., *Realism in Romantic Japan*, New York, Macmillan, 1930, p. 345, quoted in Moulton, H. G., *op. cit.*, p. 332) : '' Except in the frigid North, Japanese cultivable land has been worked with an amazing intensity, such as we hardly see in the famous vineyard regions

C. EFFECTS OF THE SMALL-FARMING SYSTEM ON THE RURAL ECONOMY

Farms in Japan are cultivated almost exclusively by hand. This involves backbreaking toil of a nature and degree that is cruel, compared to Western standards.[1] Despite the peculiar value attached to domestic rice in Japan,[2] the farmers, as hardworking as their forbears, are now faced with a struggle for their very existence. All quantitative analysis of the national economy substantiate this observation.

The Bureau of Agriculture has conducted annual investigations since 1921 in farmers' economy, and has found that for the year 1929 there was a deficit, in 32·2 per cent of the 1,475 households studied.[3] Another elaborate study of rural economy was made by the Bureau of Statistics in 1926–7 ; 670 farmers were investigated and the results corroborated the findings of the Bureau of Agriculture, showing an average deficit of 0·24 yen a month.[4] Consequently, the farmers had debts which, according to the estimate in 1928 by the Bureau of Agriculture, totalled 4,365 million yen, or 783 yen per farm. The rate of interest on such debts is usually more than 10 per cent per annum.[5]

The relative position of agriculture in the national economy of Japan can be judged to a certain degree by comparing its receipts with those of other branches of industry. According to the Bureau of Statistics, the average daily wages of factory workers and miners in 1929 was 2·064 and 1·810 yen respectively. The Bank of Japan

of southern Europe. Its wildernesses are trimmed and the deep forests combed of every twig or cone. High hills are ingeniously hollowed and mounded for water-paddies until they flash light as from a thousand faucets ; and in autumn they are studded with drying racks, on which the rice straw hangs in bundles, each tied as neatly as a Christmas present."

[1] Cf. Buchanan, D. H., "The Rural Economy of Japan," *Quarterly Journal of Economics*, Aug., 1923, pp. 558–66 ; Crocker, W. R., *op. cit.*, p. 34.

[2] See *infra*, p. 168.

[3] *Noka Keizai Chosa*, cited, 1929, p. 105.

[4] *Rodo Tokei Yoran* (Abstract of Labour Statistics), Bureau of Statistics, Japan, 1932, p. 323.

[5] Cf. *Keizai Orai*, July, 1932, p. 304 ; *Kaizo*, Dec., 1934, p. 50.

placed their wages at 1·970 yen and 1·751 yen.[1] In contrast to these figures, the returns per adjusted working day for the family labour of farmers were 0·540 yen, 0·830 yen, and 0·808 yen for the landed farmers, part-tenants, and tenants, respectively. The average for the three classes was 0·707 yen.[2]

The salient figures in the statistics, demonstrating these points, follow :

TABLE LXVIII

CASH ESTIMATE OF AGRICULTURAL ACCOUNT PROPER, REPRESENTATIVE FARMS, 1929

(Denomination Yen)

Gross receipt	1,975·004
Outlay	1,141·265
Balance : Agricultural income . . .	833·739
Interest of landed capital (per 4%) . .	264·668
Interest of other agricultural capital (per 5%)	121·695
Reward for labour (excluding hired labour) .	447·376
Adjusted days of labour (days) . . .	633·196
Reward per adjusted day of labour . .	0·707

In addition to the agricultural account proper, the income from subsidiary business and property on the one hand, and the household expenses on the other, influenced the cash account of the farmers in 1929 as follows : [3]

Income.		Outlay.	
Agriculture . . .	833·739	Household expenses.	1,074·454
Subsidiary business *	230·721	Balance, surplus. .	75·900
Domestics † . . .	85·894		
Total . . .	1,150·354		

* Includes property income.
† Gifts, sale price of garbage, etc.

This balance sheet of the average farmer shows an annual surplus of only 75·900 yen, or 6·325 yen per month. This amount must cover the unpaid labour of the family and interest on capital owned.[4]

In Japanese agriculture there is a tendency for the small

---

[1] *Rodo Tokei Yoran*, cited, 1932, pp. 172–9.
[2] *Noka Keizai Chosa*, cited, 1929, p. 51.
[3] *Ibid.*, pp. 62, 71.
[4] *Rodo Tokei Yoran*, cited, 1932, pp. 316–23.

farms to be more economical than the large farms in the use of land and other capital. Yet the extreme smallness of the former class makes their net balance inferior to that of the latter class of farms. The research conducted by the Imperial Agricultural Association in 1924 revealed the fact that the agricultural outlay of small farms, whose average size is 1·70 cho, amounts to 45·1 per cent of their receipts compared to the 49·6 per cent outlay of medium-sized farms, whose average size is 3·42 cho. In spite of this, the estimated return for family labour, after subtracting the estimated interest of borrowed capital at the annual rate of 4 per cent, was only 891·22 yen for the former and 1,375·60 yen for the latter.[1]

A study of the Bureau of Statistics, noted before, reveals additional data concerning the balance sheets of farmers, tabulated according to the size of the farms. The figures follow :

TABLE LXIX
MONTHLY SURPLUS OR DEFICIT OF FARMERS GROUPED BY FARM ACREAGE [2]

Size of Farm (Cho).	Surplus or Deficit (Yen).	Size of Farm (Cho).	Surplus or Deficit (Yen).
Under 0·5	− 5·08	1·2–1·4	1·40
0·5–0·6	− 3·88	1·4–1·6	0·53
0·6–0·8	− 2·86	1·6–1·8	7·00
0·8–1·0	− 2·19	1·8–2·0	3·86
1·0–1·2	− 3·11	Over 2·0	1·36
Average	− 2·91	Average	2·58

The above table shows that the weighted average monthly deficit of farmers cultivating less than 1·2 cho amounted to 2·91 yen, while the farmers with an acreage of over 1·2 cho realized a surplus of 2·58 yen a month. Tests made by agricultural experimental stations corroborate these findings, and show that with an acreage of less than 2·5 cho a liberal standard of farm life cannot be obtained.[3]

[1] *Nogyo Keiei Chosa Seiseki Yoko* (Abstract of the Result of the Investigation of Agricultural Economy), Imperial Agricultural Association, Japan, 1927, pp. 3–4.
[2] *Rodo Tokei Yoran*, cited, 1932, p. 322.
[3] *Keizai Orai*, July, 1932, p. 308.

In the foregoing analysis the economic significance of the small farm, a powerful factor of Japan's great rural population, has been dealt with. However, it must not be supposed that the effect of this small farm upon the national economy has been fully analysed ; it is necessary to go a step further and examine the problem, even though it may be impossible to arrive at definite conclusions, in the light of the theory of diminishing returns. Some writers assume that Japanese agriculture is now being operated at the stage of a decreasing marginal return,[1] but there is no factual basis for that opinion.

D.   Rural Economy considered in the Light of the Theory of Diminishing Returns

A purely theoretical approach to this further analysis is to apply capitalistic methods of accounting to the agricultural management, viz. to estimate the interest on the investment in farms and to apply the average rural wage scale to the corrected number of work-days of family members. This method conflicts with the general social concept of agriculture as a basic family industry, but it enables us to see agricultural economy in comparison with the general level of national economy. Applying this method of calculation, we see that, as a whole, Japanese agriculture is operated beyond the margin of profitable enterprise. The following table, which is based on the report of the Bureau of Agriculture mentioned previously,[2] shows that if the average interest rate were applied to the farm investment, and if the average farm wages were applied to the family labour, Japanese farmers would have an average deficit of about 360 yen a year. See Table LXX.

According to this Bureau, more than 70 per cent of the agricultural expenses went to purchase fertilizer, buy food for animals, and pay the taxes of landed farmers and the rent for tenants ; these expenditures amounted to 26·84

[1] Cf. Pitkin, W. B., *Must We Fight Japan ?*, New York, Century, 1921, p. 79.
[2] *Supra*, p. 145.

TABLE LXX

CASH ESTIMATE OF AGRICULTURAL ACCOUNT PROPER OF
REPRESENTATIVE FARMS, 1921–9 [1]

(Denomination Yen)

I Year.	II Agricultural Income.	III Estimated Wages of Family Labour.	IV Estimated Interest on Farm Value.	V Balance (Deficit).
1921 . .	865	940	440	− 515
1922 . .	729	830	387	− 488
1923 . .	907	915	417	− 425
1924 . .	1,082	905	421	− 244
1925 . .	1,218	909	443	− 134
1926 . .	1,023	750	462	− 189
1927 . .	915	976	405	− 466
1928 . .	881	903	407	− 429
1929 . .	952	891	421	− 360

II, Balance of agricultural receipt and cost other than III and IV ; III, Wages basis—Wage Statistics of Agricultural Labourers of the Department of Agriculture and Forestry ; IV, Rates of Interest—4 per cent of land investment and 5 per cent of other farm investment.

per cent, 20·86 per cent, and 22·52 per cent, respectively.[2] The first and third of the above items, i.e. fertilizer and land costs, will be considered in more detail.

Contrary to the statement made by Professor Crocker,[3] statistics concerning vegetable manure and manufactured fertilizers are available in Japan in recent years. Below are tabulated the data on the volume and the estimated value of vegetable manure and the cost of manufactured fertilizers paid by the farmers on the one hand, and the volume of production of rice, wheat, barley, and rye on the other. To this the value of all agricultural products is added. Among these figures, those of values are adjusted by the author to the general price index numbers prepared by the Bank of Japan, taking 1925 as the basis. In absence of systematic statistics on the total volume of

[1] Hashimoto, D., and Nagai, S., Editors, *op. cit.*, p. 81.
[2] *Noka Keizai Chosa*, cited, 1929, pp. 44–47.
[3] Crocker, W. R., *op. cit.*, p. 65.

TABLE LXX

AGRICULTURAL FERTILIZATION AND PRODUCTION, 1921–34 [1]

Year	Manure			Manufactured Fertilizer, Adjusted Value.	Total Value Fertilizer.		Production.			
	Total Amount.	Amount per Cho.	Adjusted Total Value.		Adjusted Value.	Index.	Amount of Rice.	Amount of Wheat, Barley and Rye	Value of Agricultural Produce.*	
									Adjusted Value.	Index.
	(1,000 M. Tons.)	(Metric Ton.)	(1,000 Yen.)	(1,000 Yen.)	(1,000 Yen.)	1925 = 100.	(1,000 Koku.)	(1,000 Koku.)	(1,000 Yen.)	1925 = 100.
1921	—	—	268,342	228,377	496,719	76·1	55,180	21,664	—	—
1922	—	—	274,691	261,415	536,106	82·2	60,694	21,630	—	—
1923	—	—	320,487	279,729	600,216	92·0	55,444	18,642	—	—
1924	51,519	8·50	338,192	262,298	600,490	92·0	57,170	19,083	3,653,218	90·1
1925	51,723	8·53	342,810	309,648	652,458	100·0	59,704	22,729	4,055,312	100·0
1926	52,005	8·55	382,342	382,459	764,801	117·2	55,593	21,907	3,875,257	95·6
1927	52,558	8·65	397,553	344,227	741,780	113·7	62,103	20,942	3,751,070	92·5
1928	52,564	8·64	385,230	348,649	733,879	112·5	60,303	21,121	3,654,472	90·1
1929	53,730	9·11	406,136	384,069	790,205	121·4	59,552	20,763	3,782,697	93·3
1930	54,817	9·26	416,009	359,669	775,678	118·9	66,873	19,304	3,089,060	76·2
1931	59,407	9·98	439,301	323,983	763,284	117·0	55,215	20,296	3,049,533	75·2
1932	58,931	9·83	430,198	323,590	753,788	115·5	60,390	20,627	3,510,100	86·6
1933	61,759	10·24	441,988	330,599	772,587	118·4	70,829	20,279	3,931,918	97·0
1934	63,806	10·57	451,008	344,122	795,130	121·6	51,840	22,407	3,476,560	85·7

* These figures include all agricultural products, except animal and poultry products.

[1] *Hompo Nogyo Yoran*, cited, 1935, pp. 166–175; *Hiryo Yoran* (Brief Report on Fertilizer), Bureau of Agriculture, Department of Agriculture and Forestry, Japan, 1935, pp. 24, 40.

manufactured fertilizers, this adjusted value will best meet our purpose.

It might be said that the monetary value of agricultural products fluctuates in inverse proportion to the quantity of the products and, for this reason, it cannot be regarded as a good measure of diminishing or increasing returns. To meet this possible criticism, we may add that the rice, wheat, barley, and rye, of which volume of production is cited, are by far the most important agricultural crops in Japan and occupy some 80 per cent (79·70 per cent in 1930) of all acreage. See Table LXXI.

This table reveals that the farmers in Japan use an increasingly large volume of vegetable manure. It reached over 60 million metric tons or more than 10 tons per cho in 1933. In addition to this, the farmers consume a large amount of manufactured fertilizers, monetary value of which equals the estimated value of the manure. Index numbers of the adjusted total value of fertilizers, taking 100 as the base in 1925, are 76·1 in 1921, 118·9 in 1930, and 121·6 in 1934. On the other hand, the volume of production of rice and other designated crops remains almost fixed while the adjusted value of all crops actually shows a tendency to decline. The index number of the value, again taking 1925 as the base, is 85·7 in 1934.

Other important items in agricultural expenditures, namely, taxes and rent, are directly related to the land value. The Hypothec Bank of Japan places the present value of paddy fields and that of upland fields at about ten and twenty times their respective values at the beginning of the Meiji Period.[1] Detailed statistics of land values in recent years in Japan are furnished by the Ministry of Finance, the Hypothec Bank of Japan, and the Bureau of Post Office Insurance. The average transaction prices of medium-graded paddy fields and of upland fields, as recorded by the Ministry of Finance at five-year intervals, are cited in Table LXXII.

Figures of this table evaluate paddy fields at approximately 4,000 yen and upland fields at about 2,000 yen

[1] *Bulletin*, Hypothec Bank of Japan, Investigation Section, May, 1931.

TABLE LXXII
VALUES OF THE PADDY AND UPLAND FIELDS, 1905–29 [1]
(Denomination Yen)

Year.	Paddy Field.	Index Number.	Upland Field.	Index Number.
1905–9 .	1,350	100·0	670	100·0
1915 . .	1,340	99·3	610	91·0
1920 . .	3,310	245·2	1,600	238·8
1924 . .	4,150	307·4	2,230	332·8
1929 . .	4,210	311·9	2,460	367·2

per cho in 1924 and 1929. Causes of such high land value in Japan will be analysed a little later.

Inasmuch as the paddy fields are used almost exclusively for the cultivation of rice, a consideration of the trend of the value of paddy fields in relationship to the value of the rice raised in those fields will be of considerable interest. In the following table the index numbers of land values previously noted are contrasted with the estimated value of the rice raised in the paddy fields.

TABLE LXXIII
LAND VALUES AND PRODUCE VALUES, 1905–29 [2]

Year.	Rice from Paddy Field (1,000 Koku).	Average Price (per Koku).	Total Rice Value (1,000 Yen).	Index Number.	Index Number of Land Value (Paddy-Field).
1905–9 .	46,809	14·69	687,624	100·0	100·0
1915 . .	54,591	13·02	710,775	103·4	99·3
1920 . .	61,367	48·56	2,979,982	433·4	245·2
1925 . .	58,111	41·95	2,437·756	354·5	307·4
1929 . .	58,680	29·19	1,712,869	249·1	311·9

Unquestionably, and quite naturally, there exists a definite correlation between the value of the paddy fields and the value of their products, or the income of the owner from the land. This correlation is attested to by the fact that land values decline when rentals are reduced, or when tenants' disputes cause disturbances to the security of the

[1] *Honpo Nogyo Yoran*, cited, 1931, p. 53.   [2] *Ibid.*

rental payments.[1] In other words, the high rental is a causal factor of immediate importance in the high land value in Japan. In saying this the author does not claim that the rental factor is the only cause of the fluctuation of land value. There are many others. One remote but general causal factor in the fluctuations of land values which should be mentioned in this connection is the pressure of population. This fact has received support from the study by Dr. Shiomi of Kyoto Imperial University. Professor Shiomi listed all the forty-seven prefectures of Japan proper in the order of their density of population in 1930, comparing these figures with the average rental value of the land in these same prefectures as estimated in 1926-7 by the Department of Finance. This comparison showed that of the forty-seven prefectures twenty-three were situated within a range of only three lines.[2]

Our study has been concerned, in the last few pages, with proving that Japanese agriculture is operated, compared with the general standard of national economy at least, beyond the profitable margin. Moreover, in order to maintain the present level of production the farmers must spend increasingly larger amounts upon fertilizers. The high value of agricultural land in Japan is caused both by the pressure of population and by the high rents, rather than by profits derived from agriculture. The settlement of the high rental rates, and in fact of the whole problem of tenancy in Japan, may be considered as of paramount importance in the adjustment of Japan's rural economic life. A consideration of this problem will be taken up next.

E. Land Distribution and the Tenancy Problem

The high rent of agricultural land in Japan is due to historical circumstances, and the high land value is a conse-

[1] Kawada, S., *Tochi Keizairon* (Land Economics), Gendai Keizaigaku Zenshu, Vol. XXII, Tokyo, Nihon Hyoronsha, 1931, p. 72 ; *Kosaku Sogichi ni Okeru Noson Jijo no Henka* (Effect of Tenants' Disputes on Rural Relations), Tokyo, Kyochokai, 1928, pp. 58, 73.
[2] Shiomi, S., " The Population Density and Economic Life," *Keizai Ronso*, 32 : 5, May, 1931, p. 783.

quence of the high rent instead of its cause.[1]   In any case,
whatever the cause may be, these high rentals encourage
and aggravate the agrarian disputes which at present constitute a serious threat to the stability and harmony of rural
social relations.

Land distribution in Japan has in recent decades proceeded along unsatisfactory and unfavourable lines.   Tenant
acreage, roughly supposed to have been about 20 per cent
at the beginning of the Meiji Period, increased rapidly
throughout the early years of this period.   This increase
may, perhaps, be attributed to the rapid changes in economic
life which occurred during the same period.   For example,
the removal of the ban on transactions involving land
property and the system of money payment of public dues,
instituted in 1873, are two factors which may be regarded as
causal elements.   At any rate, in 1887 the tenant acreage
was estimated by Dr. Paul Mywatt, a German expert in
the employ of the Japanese Government, at 39·89 per cent.[2]
Since 1905 we have had access to more elaborate and
accurate statistics concerning land distribution.[3]   Those

---

[1] Cf. *Saikin no Shakai Undo*, Kyochokai, cited, p. 388 ; Hashimoto,
D., and Nagai, S., Editors, *op. cit.*, p. 552 ; Nasu, H., *op. cit.*, p. 59 ;
Takahashi, K., *Nihon Noson Keizai no Kenkyu*, cited, p. 64 ; Nagai, T.,
op. cit., p. 185 ; Ono, T., " Tenant System in the Tokugawa Era," *Hogaku
Kyokai Zasshi*, 88 : 12, Dec., 1930, pp. 1–29.
[2] Hashimoto, D., and Nagai, S., Editors, *op. cit.*, p. 550.
[3] The ratios of tenant acreage since 1905 and those of tenant farmers
to total farmers since 1910 are as follows (*Honpo Nogyo Yoran*, cited,
1931, pp. 10, 33) :

PERCENTAGE OF TENANT ACREAGE TO TOTAL FARM ACREAGE, 1905–30

Year.	Percentage.	Year.	Percentage.
1905	43·9	1920	45·9
1910	45·2	1925	45·8
1915	45·4	1930	47·8

DISTRIBUTION OF LANDED AND TENANT FARMERS, IN 1910, 1920, AND
1930

(Percentages)

Farmers.	1910.	1920.	1930.
Landed	33·4	31·3	31·1
Part-tenant	27·4	28·1	26·5
Tenant	39·2	40·6	42·3

statistical data reveal the fact that somewhat less than 50 per cent of the total acreage is cultivated by tenants, an aggregate of approximately 4 million farmers who comprise about 70 per cent of the total number of farm households.

In this connection, various investigations of average rental fees have been instituted in recent years.[1] The data presented by the Bureau of Agriculture indicates that the customary rents of rice fields range anywhere from less than 25 per cent to more than 80 per cent of the value of the produce, and both the average and median rents are above 50 per cent. It must be pointed out in this connection, too, that in Japan the landlords are required to pay only the land taxes ; all other farming expenses are met by the tenants. Thus, agricultural rents in Japan, although perhaps not as extremely high as in other Oriental countries, are exorbitant when compared with those of the old agricultural nations in the West. According to the *Nihon Nogyo Nenkan* (the Japan Agricultural Year-Book), the Japanese rate is 7 times that of England, 3·5 times that of Germany, about 4 times that of Italy, and 3 times those of Denmark and Holland.[2] It is rather surprising that the vast and ever-increasing population of tenants and part-tenants have silently endured, until quite recently, the feudal heritage of such exorbitant rentals.

An indication of an upheaval in this anomalous situation of rural Japan is found in the tenants' disputes. These disputes, which emerged as one of the general mass movements during the Great War and numbered 85 in 1917, increased to 2,206 in 1925 and to 5,828 in 1934.[3] The disputes are not peculiar to any one region or locality, but, rather, are common to almost every agricultural district in Japan proper.

There were in 1930, 4,208 peasants' unions. About one-half of the tenants' disputes in that year were directed by

---

[1] See footnote, p. 156.
[2] Cf. Hashimoto, D., and Nagai, S., Editors, *op. cit.*, p. 111.
[3] *Kosaku Nenpo* (Annual Report on Tenantry), Bureau of Agriculture, Department of Agriculture and Forestry, Japan, 1930, p. 2 ; *Kaizo Nenkan* (Kaizo Year-Book), 1935, Supplement of *Kaizo*, Jan., 1935, p. 232.

[1] The Bureau of Agriculture conducted an elaborate survey of rentals which were actually paid during the period between 1915 and 1920 ; the result of this study is cited in the following tabulation. See *Kosaku Kanko ni Kansuru Shiryo* (Materials in the Customs on Tenancy), Department of Agriculture and Commerce, Japan, pp. 14 ff.   See also Nasu, H., *Kosei naru Kosakuryo* (Studies of What Constitutes a Fair Rent), Tokyo, Iwanani Co., 1925, p. 47.

AVERAGE RATIOS OF RENT OF PADDY AND UPLAND FIELDS TO TOTAL VALUE OF PRODUCTS, 1915–20 (Percentages)

I. Paddy Fields

Fields.	Rent Paid by :	High.	Usual.	Low.
One-crop fields . . .	Rice	53·3	51·0	46·9
Two-crop fields . . .	Rice	57·4	55·0	52·9

II. Upland Fields

Rent Paid by :	Percentage.	Rent Paid by :	Percentage.
Rice	40·0	Barley-beans . . .	40·6
Beans	35·0	Money	27·6
Rye	26·0		

The rents for paddy fields, with which the tenant problem is most often concerned (more than 80 per cent of the land over which tenants' disputes occurred in 1932 were over paddy fields) are tabulated below in percentage groups with 5 per cent intervals :

TOWNS AND VILLAGES GROUPED ACCORDING TO PREVALENT RENT RATIO, BY 5 PER CENT GROUPS OF PADDY FIELDS, 1915–20

Rent Groups (percentages).	One-Crop Fields.		Two-Crop Fields.	
	Number.	Per cent of Total.	Number.	Per cent of Total.
Under 25	51	—*	12	—*
25–29	25	—*	6	—*
30–34	140	2	37	—*
35–39	303	3	98	2
40–44	970	11	373	6
45–49	1,470	16	750	12
50–54	3,474	38	1,854	31
55–59	1,222	13	1,086	18
60–64	851	9	937	16
65–69	331	4	424	7
70–74	157	2	235	4
75–79	80	—*	103	2
Over 80	60	—*	120	2
Total	9,134	100	6,035	100
Median	50·2%	—	54·6%	—

* Less than 1 per cent.

left wing organizations. One foreign observer was surprised that the discontent and radical tendencies that are usually associated with an urban proletariat are in Japan more prominent among the rural population.[1] In view of the fact that the tenants enjoy a larger share in community life than do urban workers, this development is quite natural. One of the outstanding disputes, involving 250 landlords and 1,382 tenants, lasted for several years.[2] Such a conflict affects and often dislocates the traditional rural economic and social relationships.[3]

The true significance of the recent trend is seen in the development of the nature of the disputes. Originally they were limited to questions pertaining to the harvest season, and were chiefly concerned with the matter of discount on the rent in the event of a bad crop. Now many of the disputes extend over the whole year, and are most often concerned with the right of tenancy and the equity of the rent. The ratio of disputes concerned with the right of tenancy, which occupied only 1·6 per cent of all disputes in 1924, increased in a phenomenal degree, so that in 1933 it had reached 56·0 per cent.[4]

The disputes of tenants over the right of tenancy are caused by demands on the part of the landlords for the ceding back of the land either as a measure of reprisal against tenants' movements or as a means of cultivating the land previously rented to tenants.[5] The latter tendency was accorded impetus among small landlords by a new tax regulation which allowed a tax reduction on fields cultivated by owners themselves.[6] Disputes of this kind between landlords and their tenants present a graphic picture of the land hunger in rural Japan.

When landlords take fields back from their tenants they usually cultivate them on a larger scale and, not infrequently, mechanize the farming, thereby giving rise to a surplus of

[1] Cf. Crocker, W. R., *op. cit.*, p. 92.
[2] *Kosaku Sogichi ni Okeru Noson Jijo no Henka*, Kyochokai, cited, p. 5.
[3] *Ibid.*, pp. 1, 4.
[4] *Kosaku Nenpo*, cited, 1930, p. 17 ; *Kaizo Nenkan*, cited, 1935, p. 232.
[5] *Ibid.*, p. 9.
[6] Nasu, H., *Noson Shakai Mondai*, cited, p. 172.

rural labour.[1]   The reshaping of agricultural conditions as
a result of the tenants' disputes is well illustrated by the
case in Kanabashi Mura of Nara Prefecture which is cited
here.   During a serious dispute, some of the landlords in
that village pooled their lands and formed an agricultural
company to carry on large-scale production.   As a consequence of this merger, many tenants were affected ; twelve
lost their farms entirely and two of them were thereby forced
to migrate to Osaka.[2]   In 1930 there were 640 such unions
comprising 53,278 landlords and 94 agricultural companies
founded by landlords.[3]

There are two principal proposals calculated to remedy
the widespread agrarian discontent : (1) The creation of
peasant proprietorships, and (2) the establishment of right
of tenancy independent of ordinary civil lease regulations.
These proposals have been the respective platforms of the
two major political parties.   However, the creation of
peasant proprietorships on a large scale is most unlikely and
unfeasible in view of the financial difficulties involved.

F.   Fundamental Causes of Agrarian Discontent

The agrarian discontent in Japan is of such a nature and
virulence that even the settlement of the tenant problem
will not entirely solve the acute problem.   The fundamental
factor in the disturbance is the inevitable conflict between
cultural pressure conducing to a rising standard of living,
and the social and economic customs of " farmers of forty
centuries," [4] as Dr. King has aptly phrased it.   In truth,
the elevation of the standard of living can justly be regarded
as the main aim of human effort, and is a process that
cannot be inhibited.

The most important step toward raising the Japanese
farmers' standard of living is to replace by machinery the

[1] Cf. *Social Reform*, No. 108, Special Unemployment Problem Number,
p. 91.
[2] *Kosaku Sogichi ni Okeru Noson Jijo no Henka*, Kyochokai, cited, pp.
92–3.
[3] *Honpo Nogyo Yoran*, cited, 1931, pp. 145, 147.
[4] King, F. H., *Farmers of Forty Centuries, or, Permanent Agriculture
in China, Korea, and Japan*, Madison, Wisconsin, 1911.

primitive methods of human labour now employed for almost all processes of agriculture. This mechanization of agriculture would also enable the farmers to cultivate a larger acreage. Indeed, since the post-Great War period we have witnessed some progress in this direction. Oil burning and electric engines for agricultural use numbered only 2,468 at the end of 1920 ; by September, 1927, the number had increased to 51,009, and in November, 1933, there were 118,352 such machines in use.[1] However, these machines until the present time have been used almost exclusively for the " dressing up " of crops, as in the thrashing and hulling of rice, and there is almost none employed for the more arduous tilling and cultivation of the farmland. The use of machinery for the latter purpose meets with a serious obstacle in the topographical nature of Japan. Nevertheless, the employment of machine power will eventually replace the archaic system of human labour. It requires fourteen days of human labour to cultivate one acre of land, while a three-horse plough tills three acres a day, and a tractor tills eight acres a day. The relative efficiencies are 1, 42, and 112.[2] In view of the rapid inflow of modern methods into Japan, therefore, it is hardly conceivable that the Japanese farmers will permanently cling to the age-old hand-labour method of farming. Technically and economically, if not socially, a new adjustment of the man-land ratio is unavoidable.

Mechanized equipment requires capital, and, moreover, it cannot replace human labour in the intensive utilization of land usually necessary to increase yields.[3] Nevertheless, the mechanization of Japanese agriculture will progress. The development of the tenants' disputes and the rising standard of living of the farmers indicate a tendency in this direction. In the long run the rural distribution of the population will adjust itself to this changing trend of national economic life.

[1] *Honpo Nogyo Yoran*, cited, 1936, p. 114.
[2] After C. L. Alsberg. Cf. Nasu, H., *Jinko Shokuryo Mondai* (Population and Food Problem), Tokyo, Nihon Hyoronsha, 1927, p. 74.
[3] Cf. Charles Gide, *Principes D'Economic Politique*, Librairie du Recueil Sirey, 1931, p. 72.

The capacity of rural Japan to maintain numbers of people is, unquestionably, very limited ; it can, in fact, be regarded as a potential factor in the nation's future over-population. Any effective rationalization of rural economy will stimulate an overflow from this reserve of actually existing population. This development has already been intimated ; [1] it remains for us now to examine the possi-bilities and potentialities of food supply.

[1] *Supra*, p. 158.

CHAPTER VIII

PROBLEMS OF FOOD SUPPLY

A. Introduction

JAPAN to-day is dependent, in part at least, on outside
sources for the first two of the three categories of materials
indispensable for any people's subsistence, viz. food, shelter,
and clothing. It will be recalled that in 1897 the nation
turned from being a food exporter and became a food
importer.[1] Although the extent and significance of this
situation was, perhaps, not fully recognized at the time,
it has in recent years risen to considerable proportions. In
1931 and 1932 the net value of food imported amounted to
56 million yen. Furthermore, the net value of materials
imported for shelter amounted to 21 million yen in 1931
and to 13 million yen in 1932. These imports were paid
for by Japan's exportation of clothing materials, which
amounted in 1931 to 291 million yen and in 1932 to 334
million yen.[2] Incidentally, these amounts also paid for a
greater portion of the balance of Japan's international
trade.

As indicated in this brief analysis of Japan's foreign
trade, the matter of food supply cannot be regarded as the
pivotal issue in the nation's population problem. For in
this day of world commerce other factors may, and very
often do, offset a situation which, on its face, seems alarm-
ing. Nevertheless, a consideration of the relationship
between the food supply and the population problem is
justifiable for several reasons : (1) the fundamental truth

---

[1] See *supra*, p. 39 ; see also *infra*, p. 181.
[2] *Kokusei Zukai*, cited, 1933, p. 37.

of the theory of diminishing returns in agriculture and the unlimited potentiality of population increase; (2) the inelastic nature of the demand for food; (3) the necessity of adequate preparation for the emergency of war; (4) the gradual exhaustion of the possibility of commercial exploitation of agricultural countries; (5) the recent tendency toward the revival of economic nationalism, which, in brief, means national self-sufficiency with regard to the materials of industry. In view of these facts it is quite natural that the food problem should awaken the nation to an examination of the population problem. As a matter of fact, in Japan the question of the nation's food supply has assumed a position of paramount importance in the consideration of the larger problem. This is evidenced in the appointment in 1927 of a commission for the investigation of the problems of population and food supply.

B. Supply and Demand of Food

In recent years the total export value of food amounted to about half of the value of imported foodstuffs, which normally amounts to between 100 and 200 million yen. Of the items of food which Japan imported in 1931, pulse, wheat, sugar, canned and raw meat, miscellaneous crops, and rice totalled above 5 million yen in each case. In that year the chief food exports, the value of which exceeded 5 million yen in each item, were canned food, rice, sugar, aquatic products, flour, tea, and peas.[1]

Japan's import of food from her colonies is reported annually at 300 million yen. This brings the nation's annual net import of food to between 400 and 500 million yen. In addition to this, Japan each year purchases approximately 150 million yen worth of fertilizer from abroad.

Below is a table citing the production, net export or import (including to and from colonies), gross and *per capita* consumption of ordinary foodstuffs for the five-year period 1925–9.

[1] *Kinyujiko Sankosho*, cited, 1932, pp. 386–7.

TABLE LXXIV

ANNUAL AVERAGE SUPPLY AND DEMAND OF MAJOR FOOD CROPS,
1925–9 [1]

(Denomination Koku)

Crop.	Production.	Net Export or Import (−).	Consumption.	*Per Capita* Consumption.
Rice . . .	59,452,086	−10,008,266	69,460,352	1·1440
Barley . . .	7,938,560	61,562	7,876,998	0·1276
Rye . . .	7,396,441	—	7,396,441	0·1200
Wheat . . .	6,158,133	−2,889,651	9,047,784	0·1466
Soya bean .	3,217,930	− 4,735,708	7,953,638	0·1296
Small red bean	849,907	− 514,936	1,364,843	0·0222
Sweet potato .	894,284*	− 16,882*	911,166*	14·80†
Potato . . .	246,946*	4,429*	242,517*	3·93†

* 1,000 kwan.
† 1 kwan ; 1 koku equals C.1·8 hectolitre and 1 kwan equals 3·75 kilograms.

The recent trend in Japan's *per capita* consumption of the
above-mentioned major foods is depicted in the following
tabulation of three-, four- and five-year averages since 1912.

TABLE LXXV

ANNUAL AVERAGE *PER CAPITA* CONSUMPTION OF MAJOR FOOD
CROPS [2]

(Denomination Koku)

Crop.	1912–16.	1917–21.	1922–6.	1927–30.
Rice	1·060	1·133	1·127	1·102
Wheat	0·105	0·143	0·152	0·142
Barley	0·189	0·162	0·141	0·116
Rye	0·151	0·142	0·114	0·111
Soya bean . . .	0·126	0·140	0·137	0·127
Small red bean . .	0·020	0·021	0·024	0·021
Sweet potato * . . .	19·713	20·071	16·781	14·062†
Potato *	4·273	6·359	3·994	3·890†

* 1 kwan.　　　　　　† 1927–29.

Table LXXIV shows that the production of rice leads
all other crops, being 7·5 times as great as barley, Japan's

[1] *Honpo Nogyo Yoran*, cited, 1931, pp. 215–25.
[2] *Ibid.*, pp. 215–25.

second most important crop.   Moreover, rice is the nation's
most widely consumed food, occupying a position 7·7 times
as great as flour, the next most important food.
Table LXXV illustrates the rapid decline in the consumption
of all crops except rice and wheat.   The facts contained in
both tables establish the basis for the common view held by
Japanese that the rice problem constitutes, *per se*, the food
problem.

C. Supply and Demand of Rice

Japan has an unbroken series of detailed statistics deal-
ing with this crop dating as far back as 1878.   The value
of the annual production of rice was estimated recently
at 1 to 2 billion yen, depending chiefly on the price fluctuations.   Approximately half of this production is com-
mercialized and constitutes the most valuable single article
of commerce in Japan.   Adding imported rice to this,
about 40 million koku of rice are bought and sold in
the domestic market.[1]   Furthermore, since rice is the most
important food staple in Japan, the trend of its consumption is the best single measure of the nation's standard of
living.[2]   Consequently the study of Japan's rice problem
is of great interest.

The average gross and *per capita* consumption of rice
have been computed in five-year periods from the statistics
of the crop production, the balance of export and import,
and the median of the production.   In addition to these
figures, the statistics of the production of rice per unit
area and the general trend of its production and consumption
are tabulated in Table LXXVI.

These figures reveal many noteworthy facts concerning
the rice supply of Japan.   During the forty-five-year period
from 1880–4 to 1925–9 the production increased by 98 per
cent, while, it should be added, the acreage of rice increased
only to the extent of 25 per cent.   This data obviously indicates an increase in the productivity per unit acreage, which

---

[1] Hashimoto, D., and Nagai, S., Editors, *op. cit.*, p. 158.
[2] Cf. Crocker, W. R., *op. cit.*, p. 58 ; Allen, G. C., *op. cit.*, p. 180.

TABLE LXXVI

ANNUAL AVERAGE SUPPLY AND DEMAND, per CHO YIELD, AND *PER CAPITA* CONSUMPTION OF RICE, 1880–1931 [1]

(Denomination Koku)

Year.	Production.	Per Cho Yield.	Net Imp. (−) or Exp.	Consumption.	Pop. (Unit 1,000).	Per Capita Production.	Per Capita Consumption.
1880–84 . . .	29,958,186	11·59	180,139	29,778,047	37,259	0·804	0·799
1885–89	36,577,309	13·78	735,857	35,841,452	38,703	0·945	0·926
1890–94	40,355,071	14·64	− 366,755	40,721,826	40,508	0·996	1·005
1895–99	39,265,273	14·00	− 1,152,058	40,417,331	42,400	0·926	0·953
1900–04	44,643,328	15·64	− 2,739,903	47,383,231	44,964	0·993	1·054
1905–09	47,579,742	16·34	− 3,175,250	50,754,992	47,416	1·003	1·070
1910–14	51,166,907	17·06	− 2,963,764	54,130,671	50,577	1·012	1·070
1915–19	56,892,648	18·46	− 4,175,061	61,067,709	54,134	1·051	1·128
1920–24	56,339,472	18·59	− 5,907,616	62,247,088	56,798	0·992	1·096
1925–29	59,452,086	18·71	− 10,008,266	69,460,352	60,712	0·979	1·144
1930–31	61,045,399	18·82	− 8,503,000	69,548,399	64,050	0·953	1·086
Index Numbers							
1880–84 . . .	100	100	—	100	100	100	100
1925–29 . . .	198	161	—	233	163	122	143

[1] *Kome Tokeihyo* (Statistical Tables on Rice), Statistical Section, Department of Agriculture and Forestry, Japan, 1931, pp. 10, 15, 37.

amounted to 61 per cent for the period under consideration. The median population of the first and last five-year periods, 1880–4 and 1925–9, showed an increase of 63 per cent. Yet, in spite of this increase in numbers, the *per capita* production of rice increased 22 per cent. Moreover, in the 1925–9 period Japan imported over 10 million koku (net) of rice. This was in considerable contrast to the nation's previous status as an exporter of this crop ; as indicated by the above table, Japan's rice exports amounted to 180,000 koku in the first five-year period, and 735,000 koku in the second five-year period. This reversal in status is due solely to the increase in consumption. The average total and *per capita* consumption increased by 133 per cent and 43 per cent, respectively, during the entire period studied here.

It will be recalled that during the Great War Japan experienced serious disturbances arising from the mal-distribution of rice, which had not yet been adjusted to the rapid increase in consumption.[1] The *per capita* consumption increased from 1·070 koku in 1910–4 to 1·128 koku in 1915–9. The unfortunate rice riots which occurred in the summer of 1918 culminated this maladjustment in the nation's rice distribution.

During the early part of this century, Japan's annual importation of rice increased rapidly. During the period from 1908–12 to 1913–7 the net import of foreign and colonial products increased from 2·2 million koku to 2·7 million koku. In the next two five-year periods these imports grew to 5·9 and 9·3 million koku.[2] At the same time the relative positions of the sources of supply of imported rice experienced a considerable change in favour of Japan's own colonies. The amount of rice imported from Chosen, which was only one quarter of a million koku in 1912, now reaches more than 5 million koku annually. Taiwan, which supplied less than 1 million koku in 1912, now sends more than 2 million koku to Japan proper every year.

[1] Cf. Takada, Y., " Social Nature of the Food Problem," *Keizaishi Kenkyu*, No. 7, May, 1930, p. 184.

[2] *Honpo Nogyo Yoran*, cited, 1931, p. 216 ; *Kome Tokeihyo*, cited, 1931, p. 37.

Consequently, during the past twenty years the nation's rice imports from foreign countries dropped from 2 to 1 million koku.

Below are cited the figures depicting the rice consumption during the 1925–9 period in reference to the source of supply.

TABLE LXXVII

AVERAGE ANNUAL SUPPLY OF RICE CLASSIFIED BY ITS SOURCES, 1925–9 [1]

Source of Supply.	Amount (Koku).	Percentage of Total.
Japan proper . . .	57,935,000	84·635
Chosen	5,596,000	8·175
Taiwan	2,407,000	3·516
Foreign countries . .	2,515,000	3·674
Total	68,453,000	100·000

This table indicates the fact that Japan proper furnishes nearly 85 per cent of the rice consumed in the country. The remaining 15 per cent comes from the nation's colonies, which supply almost 12 per cent, and several foreign countries, which contribute slightly more than 3 per cent of Japan's rice. The principal foreign sources of supply are Siam, French Indo-China, British India, and the United States. However, in recent years these imports have been practically limited to those from Siam and the United States.[2] If we include the colonies, the Japanese Empire supplies nearly 97 per cent of the rice consumed by the nation.

D. CHARACTERISTIC PROBLEMS OF JAPANESE RICE

Rice, which is the staple food of Japan, is less marketable than wheat, the staple crop of the West. Japan is the third greatest rice-producing nation in the world, ranking next to India and China. India, Indo-China, and Siam have large export capacity, their total annual export being about 33 million koku, which corresponds to approximately

---

[1] *Beikoku Yoran* (Brief Report on Rice), Bureau of Agriculture, Department of Agriculture and Forestry, Japan, 1930, p. 4.
[2] *Ibid.*, p. 13; Hasimoto, D., and Nagai, S., Editors, *op. cit.*, p. 157.

55 per cent of the rice production of Japan proper and equals about one-fourth of the quantity of wheat that enters the world's export markets.[1]

In addition to the limited marketability of rice, there is one factor which makes the rice supply in Japan particularly rigid. Despite the fact that the quality of rice is not standardized to the extent of that of wheat, a suitable substitute for the Japanese product which is more palatable to the Japanese had not been introduced to Japanese markets until relatively recent years. The late Dr. Inagaki of Tokyo Imperial University pointed out that the difference in the quality is a negligible item compared to the fact that the " foreign rice," which for the most part comes from tropical and subtropical regions, has a coarse skin of cells which contain protein, and do not break when the rice is boiled, thereby producing a tough and unpalatable food. Dr. Inagaki maintained further that in contrast to this " foreign rice," the cell skin of the Japanese product is soft and easily broken when boiled, and the protein content therefore produces a glutinous effect which makes this rice soft and more tasteful.[2]

For this reason the rice market of Japan has been rather rigidly protected for the home-grown product; this has kept the price at a high level, thereby making it possible to increase the per hectare production regardless of the ensuing increase in the cost. Consequently both the per hectare production and the cost of production of rice in Japan are without parallel among major rice-producing countries.[3] Before the depression of 1930 the average cost of production

---

[1] *Kokusei Zukai*, cited, 1933, p. 97.

[2] Kato, Genchi, Editor, *Genka no Shakai Mondai to Shiso Mondai* (Present-Day Social Problems and Thoughts), Tokyo, Aikokusha, 1922, pp. 251–68.

[3] Average per hectare production of rice in Japan, Siam, and India at designated periods are as follows (denomination quintals) :

Country.						1924–8.	1928–32.
Japan	.	.	.	.	.	34·0	34·1
Siam .	.	.	.	.	.	18·1	16·4
India	.	.	.	.	.	14·1	14·6

See *International Year-Book of Agricultural Statistics*, Rome, International Institute of Agriculture, 1930–1, p. 177 ; 1932–3, p. 171.

in Japan was 37·00 yen per koku ; this was from 50 to 100 per cent above the production level in China and in the United States.[1] Even in 1918, the year in which the rice riots spread throughout Japan, the average price quotation of the imported crops remained at considerable variance with the quotations of Japanese rice.[2]

During 1918 the average price of Chosenese rice was quoted on the Osaka Rice Market above that of Japanese products. However, this was, undoubtedly, a special instance, for Osaka is the greatest and oldest consuming centre of Chosenese rice. In general colonial and foreign rice was regarded as a necessary supplementary supply rather than a substitute for the native product. During the following two years, 1919 and 1920, the average price of Japanese medium-grade rice was quoted in Tokyo at the exorbitant rates of 51·24 yen and 48·56 yen, respectively.[3]

E. PRESSURE OF COLONIAL PRODUCTION AND OVER-SUPPLY OF RICE IN JAPAN

In the face of such an emergency as that which arose during the Great War, the Government adopted the policy of encouraging the transplanting of Japanese rice in Chosen and Taiwan as well as the general expansion of agriculture in these two colonies. In addition, in 1919, the Reclamation Subsidy Law in Japan proper was enacted. In response to the policies of the home government, colonial govern-

---

[1] Nasu, H., *Jinko Shokuryo Mondai,* cited, p. 153. The Japanese find American rice equally palatable as their own.

[2] This is demonstrated in the following table :

AVERAGE PRICE OF JAPANESE, RANGOON, CHOSENESE, AND TAIWANESE RICE IN TOKYO, OSAKA, AND KOBE MARKETS, 1918

Rice.	Grade.	Price (Yen per Koku).	Market.
Japanese, Uncoated . .	Medium	37·94	Kobe
" Rangoon " (Indian) . .	No. 1	22·45	,,
Japanese, Coated . . .	Medium	28·84	Osaka
Chosenese, ,, . . .	Fusan, No. 3	30·90	,,
Japanese, ,, . . .	Medium	32·75	Tokyo
Taiwanese, ,, . . .	Taichu	27·34	,,

See Kawada, S., " On the Relationship of the Price of Rice and the Tariff," *Keizai Ronso,* 20 : 6, June, 1925, pp. 943–62.

[3] *Beikoku Yoran,* cited, 1930, p. 17.

ments formulated far-reaching plans designed to extend rice culture. The details of these plans will be explained later.[1] As the result of the improvement of rice culture it has become possible to substitute Chosenese rice for Japanese rice as a staple food for Japanese people. The recent success in the transplanting of Japanese rice in Taiwan is another consequence of the colonies' plans for the extension of rice culture.

When the substitution of colonial rice for Japanese rice became possible Chosenese rice began to be the dominant crop in the Osaka-Kobe area and, more recently, in the Tokyo-Yokohama area. If the market is left open, it is expected by some experts that Chosenese rice will ultimately dominate in all the rice consumption centres of Japan.[2]

A comparison of the average retail price of Japanese and colonial rice in the public retail markets of various consumption centres in 1930 showed that Chosenese rice is a strong contender with the native product in the Japanese markets, ranking in price between the second and third grades of Japanese rice. It is natural, therefore, that Chosen be encouraged to produce rice for exportation to Japan, especially since the cost of production in Chosen is considerably lower than in Japan. The comparative cost of

[1] See *infra*, p. 180.
[2] Cf. Hashimoto, D., and Nagai, S., Editors, *op. cit.*, pp. 161–2. Below is a table citing the comparative substitutability of colonial rice for Japanese rice as reflected in the retail prices of Japanese and colonial uncoated rice in the public retail markets of various consumption centres in 1930. (*Tokei Nenkan*, cited, No. 51, 1932, pp. 127–9.)

AVERAGE RETAIL PRICE OF JAPANESE AND COLONIAL RICE IN PRINCIPAL
CITIES, 1930

(Yen per 0·1 Koku)

Public Market.	Japanese Rice.			Chosenese Rice.	Taiwanese Rice.
	No. 1.	No. 2.	No. 3.		
Tokyo . . .	3·70	3·22	3·09	3·09	3·01
Yokohama . .	3·28	3·09	2·90	—	1·93
Nagoya . .	—	3·03	2·65	2·81	2·21
Osaka . . .	3·17	3·02	—	2·80	2·83
Kyoto . . .	3·00	2·85	—	2·78	2·35

production per koku in Japan proper and in Chosen was reported as follows : [1]

Date.	Cost of Production of Japanese Rice.	Date.	Cost of Production of Chosenese Rice.
1922–29	*c.* 40·00 yen	1923	26·00–29·00 yen
1926	*c.* 34·00 yen	1926	24·00–26·00 yen

In addition to the low cost of production, colonial rice is more standardized and handled by keener capitalistic interests, not infrequently under Japanese management. This higher standardization and keener business management of production contributes to the high commercial value of colonial rice as compared to the Japanese rice, which, in the main, is raised and marketed by individual farmers.[2]

Thus, while the marketability of Japanese rice is limited, the important sources of supply have been developed and exploited under Government policy. Concerning the rice supply, the relationship between the colonies and Japan has become paradoxical. Although the colonies hold the key to the solution of the problem of food supply in Japan, at the moment products of these colonies have depressed Japanese agriculture. To illustrate : since Chosenese rice is ever ready to fill the rice markets in Japan, a poor agricultural season in Japan cannot be compensated by a high price. On the other hand, a good crop may, and frequently does, ruin the farmer, since this results in a sharp decline in the price. Nevertheless, Japan proper cannot supply her own need ; she must rely on colonial products for a sufficient food supply.

In 1930, 66,876,000 koku of rice were produced in Japan. This was 12·5 per cent in excess of the average annual yield during the period 1925–9. As a result of this increase in production, the Japanese farmers were virtually ruined. As was pointed out by Dr. Nasu, the price of rice declines in a degree disproportionate to the increase in production ; thus, according to him, when the crop rises by from 10 to

[1] Yagi, Y., " The Relationship of Japan Proper to Chosen as regards the Rice Supply," *Keizai Ronso,* 33 : 3, p. 378.

[2] Cf. Hashimoto, D., and Nagai, S., Editors, *op. cit.*, pp. 161–2 ; *Keizai Orai,* July, 1932, p. 253.

20 per cent, the price declines by from 30 to 40 per cent, and the total income of the farmers is reduced to the extent of about 350 million yen.[1]

Where the crop of 1930 was extraordinarily large, we find the crop of 1934 to be the smallest since 1913, being only 51,840,182 koku. Despite this decrease in rice production, there was at the end of 1935 crop year (October 31, 1935) a carry-over to the new crop year of 9,936,000 koku, nearly double of the supposedly optimum carry-over. This is clearly revealed in the following figures : [2]

Crop Years.					Amount of Carry-over (Koku).
1920–4 Average	.	.	.	.	.	6,594,704
1925–9 Average	.	.	.	.	.	6,420,219
1930	.	.	.	.	.	5,704,871
1931	.	.	.	.	.	9,140,247
1932	.	.	.	.	.	8,907,430
1933	.	.	.	.	.	9,007,598
1934	.	.	.	.	.	16,430,872
1935	.	.	.	.	.	9,936,000

When we consider the above figures jointly with Table LXXVI we appreciate their full import. For the two five-year periods of 1920–4 and 1925–9 the average annual consumption amounted to 62 million koku and 69 million koku respectively. From the " population versus means of subsistence " point of view, neglecting for the moment the consideration of the declining *per capita* consumption,[3] this might be interpreted as indicating the bounty of nature. But the effect of this surplus supply on the present-day system of exchange economy is oppressive. Thus it is evident that the food problem involves complicated problems of value and distribution. We may consider those aspects of the problem relating to the efforts of the Government to control the price of rice.

F. Government Rice Policy

Although the Government has been determined to increase the supply of rice, particularly since the Great War, at the

---

[1] See *Kaizo*, Nov., 1930, pp. 177–81.
[2] *Beikoku Yoran*, cited, 1935, p. 5.   [3] See *infra*, p. 176.

same time it has been anxious to combat radical fluctuations in the price of rice. Only two years after the enactment of the Reclamation Subsidy Law, i.e. in 1921, Japan enacted the Rice Law. This was a measure calculated to enable the Government to institute and maintain a price high enough to stabilize agriculture. To attain this end the Government was empowered to purchase, sell, exchange, dress, and store rice. In addition, the Government was granted the power to regulate the tariff on rice as well as the importation of rice from foreign countries. In connection with the Rice Law the Special Rice Account of 200 million yen was created, ostensibly to control 3 million koku.[1] This special account was increased many times and when the Rice Law was replaced by the Rice Control Law in 1933, the sum had risen to 480 million yen for the handling 12 million koku. The failure of this Rice Law is amply evident from the fact that up to the early part of the 1933 crop year, the net loss of the Special Rice Account, which theoretically is self-sustaining—depending on the effectiveness of the control—reached the total of 200 million yen.[2]

The Rice Control Law, which has been in effect since November 1, 1933, in lieu of the Rice Law, retains the function of the open market operation in order to control the seasonal fluctuations of the price of rice. But the important feature of the new law is the economic power vested in the Government to regulate the price of rice. In December of every year and at any other time of emergency the Government may announce the minimum and the maximum standard prices. Thereupon it becomes obligatory to the Government to buy at the minimum and to sell at the maximum when there are such offers. The minimum price is based on the cost of production, and the maximum price is based on the level of the cost of living.[3] To make possible and effective this vast and important function of the Rice

---

[1] *1920–30 Seiji Keizai Nenkan*, cited, p. 98.

[2] *The Osaka Asahi*, Nov. 8, 1933, p. 2.

[3] The study of the cost of living and the cost of production of rice has progressed in Japan in recent years in connection with the administration of control over this commodity. The maximum standard price is fixed at a point designed to enable classes with monthly incomes of 50 to 100 yen to purchase rice in sufficient quantity for their needs.

Control Law, the Special Rice Account increased the fund to 700 million yen.[1] In December of 1933 the maximum and the minimum standard prices were fixed at 30·50 yen and 23·30 yen, respectively, for the 1934 rice year.

In the event the Government is compelled to purchase at the minimum standard price the estimated surplus of the rice supply in the 1934 crop year, which amounts to about 11·5 million koku above the ideal carry-over, the greater part of the net operation fund of the Special Rice Account would, of necessity, be spent immediately. This impelling condition led the legislature in the spring of 1934 to raise the special account to 850 million yen, and at the same time to provide for an allowance up to 300 million yen to take care of the accrued loss in the account. In effect the legislature had appropriated over a billion yen to the Special Rice Account.

With these large funds at their disposal, the Government was prepared to meet offers to buy at the minimum standard price. Thus, by May, 1934, more than 10 million koku were purchased at prevailing minimums, in addition to purchases made in the open market in an attempt to control the seasonal fluctuations of the market. This determined effort on the part of the Government to regulate the rice market was the first effective venture in the Government's rice policy ; after April, 1934, the market price of rice rose, reaching a higher level than that of the Government's purchase price.

However, it was obvious that another year with bountiful crop would have easily smashed this control structure. In view of this difficulty, the Government drafted a supplementary Autonomous Rice Control Law as early as the first of 1935. This supplementary law was finally passed by the Diet in May, 1936, after a year's delay caused by antagonistic manœuvres of the rice traders throughout the nation. Under this law, the Government in effect shifted the main burden of eliminating the surplus stock from the market

---

[1] This sum includes the accrued loss of about 200 million yen and also 70 million yen invested for equipment. The net working fund is therefore 430 million yen. Cf. *The Osaka Asahi*, Nov. 1, 1933 ; *Central Review*, Dec., 1933, p. 110.

to specially created local rice control co-operatives or other specified organizations in Japan proper, Chosen, and Taiwan and confined itself to the guarantee of the costs and losses incidental to the storing. In December of every year the Government will announce the amount, if any, of the excessive supply of rice which should be stored by recognized organizations.

Skilful administration of two existing major laws mentioned above, viz. the Rice Control Law and the Autonomous Rice Control Law, will satisfy the need of the nation for the moment. Nevertheless, these laws, concerned merely with the distribution of rice, do not attack the main causal issue of supply. Consequently, a few successive years of good crop will again threaten the foundation of these laws. It may be added, moreover, that in time these colossal schemes of rice control will prove but a disguised form of " work relief " administration, offering on the one hand a guarantee of production cost to domestic growers and, on the other, a considerable margin of profit to colonial producers. The ultimate practicability of the rice policy of the Government may, therefore, be questionable.

In anticipation of these situations, there are many proposals designed either to replace or to supplement the present measures. Some have favoured a Government monopoly of the distribution of rice ; others a restriction of the acreage devoted to rice cultivation ; and still others the control of the import of rice from colonial possessions. A measure to encourage storing of a limited amount of paddy by granting a subsidy to local co-operatives has been in operation since the fall of 1933.

Another device calculated to relieve the situation is the encouragement of rice consumption in Chosen as a means of preventing the flow of Chosenese rice to Japan proper. The three-year average *per capita* consumption of rice for 1930–2 was 0·473 koku in Chosen, as compared to 1·073 koku in Japan proper. Should the Chosenese *per capita* consumption of rice reach the Japanese level, Chosenese production for 1930–2, 16,250,000 koku, would have been deficient by 5 million koku. The Government formulated various means to encourage the consumption of rice by Chosenese.[1]   However, the anticipated effects of this policy cannot be realized very soon, for the export of rice to Japan proper is profitable especially since the Rice Control Law became effective at the close of 1933.   Moreover, should the policy of encouragement of consumption of rice in Chosen once be realized, it would disorganize the food policy of Japan, which is to supplement the domestic supply by rice from her colonies.

The influence of the consumption power of rice on the rice market is not limited to colonies.   The *per capita* consumption of rice, which is regarded as the best single measure of the standard of living in Japan,[2] reached its peak in 1921 and 1923, when the amount was recorded as 1·153 koku. Compared to this, the *per capita* consumption in 1932 and 1933 was 1·014 and 1·095 koku, respectively.   Had the *per capita* consumption in 1932 reached the level set in 1921 and 1923, the total consumption in 1932 would have been increased 9,161,490 koku.   This would have resulted in a shortage of almost one-quarter of a million koku instead of a surplus of 8·9 million koku which was carried over on October 31, 1932.   These figures assume, of course, that the import from the colonies would have remained.   Undoubtedly the decline in rice consumption in recent years has been a contributing factor to the nation's present over-supply of rice.

Other remedies proposed for this over-supply are the encouragement of the utilization of rice for the production of alcohol or fuel and the encouragement of rice exportations to foreign countries.   But the utilization of rice by the chemical industries cannot be regarded as being on a permanent economic basis ; and the possibility of large-scale exportation of Japanese rice is also very much limited.[3]

[1] *The Tokyo Nichi Nichi*, Nov. 13, 1933 ; *The Osaka Asahi*, Nov. 14, 1933.
[2] *Supra*, p. 172.
[3] E.g. at the only nominal price of 9·00 yen per koku the Government was unable to dispose of the rice carried over under the Rice Law in foreign lands at any year.   See Takahashi, K., " Failure of the Rice Policy : a Menace to the Rural Districts," *Keizai Orai*, May or June, 1931, p. 37.

Among the various proposals mentioned above, greater attention is now being centred on the possibilities of controlling the importation of colonial products. This attention is well founded, for if the importation of colonial rice remains uncontrolled, colonial rice will flow into Japan's markets in increasingly large quantities even at the minimum standard price announced under the Rice Control Law. The reason for this is simple ; since the minimum standard price is based upon the cost of production of rice in Japan proper, this price leaves a considerable margin of profit for colonial products, due to the lower cost of production in the colonies.[1]

However, inasmuch as Japan regards her colonies as sources of supply for both present and future increased demands for rice,[2] the colonial governments, including the Department of Overseas Affairs, are, of necessity, careful not to alienate the sympathies of the native colonial farmers.[3] Consequently a radical solution to the problem of regulation of colonial products may not at the present time be expected.[4]

Because of the small crop in 1934, the question of the control of the rice supply remained less acute in 1935. But the principal problem, that of the status of colonial rice in the Japanese market, still remains unsolved. Closely interwoven with this question is the problem of urban-rural relations.

Theoretically, the causes for these difficulties are on the one hand the uncontrolled supply of rice from the colonies, produced at a less cost than the rice grown in Japan proper, and, on the other, the nation's desire and necessity to protect rice growers in Japan proper. Briefly,

[1] As a matter of fact, with the approach of the enforcement of the Rice Control Law, the price of Taiwanese rice rose 75 per cent between August and November, 1933. Compared to this the price of Japanese rice rose only 50 per cent during the same period. See *The Osaka Asahi*, Nov. 10, 1933. For the comparative cost of Japanese and Chosenese rice see *supra*, p. 171.

[2] See *infra*, p. 180.

[3] Farmers numbered 82·1 per cent of the entire native workers in Chosen in 1930.

[4] Even the proposed plan for uniform reduction of rice cultivation for 1934 in Japan proper, Chosen, and Taiwan, was forcibly abandoned due to the determined opposition of the colonial authorities.

then, the problem is primarily how to preserve agricultural Japanese standards which can be maintained only at a high cost. Two additional objectives must be considered in any policy adopted, viz. the preservation of the agricultural population, and, thereby the preservation of rural markets for home industries.

It has been demonstrated that any substantial increase in the agricultural population of Japan cannot be expected.[1] This, however, does not imply that the preservation of the existing rural population is not to be desired, especially as a means of conserving the national morale. From the purely economic point of view, rapid urbanization, when accompanied by a large-scale desertation of the rural population, is likely to foreshadow an acute over-population problem. Concerning the second point, relative to the preservation of rural markets, the question arises : to what extent will the national profit of industry, dependent on the preservation of the rural markets in their present state, compensate for the increasing cost of food ? The food problem thus becomes the problem of affecting a healthy balance of national economy.

We have already surveyed the present food situation in Japan with a due reference to the historical background. Two other aspects of the problem remain to be considered, i.e. the future prospects of the food supply and the present nutritive value of Japanese food. Both, as will be seen, are essential for the formulation of any satisfactory food policy.

G. Estimate of Future Supply and Demand of Food

It has been shown that during the next thirty years the Japanese population will probably increase by about 20 million and that by 1960 the total population should reach about 90 million. Mr. Takeo Soda estimated that the population in 1957 would be 87,291,000 and 90,351,000 by 1960.[2] Meanwhile the *per capita* consumption of rice may increase. The agricultural authorities estimate the *per capita* con-

---

[1] See *supra*, p. 160.   [2] *Supra*, p. 133.

sumption in 1957 at 1·25 koku.[1] The spread of scientific
knowledge concerning the desirability of a variety in diet
may, of course, affect this estimate ; nevertheless, in view
of the improbability of a rapid and universal adoption of a
meat diet as in the West, and in view of the present tendency
toward a rapid decline in the consumption of cereals other
than rice and wheat, the above estimate may have a high
degree of accuracy. According to the estimates just cited of
population and of *per capita* consumption of rice, the total
rice consumption will reach 109,113,750 koku in 1957.

This amount roughly coincides with the estimate based
upon the past trend of gross rice consumption made by
Dr. H. Ando, Director of the National Agricultural Experimental Station. Following are Dr. Ando's figures of the
estimated rice consumption, together with the other commonly used cereals, in ten-year periods up to 1957.

TABLE LXXVIII

CONSUMPTION OF RICE, WHEAT, BARLEY AND RYE AS ESTIMATED
BY DR. ANDO, IN 1937, 1947, AND 1957 [2]

(Unit 1,000 Koku)

Year.	Rice.	Wheat.	Barley.	Rye.
1937	78,900	14,090	6,450	5,380
1947	90,110	17,370	5,180	4,290
1957	102,292	19,940	4,090	3,410

From the above estimates it may be fairly concluded
that the demand for rice in Japan will reach about 100
million koku within the next twenty-five years. The study
of the food problem, which was treated with much enthusiasm from the Great War period to about 1927 (when the
Population and Food Commission was organized), received
considerable impetus because of the dual factors of the
future demand for and the possible maladjustment of the
food supply. Under these circumstances the extension of
rice culture in Japan proper as well as in the colonies was
widely advocated.

[1] Hashimoto, D., and Nagai, S., Editors, *op. cit.*, p. 39.
[2] Nasu, H., *Jinko Shokuryo Mondai*, cited, p. 140.

According to this measure, 2 million cho devoted to agriculture are to be added in Japan proper. This additional area, combined with the probable increase of the per unit area productivity, which was estimated at 25 per cent, the total increase in production will reach 36 million koku. In Chosen 350,000 cho of land will be irrigated, and 200,000 cho of this new area will become paddy fields. With the improvement in productivity, the net increase of rice production will be 8,200,000 koku, of which 5 million koku will be exported to Japan, thereby bringing the nation's total import from Chosen to 10 million koku. In Taiwan the paddy acreage will be increased by 130,000 cho. Taking into consideration other improvements, an additional 3 million koku will be exported to Japan, making the total import from Taiwan 5 million koku.[1]

The above three plans will, together, increase the supply by 35 million koku. This would seem to be sufficient to meet the estimated demand in 1960. As for wheat, which is the only other major crop for which the demand is constantly increasing, Dr. Ando maintains that if the lands now used for the cultivation of barley and rye were used for raising wheat, the domestic crop would be increased to 20 million koku, which would be enough to supply the demand in 1960.[2]

According to these proposals, Japan, within the next thirty years, can be made self-sufficient with regard to her food. However, these proposals overlook many obvious difficulties. First, although the colonial cultivation of rice is at present expanding and its free flow into Japan proper is upsetting agriculture in the latter, it is perhaps erroneous to expect the colonies to remain rice exporters at the rate proposed for the coming thirty years. The living conditions in the colonies are improving rapidly. In the event that the *per capita* consumption of rice in Chosen reaches the Japanese level, Chosenese consumption would be 21,250,000 koku. This is 5 million koku above the three-year average yield in Chosen during 1930–2. As a means of relieving the pressure of Chosenese rice, the Japanese

[1] Nasu, H., *Jinko Shokuryo Mondai*, cited, p. 150.   [2] *Ibid.*, p. 150.

Government decided, by concrete means, to encourage the consumption of rice in Chosen.[1] This process will be slow to take effect. Nevertheless, in addition to the population increase in Chosen, the increase in the *per capita* rice consumption is certain to affect the rice exports of that colony. The same is true of Taiwan. It will be recalled that the increased population and the increased *per capita* consumption of rice were instrumental in changing Japan from a rice-exporting to a rice-importing nation in 1897. It is also well to remember that in 1895 Baron—later Count—K. Kaneko studied European markets of Japanese rice because he believed that rice would remain an important export commodity.[2]

Another vital question relative to the practicability of the plans to increase the supply of rice concerns the probability of the extension of acreage in Japan proper. At the end of 1918 it was estimated that 2,032,000 cho could be added to the agricultural land then in use. Of this total it was expected 770,000 cho were fit for paddy cultivation and 1,262,000 cho were suitable for upland field agriculture. This total represents 5·2 per cent of the entire land area in Japan proper. The prospective agricultural land surveyed in 1918 is reported as follows under its proper classification :

TABLE LXXIX

ESTIMATED ACREAGE OF LAND RECLAIMABLE FOR AGRICULTURAL PURPOSE [3]

(Denomination Cho)

Classification.	Paddy Field.	Upland Field.	Total.
Reclamation of land . . .	333,122	1,249,515	1,582,637
Reclamation from sea and lake.	61,897	11,453	73,350
Alteration of land class . . .	374,777	1,186	375,963
Total	769,796	1,262,154	2,031,950

[1] *Supra*, pp. 175–6.
[2] Collected in Kaneko, K., " Japanese Rice in Europe," *Keizai Seisaku* (Economic Policy), Tokyo, Okura Shoten, 1902, pp. 152–70.
[3] *Kochi Kakucho Kairyo Jigyo Yoran*, cited, 1932, p. 75.

The central government has employed various means to encourage the utilization of these prospective farms. Subsidies for reclamation work, for settlement of such newly opened areas, and Government ventures in major irrigation and drainage works are only a few examples of these measures.[1]

In spite of these measures, the extension of arable land in Japan has progressed very slowly. From 1919, when the Reclamation Subsidy Law went into effect, to the end of 1931, only 3,189 permits were issued under the law, embracing a total area of but 85,960 cho. The estimated cost of this work was reported at 182,965,913 yen, or 2,128·50 yen per cho.[2] This unit cost is lower than the usual price of farm land in the same category.[3]

Statistics relative to the extension and contraction of acreage in Japan since 1918 are cited in the following table.

TABLE LXXX

ANNUAL EXTENSION AND CONTRACTION OF ARABLE LAND, 1918–30 [4]

(Denomination Cho)

Year.	Extension.	Contraction.	Net Increase or Decrease (−).
1918–20 Average . .	67,890·9	24,754·3	43,136·6
1921–25 Average . .	38,584·9	44,225·7	− 5,640·8
1926	34,168·1	39,817·3	− 5,649·2
1927	41,323·1	41,212·1	111·0
1928	54,156·5	46,949·7	7,206·8
1929 . . . . . , .	73,657·9	101,651·6	27,993·7
1930	53,772·4	35,493·1	18,279·3
1926–30 Average . .	51,415·6	53,024·8	− 1,609·2

The above table shows that throughout Japan proper new

[1] The Reclamation Subsidy Law of 1919 empowered the Government to furnish part of the principal and interest cost of reclamation works. There is an agency for the dissemination of information regarding reclamable land ; the transportation fees to these lands are reduced, and a subsidy is given to families settling there. This is, of course, accomplished in co-operation with the local governments. Another measure designed to encourage utilization of these new lands is the Government grant to buy machinery for reclamation purposes and the use of these machines by the farmers free of charge. See *ibid.*, pp. 30–2.

[2] *Ibid.*, p. 64.　　　　[3] Cf. *supra*, pp. 151–2.

[4] *Honpo Nogyo Yoran*, cited, 1931, p. 20.

acreage was added to the extent of but 38,585 cho during the five-year period 1921–5, and 51,416 cho during the period 1926–30. During these two periods, 44,226 and 53,025 cho, respectively, were retired. Consequently, the acreage declined during these two quinquennial periods.

This tendency indicates, in a measure, the overwhelming difficulty attendant upon the proposed project for extension by 2 million cho. The programme would be more feasible, perhaps, if the population remained unenlightened and if external trade were completely cut off. This, however, would result in a high cost of food and a low scale of real wages, thereby inducing a low standard of living among the general population. Dr. Yasuma Takada, a noted sociologist of Kyoto Imperial University, contends that the difficulty of Japan's food supply is contingent on the supply of rice cultivated under the present-day high standard of living among the farmers. He believes that the food problem can be solved only by substituting some more economical food, such as potatoes, for rice, or by lowering the standard of living of the agricultural population so as to enable them to cultivate lands which at present, because of their low yield, lie unused.[1] However, the maintenance of the standard of living is the fundamental basis of all Government efforts ; consequently such a remedy as that suggested by Dr. Takada negates the all-important principle of economic policy. Moreover, Dr. Takada's suggestion is merely a palliative, or, at best, a temporary relief measure, since it would only post-pone the ultimate solution of the food problem by a few decades at most, and does not solve the problem—either temporarily or permanently.

Japan, whose population has undergone a somewhat rapid process of political enlightenment, will not take the course of extreme isolation, the writer believes. In spite of the present universal tendency toward economic nationalism, Japan's national economy will tend to adjust itself to the world's economic level. The recent effort to strengthen economic and political relations with Manchuria is an indication of Japan's effort to maintain her standard under the anomalous

[1] Takada, Y., " Social Nature of the Food Problem," *op. cit.*, p. 187.

economic nationalism universally prevalent. As noted before, Japan's immediate food supply can be met by effecting
a healthy balance of national economy; the future food
supply is in no small measure dependent on the international
aspects of Japan's economic development.

H.   Nutritive Aspect of the Food Problem

Now we have finally to make a few observations concerning the food habits of the Japanese people with a view to
determining the future food policy of the nation.

Below are two tables, one citing the ideal food value for
the Japanese people and the other the actual nutritive value
of food consumed daily. The former was determined by
three different food experts, while the latter is based on the
actual present-day conditions of nutrition as revealed by
the investigations of the Bureau of Statistics and by Dr.
Egerton C. Grey of the League of Nations. The survey of
the Bureau of Statistics was conducted daily during the
entire months of October, 1926, and May, 1927, and covered
5,454 families embracing 23,400 persons. Dr. Grey's survey
was made by the computation of Japan's food consumption
in 1925.

TABLE LXXXI

STANDARD NUTRITIVE REQUIREMENTS FOR JAPANESE AS ESTIMATED
BY DRS. SAWAMURA, MORI AND TAWARA [1]

(Grammes per Day, Dry Weight)

Nutritive Element.	Dr. Sawamura.		Dr. Mori.		Dr. Tawara.	
	Gm.	Per-centage.	Gm.	Per-centage.	Gm.	Per-centage.
Protein . .	74	13·10	71	11·66	96	16·96
Fat	15	2·65	14	2·30	20	3·53
Carbohydrate .	476	84·25	524	86·04	450	79·51
Total . .	565	100·00	609	100·00	566	100·00
Calories. . .	2,400	—	—	—	—	—

[1] Sawamura, M., *Eiyo to Shokumotsu* (Nutrition and Food), Tokyo,
Seibido, Revised Edition, 1925, p. 210; *Encyclopædia Japonica*, Vol. I,
p. 1135, " Nutrition."

TABLE LXXXII

NUTRITIVE VALUE OF FOOD CONSUMED BY JAPANESE, AS ANALYSED
BY THE BUREAU OF STATISTICS AND DR. GREY [1]

(Grammes per Day, Dry Weight)

Nutritive Element.	Bureau of Statistics.						Dr. Grey.	
	Salaried Men.		Labourers.		Farmers.		Gm.	Per-centage.
	Gm.	Per-centage.	Gm.	Per-centage.	Gm.	Per-centage.		
Protein . .	68	11·11	72	11·22	98	12·08	88·5	13·75
Animal .	21	3·43	20	3·12	13	1·60	—	—
Vegetable .	47	7·68	52	8·10	85	10·48	—	—
Fat . . .	22	3·59	20	3·12	18	2·22	17·7	2·75
Carbohydrate	493	80·56	521	81·15	658	81·14	537·6	83·50
Inorganic matter .	29	4·74	29	4·51	37	4·56	—	—
Total . .	612	100·00	642	100·00	811	100·00	643·8	100·00
Calories . .	—	2,506	—	2,614	—	3,265	—	—

The nutritive survey conducted by the Bureau of Statistics
and the *per capita* average consumption of nutrition computed by Dr. Grey compare favourably with the standard
requirements and demonstrate the fact that the Japanese
population is sufficiently well fed. While the standard food
requirement is about 2,400 calories per person per day, with
variations of about 20 per cent, depending on the different
types of occupation, the calories consumed by salaried,
labour, and farmer classes in Japan numbered 2,506 ; 2,614 ;
and 3,265, respectively. In terms of dry weight the actual
consumption varied from 612 grammes to 811 grammes.
This is somewhat above the ideal requirement as calculated
by the food experts mentioned above, whose calculations
ranged between 565 and 609 grammes.

Dr. Grey found that in 1925 the importation of food
amounted to 4·04 per cent of the total consumption, and

[1] *Kakei Chosa Hokoku* (Report on the Investigation of Household
Economy), Bureau of Statistics, Japan, Section of Statistical Tables on
Nutrition, 1931, pp. 5, 21, 35 ; Grey, E. C., *Food of Japan*, League of
Nations Publication, 1928, Series III, No. 2, pp. 39–40.

that during the period of 1915–25 the maximum variation
of the rice production was 8·3 per cent above and 4·6 per
cent below the average yield.   He also found that there is
no trace of the influence of crop yields reflected in the vital
statistics of the nation during the same period.   The *per
capita* available food in Japan in 1925 was estimated by the
same authority as follows :

TABLE LXXXIII

ANNUAL AND DAILY *PER CAPITA* FOOD AVAILABLE IN JAPAN, 1925 [1]
(Dry Weight)

Food.	Per Year (Kg.).	Per Day (Gm.).
Cereal	217·45	595·8
Fresh vegetables and fruit .	23·87	273·0
Root and crops . . .	91·91	251·8
Fish	99·64	91·5
Dry legumes . . .	2·62	65·4
Sugar	3·75	35·3
Farm produce . . .	33·41	10·3
Meat . . .	12·88	7·2
Total.	485·53	1,330·3

From the above data Dr. Grey maintains that the quantity
of available food suffices for the present needs of Japan's
population.   A detailed analysis of the content of foods
consumed in Japan, however, reveals some disadvantageous
points.   Dr. Grey found that the preponderant consumption
of rice resulted in a low proportion of mineral salts, lime,
iron, and alkali, and that the concentration on carbohydrate
was augmented by the presence of legumes, chiefly in soy
beans, fish, green vegetables and fruits.   He also found an
absence of milk, dairy products, flesh and animal fat.[2]
While the Japanese consume sufficient protein, viz. more
than 10 per cent of all nutrition elements, they take only
from 13 per cent (farmers) to 31 per cent (salaried persons)
of protein derived from animal sources.   This is a very low
percentage when compared to the 50 per cent of animal
protein consumed by Americans.[3]

[1] *Kakei Chosa Hokoku*, p. 19.   [2] *Ibid.*, pp. 39–40.
[3] Sawamura, M., *op. cit.*, p. 209.

From the foregoing study it can be fairly concluded that at present the Japanese people have a sufficient supply of food. Nevertheless, with regard to the quality of food, there is a great need for improvement. Dr. Grey maintains that in the long time view of racial hygiene it is more dangerous to have a sufficient food supply of an unsatisfactory quality than to have a situation of imminent starvation.[1] The promotion and dissemination of scientific knowledge regarding dietetics is of utmost importance and value in the creation of a satisfactory food policy for the nation.

[1] Grey, E. C., *op. cit.*, pp. 39–40.

CHAPTER IX

COLONIZATION AND IMMIGRATION

DURING the past few centuries the world has witnessed great movements of colonization and immigration. Whatever the actual effect of these movements on a particular country may be, an account of colonization and immigration is at least of academic interest, for it may throw light on the influences which determine and control the population movement. Let us now consider these movements as they affect Japan.

A. HISTORICAL BACKGROUND

The first decades of the sixteenth century in Japan were a period characterized by almost incessant turmoil, for both civil and foreign wars were rife. It was then that the Japanese people first came into contact with European adventurers, and at that time there were indications of a rapid overseas expansion of the nation. Within a short period the Japanese developed into hardy pirates, merchants, and colonists, and wandered over all the Orient—the Philippines, Siam, Cambodia, and Java. In 1606 there were 3,000 Japanese colonists in Manila and 15,000 in Dilao, which includes Manila. It is said that about 1619 there were more than 8,000 Japanese in the towns of Siam.[1] There are many well-known romances concerning Japanese adventurers who became princes in Siam.

However, with the Government's adoption of the policy of seclusionism in 1631–9, Japanese overseas expansion came to an abrupt end. Under the prolonged Tokugawa regime,

---

[1] Cf. *International Migrations*, New York, National Bureau of Economic Research, Vol. II, 1931, p. 626 ; Takekoshi, Y., *op. cit.*, Vol. III, Chap. VI.

emigration was considered and treated as a capital offence.[1]
Thus, for more than 200 years, Japanese immigration and
colonization were at a standstill.

The Government of Meiji accomplished many reforms, and
colonization became an integral part of the Government's
programme. Hokkaido was the first territory to come under
this programme of development. As early as the second
year of Meiji, or 1869, the Colonial Development Office was
established in Hokkaido. In that year the population of
Hokkaido was estimated at about 58,000, or 2 persons per
square mile. Colonization was rapidly accomplished after
the effective institution of the system of colonial militia.[2]
To what extent the present development of Hokkaido is
due to this organized plan of colonization cannot, of course,
be determined. However, it is certain that the Government's policy encouraged in no small degree the settlement
and growth of Hokkaido. To-day that region is one of the
most important agricultural centres of the nation, having
the highest standard of farming within Japan proper.

The colonization of Hokkaido was encouraged as an urgent
national policy partially because there was a threat of
Russian penetration into that unsettled territory. It was
also regarded as a measure calculated to relieve the condition
of the *samurai* class which had but recently lost its position
in the course of the fall of feudalism.

The colonization of Hokkaido absorbed the attention of
the government and of the people during the early Meiji
Period, and consequently they remained practically in-
different to the possibilities of emigration to foreign lands.
It was not until 1885 that freedom of emigration was
legalized.

Japan emerged a colonial power after the Sino-Japanese

---

[1] After 1636 not only emigration but the return of Japanese who
emigrated abroad was prohibited under the penalty of death. Many
attempting to return home were executed when the policy of seclusionism
was strengthened during the years toward 1639. Cf. *ibid.*, pp. 334, 546.

[2] Under the scheme of colonial militia, 7,337 families, consisting of
39,901 members, settled in Hokkaido between 1873 and 1899. The cost
was 9,209,648 yen, or 1,255 yen per family and 230 yen per person settled.
Cf. Uehara, *Hokkaido Tondenhei Seido* (Colonial Militia System of Hokkaido), cited in *Social Reform*, No. 140, May, 1932, Special Manchurian
Migration Number, pp. 46–9.

War. However, there existed various obstacles to the rapid migration of Japanese nationals to the new overseas territories. This situation will be analysed in greater detail later in this chapter.[1] Concurrently, the Sino-Japanese War also marked the nation's first step toward industrialization —a development that ultimately led to an absorption of vast population numbers in urban districts. Because, perhaps, of the rapidly growing interest in the industrial development of the nation, neither colonization nor emigration was actively encouraged by the Government, nor were individuals interested, to any extent, in leaving the country.[2] This general lassitude toward colonization and emigration prevailed until the period immediately following the Great War. Not until then did Japan awaken to the possibilities in an extensive overseas population movement, and only then did the Government manifest an active interest in overseas expansion.[3]

B. Japanese in Overseas Territories

There are certain demographic considerations, such as the sex and occupational distribution of the colonists and emigrants, that have a great bearing on the question in hand. Those factors are not only indicative of conditions among colonists and emigrants but also are important in determining their future course. In the case of colonies there is another important factor, viz. the ratio of the number of colonists to the total number of inhabitants. This ratio may be regarded as an important indication of the status in which the colonies and home country place each other.

In the following table are set forth the total number of Japanese in colonies or semi-colonies, the sex ratio, i.e. the ratio of males to 100 females, and the ratio of the Japanese to the total population in the respective area.

[1] Cf. *International Migrations*, National Bureau of Economic Research, cited, Vol. II, p. 618 ; *Encyclopædia Japonica*, cited, Vol. I, p. 1,809, " Colonization."
[2] Cf. Nagai, T., *op. cit.*, pp. 57, 198 ; Yamamoto, M., " The Question of Population in Japan," *Kyoto Imperial University Economic Review*, July, 1927, pp. 52–62.
[3] See *supra*, p. 41, and *infra*, p. 199.

TABLE LXXXIV

NUMBER OF JAPANESE IN COLONIES AND LEASED AND MANDATED
TERRITORIES, 1929 AND 1930 [1]

I Area.	II No. of Japanese.	III Males per 100 Females.	IV Per cent of Total Popula- tion of the Area.
Chosen	501,867	108·1	2·5
Taiwan	232,299	108·1	5·0
Karafuto	277,279	125·0	97·3
Kwantung *	215,463	107·7	16·7
South Sea Mandatory .	19,835	174·1	28·5
Total	1,246,743	111·4	4·7

Soldiers are excluded.
* Kwantung Leased Territory and South Manchuria Railway Zone. Dates:
II and IV, October 1, 1930 ; III, December 31, 1929.

Table LXXXIV shows that on October 1, 1930, the total
number of Japanese in the colonies and South Sea Mandated
Islands amounted to 1,246,743. The percentage of Japanese
inhabitants to the total population of the individual colonies
ranged from 2·5 per cent in Chosen to 97·3 per cent in Karafuto. Because of the vast population of Chosen and Taiwan,
however, the ratio of the total Japanese colonial population
to the total population in all the colonies falls as low as 4·7
per cent. It is unquestionably to the high percentage of
Japanese residents in Karafuto that we can attribute the
fact that the region rapidly became assimilated with Japan
proper. In the colonies the ratio of males per 100 females
is not seriously high. At the end of 1929 the average
ratio was 111·4.[2]

In 1910, the year of annexation, there were 171,543
Japanese in Chosen. This was 1·3 per cent of the total
population. In 1930 there were 501,867 Japanese, aggre-
gating 2·5 per cent of the total population in that colony.

[1] II, IV : *Asahi Nenkan*, cited, 1933, p. 478 ff. ; III : *Ibid.*, p. 478 ff. ;
Financial and Economic Annual of Japan, Department of Finance, Japan,
1932, p. 2 ; *Taiwan Jijo*, cited, 1931, p. 19.
[2] Kanaji, I., *Shokumin Seisaku* (Colonial Policies), Gendai Keizaigaku
Zenshu, Vol. XXII, Tokyo, Nihon Hyoronsha, 1931, p. 401 ; Asami, N.,
Nihon Shokuminchi Tojiron (Colonial Government of Japan), Tokyo,
Ganshodo, 1928, p. 272.

At the beginning of the Japanese administration in 1895 the number of Japanese in Taiwan was 59,668, or 2·0 per cent of the total population of the colony. By 1930 the figures had risen to 232,299, or 5·0 per cent. The number of Japanese in other colonies at the beginning of Japanese administration are as follows : Karafuto, 10,606, 87·4 per cent (1906) ; [1] Kwantung Leased Territory, 16,613, 4·3 per cent (1906) ; the South Sea Mandatory, 3,310, 6·5 per cent (1922). [2]

From comparison of these ratios with those of 1930, it can be seen that the Japanese portion of the population of the colonies has increased at a more rapid rate than the native population. Despite this tendency, however, the absolute number of Japanese in colonies or semi-colonies still remains very small.

At this point it is pertinent to consider the occupational distribution of the Japanese in colonial territories. The table on page 193 cites the number of Japanese residing in Japan's overseas possessions and leased and mandated territories at dates noted, and classifies them as to the occupations of the main workers of the families. As is demonstrated, the leading occupational fields of the Japanese settlers in Chosen are official and professional services, and commerce and transportation. In Taiwan, manufacturing and mining are added to the above two fields. This occupational distribution sheds considerable light on Japan's political and capitalistic interests in these possessions. In Kwantung Leased Territory and the South Manchuria area, transportation ranks first, followed by manufacturing, official and professional services and commerce. This again reveals the dominant activities of the railway and industrial interests under the aegis of the South Manchuria Railway Company. Only in Karafuto and in the South Sea Mandatory does agriculture lead all other occupations. In view of the dominant position of agriculture and the high proportion of Japanese in the total population, notwithstanding the high ratio of males, the

[1] Chosenese included in 1906 figures.
[2] *Tokei Zensho*, cited, pp. 272–4.

TABLE LXXXV

OCCUPATIONAL DIVISION OF JAPANESE IN COLONIES AND LEASED AND MANDATED TERRITORIES [1]

Occupation.	Actual Number.					Percentage Distribution.				
	Chosen.	Taiwan.	Karafuto.	Kwantung.*	S. Sea Mandatory.	Chosen.	Taiwan.	Karafuto.	Kwantung.*	S. Sea Mandatory.
Agriculture	54,696	10,091	46,649	2,781	7,457	10·9	6·1	18·6	1·3	46·0
Aquatic industries		—	29,715	940	373	—	—	11·8	0·4	2·3
Mining	72,434	44,823	6,193	6,460	153	14·4	27·3	2·5	3·0	1·0
Manufacturing	147,438	47,864	29,111	45,578	1,853	29·4	29·1	11·6	21·2	11·5
Commerce			46,494	41,958	1,501			18·5	19·0	9·3
Transportation			10,098	50,758	637			4·0	23·5	3·9
Official and professional	176,795	57,677	23,939	48,901	1,430	35·2	35·1	9·5	22·7	8·8
Miscellaneous	31,892	672	55,618	10,360	2,760	6·4	·4	22·5	4·8	17·0
Those who subsist on unearned income	18,612	3,139	2,496	7,727	38	3·7	1·9	1·0	3·6	0·2
Total	501,867	164,266	251,313	215,463	16,202	100·0	100·0	100·0	100·0	100·0

* Kwantung Leased Territory and South Manchuria Railway Zone. Dates: Chosen and Kwantung, December 31, 1930; Karafuto, December 31, 1929; South Sea Mandatory, October 1, 1929; Taiwan, October 1, 1920.

[1] Chosen: *Asahi Nenkan*, cited, 1933, p. 479; Taiwan: *ibid.*, 1931, p. 449; Karafuto and the South Sea Mandatory: *Jiji Nenkan*, cited, 1931, pp. 628, 636; Kwantung *Manchuria Year Book*, Tokyo, East Asiatic Economic Investigation Bureau, 1932–3, p. 443.

South Sea Mandatory gives promise of further and more effective assimilation. The relatively low ratio of males in the other areas under consideration, with the possible exception of Karafuto, may be attributed to the fact that a considerable number of the Japanese are native born and also to the fact that most of the government officials are accompanied by their families.

C. Emigration Movement

The story of the delayed awakening of Japan to emigration has been narrated in the early part of the present chapter. There, it was pointed out that not until 1885 was the freedom of emigration of the nationals legalized.[1] Subsequent developments proved that the outside world has not been hospitable in receiving these late-comers in immigration. Causes for such situation will be further analysed later.[2]

In brief, the history of Japanese emigration is, in its essence, a history of restriction. Even before the people migrated to any considerable extent they had to meet with antagonism and restriction. No considerable number of Japanese people had migrated to Australia when that prospective new land for settlement was closed to Asiatic races by the First Session of the Parliament of that Commonwealth, in 1901, through the institution of the tactful " dictation test." [3] Toward the end of the nineteenth century, any emigration worthy of note went to Hawaii as contract labour. By 1894, 30,000 Japanese had moved to these islands.[4] In 1900, three years after Hawaii was annexed by the United States, the system of contract

---

[1] See p. 185.   [2] See p. 209.

[3] Immigration Restriction Act No. 17, 1901, § 3. The Act stipulates that permission to enter the country shall be withheld from any person who, upon request to do so, fails to write at dictation and sign " a passage of 50 words in length in an European language." By the discretionary application of this regulation any person can be prohibited from entering Australia. According to Professor Yanaihara, the exclusion of Asiatic immigrants was the direct motive for the federation of the commonwealths of Australia. Cf. Yanaihara, T., *Jinko Mondai* (Population Problem), Tokyo, Iwanami Co., 1928, p. 217.

[4] *Takumu Yoran* (Abstract of Overseas Affairs), Department of Overseas Affairs, Japan, 1931, pp. 533–7.

immigration was forbidden. This affected Japanese movement toward Hawaii, for many of them were brought there
under that system.

In 1907, when there were far less than 100,000 Japanese
in the United States, Japan and the United States entered
into a " Gentlemen's Agreement." This was a measure to
restrain, through the co-operation of the Japanese Government, the migration of Japanese labourers to Hawaii, continental United States and the contiguous areas, viz. Canada
and Mexico. In 1908 the Canadian Government limited the
entry of Japanese immigrants to 400 a year. In 1913 the
Union of South Africa prohibited not only the entry of
Japanese labourers and merchants but also prohibited
permanent settlement of any Japanese in the Union. Thus,
after the Great War, when the Japanese public had awakened
to the realization of the necessity for emigration, all potential fields were occupied by the Anglo-Saxon race and had
long been closed to Asiatic peoples.

On the other hand, in 1908, in the same year that Canada
inaugurated the restriction of Japanese immigration, Japanese
immigrants found their way to South America, particularly
to Brazil and Peru. This new field for Japanese immigration
has since proved productive. From the time of the Russo-
Japanese War, Japanese traffic to China and Chosen, which
was then an independent country, was unhampered to the
extent that passports were not required.[1]

Statistics concerning the number of permits issued to
emigrants and statistics of home-coming emigrants are
available. It must be noted that Japanese statistics of
emigration exclude those who go to China and Manchuria.
The figures for the past seven years, exclusive of officials,
students, and merchants, are presented in Table LXXXVI.
In this statistical table the amount of the remittances by
Japanese living abroad, as presented in the *Tokei Nenkan*,
is included.

This table shows that during the course of the five years
between 1926 and 1930 the average annual number of
permits issued to emigrants was 20,322. The average

[1] Ichihashi, Y., *op. cit.*, pp. 7–8.

TABLE LXXXVI

Number of Emigrants, Number of Japanese Returning to Japan, and Amount of Remittances from Emigrants Abroad [1]

Year.	Emigration.	Those returning to Japan.	Net Emigration.	Amount of Remittance (Denomination Yen).
1926	16,184	14,549	1,635	24,944,716
1927	18,041	14,735	3,306	24,440,895
1928	19,850	15,004	4,846	27,613,463
1929	25,704	14,073	11,631	28,144,875
1930	21,829	15,432	6,397	23,195,481
Average . .	20,322	14,759	5,563	25,667,886
1931	10,384	12,965	− 2,581	17,914,225
1932	19,033	13,170	5,863	20,065,725
1933	27,319	14,141	13,176	20,306,663
1934	28,087	—	—	20,531,852

annual number of home-comers was 14,759. Assuming that all those who secured permission emigrated, the average annual surplus of emigrants over home-comers amounted to only 5,563. However, it is necessary to add the number of emigrants to China and Manchuria if an estimate of the total number of emigrants is desired. As will be shown shortly, emigration to China is very limited, while emigration to Manchuria, outside of Kwantung Leased Territory and South Manchuria Railway Zone, was also negligible until quite recently, and these together do not by any means reverse the above observations. The seasonal migration of Japanese people to foreign lands is similarly insignificant. The only noteworthy movement of this kind is that of a few hundred fishermen who migrate to the Russian Far East during the summer months.[2] Further details of the trends of Japanese migration, considered from various angles, will follow.

On October 1, 1930, there were 509,754 Japanese in foreign territories. This figure was arrived at from data submitted to the Japanese consuls in their respective districts. How-

[1] *Tokei Nenkan*, cited, No. 52, 1933, p. 65.
[2] *Kokusei Zukai*, cited, 1931, p. 259.

ever, since there is no legal means of enforcing registration with these consuls,[1] omissions, and a consequent depression in the total figure, are to be expected. Table LXXXVII shows their distribution according to continents and countries.

TABLE LXXXVII
Number of Japanese in Foreign Countries, 1930 [1]

Country.	Male.	Female.	Total.
Asia	66,183	43,683	109,866
Russian Far East	2,483	307	2,790
Manchuria *	6,854	6,234	13,088
China	29,924	25,041	54,965
Hong Kong	1,751	975	2,726
Siam	232	104	336
French Indo-China	179	167	346
British India and Ceylon	1,633	597	2,230
British Malay States and Straits Settlements	3,974	2,859	6,833
British N. Borneo and Sarawak	374	218	592
Persia	13	6	19
Dutch E. Indies	4,188	2,181	6,369
Philippines	14,578	4,994	19,572
Oceania	69,257	55,953	125,210
Hawaii	65,452	55,456	120,908
Others	3,805	497	4,302
North America	77,519	50,445	127,964
U.S.A.	60,467	39,661	100,128
Canada	12,537	8,452	20,989
Mexico	3,749	2,083	5,832
Panama	171	57	228
Cuba	595	192	787
South America	81,539	61,109	142,648
Brazil	64,346	52,301	116,647
São Paulo State	62,537	51,021	113,558
Other States	1,809	1,280	3,089
Argentine	2,959	1,068	4,027
Peru	13,200	7,335	20,535
Others	1,034	405	1,439
Europe	3,047	950	3,997
Africa	42	27	69
Total	297,587	212,167	509,754

*Excludes Kwantung Leased Territory, the South Manchuria Railway Zone.

[1] *Tokei Nenkan*, cited, No. 52, 1932, p. 65.

From this table we learn that in each of four continents, namely, South America, North America, Oceania, and Asia, there are more than 100,000 Japanese immigrants. In none, however, is there more than 150,000. In two of the above-mentioned continents the ratios of males are above 150, viz. in North America (155·0) and Asia (151·5) ; in South America and Oceania the ratio is 138·4 and 123·8 respectively. Territories in which there are more than 10,000 Japanese are Hawaii, Brazil, the United States, China, Canada, Peru, the Philippines and Manchuria. Among these eight territories only the three first-mentioned contain more than 100,000 Japanese.[1]

The following table illustrates the occupational distribution and thereby indicates in further detail the situation of Japanese immigrants in foreign territories :

TABLE LXXXVIII

OCCUPATIONAL DISTRIBUTION OF JAPANESE IN FOREIGN
COUNTRIES, BY CONTINENTS, 1930 [2]

Occupation.	Asia.	Oceania.	N. America.	S. America.	Europe.	Africa.	Total.
Agriculture . .	8,384	16,515	24,376	51,719	10	—	101,004
Aquatic indus- tries . . .	2,783	1,964	2,662	123	1	—	7,533
Mining . . .	905	99	697	14	3	—	1,718
Manufacturing .	9,684	11,289	8,077	3,025	91	1	32,167
Commerce . .	16,554	7,522	15,345	9,355	270	15	49,061
Transportation	3,634	2,422	1,751	486	274	—	8,567
Public and pro- fessional . .	11,534	3,041	2,800	664	1,387	21	19,447
Domestic em- ployment .	1,254	1,959	1,991	377	47	2	5,630
Miscellaneous .	612	2,391	1,376	396	8	—	4,783
Not employed .	56,083	77,654	68,159	76,244	1,342	30	279,512

Among the occupations followed in foreign territories classified by continents, commerce dominates in Asia and agriculture leads in the other three important continents,

---

[1] The writer, however, is uncertain of the exact legal status of census conducted by the Japanese authorities in China where Japan has extra-territorial rights.

[2] *Tokei Nenkan*, cited, No. 51, 1932, p. 65.

viz. Oceania, North America, and South America. In the vast area of Asia agriculture is the leading occupation only in the Philippine Islands. In view of the fact that agriculture is the occupation most conducive to stability and permanence of settlement, it is significant that the two important continents which absorbed Japanese farmers, viz. Oceania and North America, are now practically closed to Japanese immigrants.

D. IMPORTANT OUTLETS FOR JAPANESE EMIGRANTS

The preceding pages have summarized colonization and immigration movements of the Japanese people. At this point the present situation concerning Japanese immigration in the two major territories that are still open to Japanese agricultural settlers, namely, Brazil and the Philippines, will be examined. The condition that prevails at the present time in Manchuria, which is generally regarded as the natural outlet for Japanese emigration, will also be considered here in further detail.

Brazil.—Japanese emigration to Brazil began in 1908. Since 1917 the State of São Paulo has offered a subsidy to some 5,000 Japanese yearly, in addition to immigrants of some other nations. However, during the period when this subsidy was effective, the number of Japanese immigrants actually reached this maximum only once—in 1918. This State subsidy has been gradually diminishing since 1921 ; [1] but in 1923 the Japanese Government undertook to subsidize, by paying all transportation expenses, those refugees of the great earthquake who desired to settle in Brazil. The following year the subsidy grant was extended practically to all who sailed to Brazil.

This encouragement, occurring as it did at a period of great public interest in emigration, resulted in a phenomenal

[1] The State of São Paulo subsidy increased from £9 per immigrant aged over 12, £4 10s. per immigrant aged 7 to 11, and £2 5s. per immigrant aged 3 to 6 at the beginning, to £17 per immigrant until the abolition of the subsidy to Japanese in 1925. Cf. *Brazil Nenkan,* or *Annuario do Noticias do Brazil*, São Paulo, The Brazil Nenposha, 1933, Part II, pp. 12–13.

increase in the number of emigrants to Brazil. Twelve
thousand Japanese emigrated to that country in 1928. In
the past few years Brazil has adopted a quota system of
immigration. However, the Japanese quota was higher
than that of any other nation and it permitted entry to a
greater number than could actually go. The Japanese
Government attempted to stimulate emigration to Brazil,
for it was feared that should the number of immigrants
remain below the quota for a considerable length of time,
the quota would be reduced.

In addition to the transportation fees, the Japanese
Government in 1932 instituted a subsidy to aid the outfitting
of emigrants to Brazil ; this amounted to 50 yen per adult, 25
yen per minor aged seven to twelve and 20·50 yen per infant
under seven years. The numbers of emigrants in the past
seven years were as follows : [1]

Year.	Emigration to Brazil.	Year.	Emigration to Brazil.
1927	9,625	1931	5,565
1928	12,002	1932	15,108
1929	15,597	1933	23,152
1930	13,741	1934	22,960

As has been shown in Table LXXXVII, Japanese residents
in Brazil numbered 116,647 on October 1, 1930. This
number amounts to less than 10 per cent of the Italian
and Portuguese populations in Brazil. Of these 116,647
Japanese, 113,558, were residents of the State of São Paulo.
Of the 51,851 Japanese in Brazil gainfully employed in
1930, 48,571, or 93·7 per cent, were engaged in agriculture.
The only other occupation which embraces more than
1,000 Japanese is commerce ; in this field there are 1,388. [2]
About 50 per cent of the Japanese engaged in agriculture are
tenant or landed farmers. [3] Owing to the policy of public
subsidies which favoured immigration of farmers by family

[1] *Takumu Yoran*, cited, 1931, p. 537 ; *Asahi Nenkan*, cited, 1935,
p. 471.
[2] *Tokei Nenkan*, cited, No. 51, 1932, pp. 66–7.
[3] *Asahi Nenkan*, cited, 1934, p. 494.

units, proportionately a rather large number of women emigrated. In 1930 there were 100 females for every 123 males.

The new constitution adopted by the post-revolutionary Constituent Assembly of Brazil, which took effect on July 16, 1934, placed the control of immigration under the Federal authority and provided that the annual number of immigrants from any nation should be limited to 2 per cent of the total number of immigrants from that nation who had settled in Brazil in the past fifty years. Under this constitutional provision the annual entry of Japanese will be limited to 2,755. With this limited number, Brazil still remains one of the major outlets for Japanese emigrants.

Philippine Islands.—Next to Brazil the most important outlet for Japanese emigration at present is the Philippines. Japanese emigration to the Islands in the post-Reformation period began in 1900. In contrast to the situation that prevails in other Pacific possessions of the United States, there are no restrictions against Japanese emigration to the Philippines. During the last seven years emigration to these islands has been as follows : [1]

1928	2,077
1929	4,535
1930	2,685
1931	1,109
1932	746
1933	941
1934	1,544

The Japanese population in the Philippines, as of October 1, 1930, numbered 19,628, and was distributed in this manner : [2]

In the City of Manila	3,984
In Luzon excluding Manila	3,052
In Davao and Cotabota States	12,592

Among the 12,714 Japanese gainfully occupied at that

[1] *Tokei Nenkan*, cited, No. 51, 1932, p. 63 ; *Asahi Nenkan*, cited, 1935, p. 471.
[2] *Ibid.*, 1934, p. 494.

date, the occupations, which embraced more than 500, were
as follows : [1]

Agriculture	7,271
Aquatic industries	983
Manufacturing	1,855
Commerce	1,790

Fifty-seven per cent of all Japanese gainfully employed
in the islands are engaged in agriculture and the majority
of these in hemp culture. As a matter of historical fact,
it was a Japanese immigrant who first started the cultivation
of hemp in Davao.[2] The ratio of males per 100 females is,
however, very high ; on October 1, 1930, it was 299·6.

Manchuria.—Our final consideration will be given to the
Japanese immigration to Manchuria. Manchuria, now
Manchoukuo, consists of 1,303,143 square kilometres, or
3·41 times the area of Japan proper. At the end of 1933
the population was estimated at 30,879,717, which is about
46 per cent of the population of Japan proper estimated
for the same date. The population density is, therefore,
less than one-seventh of Japan, the actual figure being
23·6 per square kilometre. The latter figure is very low
compared with the density in Taiwan and Chosen when
these territories were first included in the Japanese Empire.
The figures were 76·4 and 60·3 per square kilometre respectively.

The South Manchuria Railway Zone, which has been
considered in this chapter as an integral part of the Japanese
colony of " Kwantung Leased Territory and South Manchuria Railway Zone," is included in the above-mentioned
Manchoukuo domain. Under the terms of the Japan-
Manchoukuo Treaty of June 10, 1936, Japan agreed to
relinquish gradually its special privileges in the Railway
Zone, as well as the extra-territorial rights elsewhere in
Manchoukuo, in favour of Manchoukuo. Therefore, technically the status of the Railway Zone is now in transition
from that as a Japanese colony to that of a foreign territory, pure and simple. Area of the Railway Zone is 290

[1] *Tokei Nenkan*, cited, No. 51, 1932, p. 67.
[2] *Asahi Nenkan*, cited, 1934, p. 494.

square kilometres, or 12 per cent of the area of " Kwantung Leased Territory and South Manchuria Railway Zone." The status of Kwantung Leased Territory remains the same as before.

In spite of the legal demarcations which have been established, we may here consider the Manchurian region, including Kwantung Leased Territory, as a whole, for it is extremely difficult to follow closely the territorial limits when considering Japanese activities in the Manchurian region.

Since 1905, when Japan acquired her first foothold, the development of Manchuria and the extension of Japanese interests throughout that region has been remarkable. At the close of 1930 Japanese investments in Manchuria reached 1,617 million yen. Foreign trade in Manchuria increased by 37·5 per cent between 1913 and 1930 as compared to 20·3 per cent in China proper. In 1930 Manchuria's foreign trade amounted to 538 million yen ; of this amount the Japanese Empire absorbed 54 per cent of the exports and furnished 58 per cent of the imports.[1]

The economic expansion of Manchuria was closely related to the industrial development of Japan and thereby was a contributive factor to the rapid increase of the Japanese population and to a higher standard of living. However, the actual settlement of that region by Japanese was an ever-present desire among the Japanese. The temporary and transitory nature of the commercial and industrial exploitation of new territories is generally recognized.[2] For the permanent effective control of any land the settlers' feet must first be firmly lodged in the soil.

At the beginning of Japanese expansion in Manchuria it was universally expected that this rather undeveloped region would be rapidly settled by the Japanese.[3] Several pro-

---

[1] *Manchuria Year Book*, cited, 1932–3, pp. 329–37, 426.

[2] For an excellent exposition of the permanent and transitory types of colonization, see Keller, A. G., *Colonization*, Boston, Ginn & Co., 1908, Chap. I.

[3] *Appeal by the Chinese Government, Supplementary Document to the Report of the Commission of Inquiry*, Geneva, League of Nations, 1932, Part III, Study No. 2, " What is the Economic Importance of Manchuria for Japan ? " (E. Dennery), p. 71.

posals were even made to the home government to send
from one to two million Japanese settlers to Manchuria.[1]
Nevertheless, although the gross population of Manchuria,
exclusive of Jehol, increased from 16,778,000 to 29,575,000,
or by 12,797,000, during the period between 1907 and 1930,
the Japanese population throughout Manchuria numbered
only 228,551 in 1930.[2]

Various causes are attributed for this slow rate of migration into Manchuria. Climatic conditions, especially the
severe winters, are a contributing cause. The hostile attitude of the former Manchurian authorities, particularly as
reflected in their unwillingness to grant land leases to the
Japanese, was a discouraging factor. Moreover, the prevalence of banditry made life and property insecure in the
interior. Lastly but no less significantly, the relatively
low standard of life prevailing among the native farmers
and other inhabitants compared with that in Japan must
be mentioned.[3]

---

[1] *Manshu Tokuhon* (Manchuria Reader), Tokyo, East Asiatic Economic
Investigation Bureau, 1930, p. 113.

[2] *Manchuria Year Book*, cited, 1932–3, p. 13.

[3] Because of the lack of precise statistical data on the comparative
productivity and earnings of Chinese and Japanese farmers in Manchuria,
we are forced to base our conclusions as to standards of living on a comparison between city labourers. The efficiency of Chinese urban workers
in Southern Manchuria is estimated at 60 or 70 per cent of that of the
Japanese. On the other hand, a comparison of the wages of the two
groups, investigated by the Investigation Section of the South Manchuria
Railway Company, revealed that in carpentry and nine other trades the
Chinese earn on the average only one-third to one-half as much as the
Japanese workers earn. This low wage standard existing among the
Chinese more than compensates for their relatively lower efficiency. Thus
we are not surprised to find, in the light of these comparisons, that the
Japanese workers depended in the main for their employment on the highly
productive capitalistic enterprises, or on Japanese communities which
patronize them for some indispensable capacities.

The situation of the farmers is hardly so complex. Agriculture in
Manchuria is, as well as that in Japan, operated as a family enterprise.
Hence its economic basis is both rigid and direct. Unless new colonists
in Manchurian plains manage to revolutionize the traditional standard of
agricultural economy either through superior technical skill or by enlarg-
ing the scale of enterprise, they are bound to conform to the standard of
living prevailing among the old settlers. Japanese farmers were unable
and unwilling to accept either alternative. The inevitable result was the
failure of the Japanese to settle on the soil of Manchuria.

The comparative figures of daily wages of Chinese and Japanese
labourers in Southern Manchuria given by the above-named authority
are shown at the foot of the facing page (*ibid.*, p. 448):

Since the establishment of Manchoukuo in March, 1932, the government is gradually reforming every aspect of her political and economic systems. Favoured by a relatively fertile soil and hitherto untouched natural resources which now have been opened to full exploitation, the economic development of that region seems to be assured. The low population density of the region has been noted before. Hence, from now on, appropriate government assistance by such means as liberally reserving large tracts of uninhabited land for the future settlers and training them for large-scale farming will undoubtedly prove to be effective.

In fact, the number of Japanese in Manchuria (exclusive of soldiery) is increasing rather rapidly in the past few years. Japanese residents in Kwantung Leased Territory and South Manchuria Railway Zone, where the majority of Japanese in Manchuria settle at present, were reported in June, 1936, as 362,911 compared with 215,463 at the end of 1930. In such a changing situation, it is not merely incidental that the Japanese leaders in 1936 are promoting a project for settlement of 1,000,000 families during the next twenty years. In this plan, which is not yet fully formulated, the policy of national defence as well as that of forming a closer racial tie between Japan and Manchoukuo is envisaged. However, it is an established prin-

AVERAGE DAILY WAGES OF CHINESE AND JAPANESE WORKERS IN
SOUTH MANCHURIA, N.D. (*c.* 1930)
(Denomination Yen)

Occupation.	Chinese.			Japanese.		
	High.	Low.	Average.	High.	Low.	Average.
Carpenters	2·00	·80	1·29	4·50	2·70	3·53
Plasterers	2·80	·80	1·56	6·00	3·00	3·91
Mat-makers	2·40	·90	1·53	4·20	2·80	3·48
Paper-hangers	2·40	·80	1·27	4·00	2·00	3·29
Glass factory workers . .	1·80	·60	1·21	4·00	2·00	3·19
Tailors	3·50	·80	1·90	4·10	2·00	3·13
Shoemakers	2·00	·50	1·19	3·50	1·50	2·61
Bricklayers	2·00	·80	1·19	4·00	2·70	3·42
Printers	2·50	·50	1·19	4·00	1·00	2·72
Odd job men	0·80	·30	0·54	2·50	1·00	1·9?

ciple that modern immigration is essentially an individualistic movement, motivated by a desire for self-improvement. No war-time devotion or racial loyalty, no government stimulation can permanently dislodge a great mass of the population in opposition to their individual desires.[1] Therefore, in order to make the present emigration plan successful, Japan at first must co-operate with Manchoukuo to secure their confidence in the possibilities of improving their living conditions in the new country. We may refer in this connection to Professor E. F. Penrose, who aptly pointed out that after European peoples had acquired relatively empty lands they were able to send emigrants to these lands in large number only when, as a result of the industrial revolution, they, particularly England, had a large savings available for investment abroad.[2]

E.   CHINESE AND CHOSENESE MIGRATION TO JAPAN PROPER

It has been already intimated that no passport is required by either nation for nationals going between China and Japan. Actually, however, under the provisions of an Imperial Ordinance, there are some restrictions placed on the free movement of Chinese common labourers other than cooks and servants. This ordinance prescribes that foreigners who wish employment as common labourers in areas outside the former foreign settlements must secure permission from the local (prefectual) governments.[3] A similar rule is in force in Taiwan and it is planned to extend this regulation to Chosen.[4] Labour organizations in Japan have, thus far, demonstrated no antagonism to Chinese immigrants. On October 1, 1930, there were 39,440 Chinese in Japan, a figure representing 73 per cent of the total foreign population.

[1] Cf. Fairchild, H. P., *Immigration*, New York, Macmillan, Revised Edition, 1926, p. 25.

[2] Penrose, E. F., *Population Theories and Their Application*, Food Research Institute, Stanford University, 1934, p. 250.

[3] Cf. Akiyama, O., " The Unemployment Problem and Chosenese Workers," *Social Reform*, No. 111, Dec., 1929, p. 120 ; Nitobe, I., Editor, *Taiheiyo Mondai* (Problems of the Pacific), Kyoto Conference, Tokyo, Institute of Pacific Relations, 1929, p. 167 ; Harada, S., *op. cit.*, p. 104.

[4] *Nihon Rodo Nenkan* (Labour Year Book of Japan), Osaka, Ohara Institute for Social Research, 1929, p. 81.

The Chosenese migration to Japan proper constitutes one of the most interesting and important inter-territorial population movements of present-day history. Every year more than 200,000 Chosenese cross the Korean Straits to and from Japan. The extent of this movement during the five years between 1924 and 1928 has been reported as follows :

TABLE LXXXIX

ARRIVAL, DEPARTURE, AND NET INCREASE OR DECREASE OF CHOSENESE IN JAPAN PROPER, 1924–8 [1]

Year.	Arrivals.	Departures.	Net Increase or Decrease (−).
1924 . .	122,215	148,578	− 26,363
1925 . .	131,273	112,471	18,802
1926 . .	91,092	83,709	7,383
1927 . .	138,016	93,991	44,025
1928 . .	166,286	117,563	48,723

The above figures demonstrate the fact that in 1928 nearly 284,000 Chosenese crossed the Straits to and from Japan. This traffic amounted to approximately 800 per day. During that year the net increase of Chosenese in Japan was 48,723. In view of this it is not surprising to see that Chosenese residents in Japan proper, who numbered 40,755 on October 1, 1920, had increased tenfold to 419,009 by October 1, 1930. These Chosenese settlers in Japan proper are distributed in all prefectures, but in 1929 more than half of them were concentrated in the five prefectures in which the great industrial cities are located.

Investigations have revealed that about 90 per cent of the Chosenese in Japan were formerly either tenant peasants or unskilled casual labourers. The occupational classification of 271,278 Chosenese in Japan proper was recorded in June, 1929, as follows : [2]

Coolies	127,630
Miners	5,473
Factory operatives	47,943
Apprentices	9,248
Students	8,443
Miscellaneous workers and dependents .	72,541

---

[1] Yoshio, E., " Chosenese Migration to Japan Proper," *Revue Diplomatique*, March 15, 1930, pp. 173–7.
[2] Akiyama, O., *op. cit.*, pp. 98, 110.

Until about 1923 the wage level of Chosenese labourers in Japan differed from that of the Japanese workers, but since that date this disparity has gradually disappeared. Most of these migrants enjoy a higher plane of living in Japan than they do in their homeland, and, according to the report of the Kyochokai, about 60 per cent of them save money and frequently send some of their savings to relatives at home.[1] The motive of Chosenese migrations to Japan is purely economic—to partake of the real or imagined superior material opportunities in Japan.[2]

During the time that they remain in Japan proper, the Chosenese enjoy all the political rights and privileges of the Japanese.[3] They often adopt Japanese names and Japanese-Chosenese intermarriages are not infrequent.[4] The adequate adjustment of the Chosenese to the Japanese scheme of life presents no serious problem. It is expected that, in the long run, they will be absorbed into the Japanese blood, as has been the case in Japanese history from time immemorial.[5]

As an immediate and actual effect of the Chosenese influx, the labour markets of Japan are disturbed.[6] However, our chief interest in the above observation lies in its theoretical significance as a reflection of the fundamental nature of the population movement : while the Japanese Government was spending millions of yen in encouraging emigration which annually amounted to less than 20,000 persons, more than twice that number of Chosenese migrate to Japan proper and settle there every year.

[1] *Saikin no Shakai Undo*, Kyochokai, cited, p. 195.
[2] Akiyama, O., *op. cit.*, p. 101.
[3] Since the second general manhood election of 1930 Chosenese writing was legalized in vote, and in 1932 a Chosenese was elected to the Parliament.
[4] Yoshio enumerated 444 known cases. Yoshio, E., *op. cit.*, p. 176.
[5] Cf. *ibid.*, p. 176 ; Nitobe, I. Editor, *op. cit.*, p. 168.
[6] This will be seen from the fact that not infrequently the great majority of labourers employed under the winter unemployment relief public works of great cities in 1929 were Chosenese. Some of these workers come every year from Chosen to large cities of Japan at the registration time to participate in these public works. Akiyama, O., *op. cit.*, p. 114.

F. CONCLUSIONS

In this study the writer has repeatedly stressed the economic factor as the predominating influence in colonization or immigration movements. The expression of this basic economic factor is, however, conditioned by the given historical, political and social background of the nation. It will be convenient therefore to consider more specifically certain aspects of the stagnant condition of overseas Japanese expansion. The three most important contributive factors in this situation are :

1. The prolonged policy of isolation under the Tokugawa regime suppressed the earlier tradition and ambitions of overseas activities, and thereby devitalized Japanese ventures in colonization and emigration.

2. When, after the Russo-Japanese War, Japan entered the field of international activity, she found that all undeveloped territories were already occupied by the Caucasian peoples. In particular, the Anglo-Saxon peoples were in possession of those territories which, for many reasons, seemed most desirable for Japanese colonization. Racial prejudice, accompanied, of course, by economic ambitions, destined the exclusion of Japanese in these regions.

3. Most of the colonies and dependencies secured by Japan in recent decades were already densely populated, long before their inclusion into the Japanese Empire, by peoples of relatively inferior standards of living.

In the preceding pages an attempt has been made to present a brief account of the 1,246,743 Japanese living in the colonial territories and the 509,754 residing in foreign countries. In short, on October 1, 1930, there were 1,756,497 Japanese living outside of Japan proper, representing 2·7 per cent of the population of Japan proper. Nor have all of these limited numbers actually migrated from Japan ; of the " Japanese " in Hawaii in 1930, for example, 65·3 per cent were born in Hawaii. Professor Ichihashi estimates that about 50 per cent of " Japanese " in continental United States and Canada are second generation, children of immigrants.[1] From such data it may be concluded that,

[1] Ichihashi, Y., *op. cit.*, p. 14.

P

of the total Japanese population in colonies and foreign
countries, less than 1,000,000 have actually migrated from
Japan.   In other words, after a considerable effort extending over several decades the number of Japanese emigrants
abroad, including colonies, equals only the number of one
year's natural increase within the nation.

Nevertheless, this need not necessarily be regarded as
disadvantageous to the homeland.   Indeed, in regard to
the ultimate effects of a colonization or emigration movement on the population in the mother country, the paradox
as expressed by an old writer, "leave a few breeders, and
you will have more people than if there were no emigration," [1] is now subjected to close scrutiny.   Not only that
aspect, but also the adverse economic effect of emigration
movement to the homeland has been subjected to a re-
evaluation. [2]

The percentages of Japanese in colonies are gaining somewhat.   On the contrary, in view of the relatively small
number of Japanese in those Western countries regarded,
at one time or another, as important outlets for Japanese
nationals, and the virtual cessation of such migration to
these countries, the ethnical and cultural identities of the
Japanese immigrants will eventually become indistinguish-
able, as was the case of the Japanese movement to the
South Sea regions in the sixteenth century. [3]

Our study in this chapter has brought to light many
important factors affecting the population movements of
a nation.   As far as Japan is concerned, we are forced to
conclude that colonization and immigration as a remedy
for over-population are definitely limited in their application.   The scheme of mass emigration to Manchuria which
is now being formulated is animated by a desire to cultivate

---

[1] This subject was discussed at the Literary Club of Samuel Johnson
in 1778.   The above remark is attributed to Edmund Burke.   See Hill,
G. B., Editor, *Boswell's Life of Johnson*, New York, Harper, 1891, Vol.
III, p. 263.   It is doubtful if a similar paradox voiced by David Hume
about the same time (1752), that a restriction in the size of the family
(to Hume it meant the exposure of infants) results only in an even larger
population, will any longer hold water.   See *Philosophical Works of David
Hume*, Boston, Little, Brown & Co., 1854, Vol. III, p. 431.

[2] Cf. Penrose, E. F., *op. cit.*, p. 259.   [3] See *supra*, p. 188.

closer racial and social ties with Manchoukuo. In order to attain the objectives, the economic principles of population movement must be followed and the nation must co-operate with Manchoukuo to make the living conditions there attractive.

CHAPTER X

INDUSTRIALIZATION AS A REMEDIAL MEASURE

A. Introduction

INDUSTRIALIZATION has been proposed by many writers as an economic measure calculated to relieve Japan's population pressure. This policy has been widely advocated and acclaimed by political leaders, business men, militarists, economists, and others. One business leader pointed out that if Japan were to promote industry to such an extent as to absorb a ratio of the population comparable to the proportion in industry in the United States, the nation would, under such industrialization, be able to support not only her present population but an additional 10 million as yet unborn.[1] A leader in politics maintains that if the ratio were brought up to the level of England or Belgium, Japan's population could be increased to the extent of 15 millions.[2] A consideration of the feasibility and practicability of the policy of industrialization as a solution to Japan's population problem will be the subject of this chapter.

In the previous pages the rapid growth of the Japanese population during the past few decades has been demonstrated to have been a phenomenon concomitant with that of urbanization, which, itself, was an incident of the nation's industrial progress.[3] In reality, there was a definite paucity of industrial workers during the period of industrial expansion immediately following the Sino-Japanese War.[4] This

[1] Fujiwara, G., " A Forgotten Population Policy," *The Chugai Shogyo Shinpo*, Oct. 1-4, 1926.
[2] Yamamoto, J., *Keizai Kokusaku no Teisho* (Proposals regarding the National Economic Policy), Tokyo, Nihon Hyoronsha, 1930, p. 220.
[3] See *supra*, pp. 71-4.
[4] Cf. Takahashi, K., *Saikin no Nihon Keizaishi*, cited, p. 407.

situation was a contributing factor in the relative indifference of the Government and people toward overseas colonization and emigration prior to the Great War.[1] Only since the post-War depression set in has Japan encountered the problem of unemployment, and only very recently has the nation been forced to take cognizance of the various socio-economic ramifications of the question as it relates to that of population growth.

B. Industrial Progress of Japan

The post-War economic dislocation was prolonged in Japan. The consequent concentration of capital intensified the effects of this maladjustment. The situation was further aggravated in 1930 by the nation's return to the gold standard at the old par of yen ; since the exchange rate of the yen had been greatly depressed during the protracted period of the gold embargo, its removal at the old par resulted in a substantial fall of prices in general.[2]

Nevertheless, although these developments placed a great burden on the people of the nation, concrete efforts toward a " rationalization " of industry were instituted ; the unification of enterprises growing out of this period resulted in a considerable elimination of waste in industry through the adoption of efficient machinery. Thus in a great many lines Japanese industrial enterprise attained the level of technical efficiency reached by the most advanced Western nations. This development is well illustrated in the case of the textile industry, in which Japan now holds a competitive advantage over the Lancashire mills solely on the basis of superior technical efficiency. Hence, in spite of the universal economic and social instability of the past decade and a half, Japan has steadily advanced in most of the manufacturing industries and has developed techniques therein comparable to those of Western nations.[3]

In the following table are cited figures showing coal and electric power consumption in factories, the index numbers

---

[1] See *supra*, p. 190.   [2] See *supra*, p. 22.
[3] Bisson, T. A., " Japan's Trade Expansion," *Foreign Policy Reports*, 10 ; 16, Oct. 10, 1934, p. 205.

of manufactured products, and the adjusted value of these goods.

TABLE XC

FACTORY CONSUMPTION OF COAL AND ELECTRIC POWER, INDEX NUMBERS OF INDUSTRIAL OUTPUTS, AND ADJUSTED VALUE OF MANUFACTURED PRODUCTS, 1914–33 [1]

I Year.	II Coal (1,000 Kg.).	III Electric Power (1,000 K.W.H.).	IV Index Number of Output.	V Adjusted Value of Products.
1914 . .	3,848,487	392	100·00	1,371,608
1919 . .	8,890,028	1,130	177·84	2,721,176
1920 . .	8,692,990	1,282	178·69	2,192,345
1921 . .	—	—	169·72	2,003,358
1922 . .	—	—	200·95	2,662,541
1923 . .	—	—	209·59	2,902,606
1924 . .	—	—	226·77	2,691,874
1925 . .	11,316,394	2,087	325·28	3,195,621
1926 . .	11,905,722	2,293	269·23	3,304,104
1927 . .	12,633,084	2,045	274·18	3,586,316
1928 . .	13,180,895	3,050	304·86	3,936,629
1929 . .	10,404,007	3,319	329·08	4,301,448
1930 . .	9,358,874	3,577	299·36	3,410,505
1931 . .	8,705,128	3,833	294·10	4,265,350
1932 . .	9,059,973	3,834	—	4,691,765
1933 . .	10,513,772	3,256	—	5,539,703

IV. Nagoya Commercial College Index Numbers. V. The actual value of products adjusted to the Tokyo wholesale price index numbers, 1914 taken as base.

The above statistics illustrate the important fact that the volume of Japan's factory consumption of coal increased from 3,848,000 tons in 1914 to 10,514,000 tons in 1933. Moreover, this latter figure is lower than those of the 1925–8 period, due to the steady increase in the annual consumption of electric power during the period under discussion. Taking 100 as the production index in 1914, the figure in 1931 stood at 294. The value of manufactured products, when adjusted to the price index (thereby eliminating the

[1] II. *Kinyujiko Sankosho*, cited, 1933, pp. 245, 251; III. *Tokei Nenkan*, cited, No. 43, 1924, pp. 199, 201. *Financial and Economic Annual of Japan*, cited, 1933, p. 101; IV. *1920–30 Seiji Keizai Nenkan*, cited, p. 316; V. For actual value of production, *Tokei Nenkan*, cited, No. 52, 1933, p. 3. For price index, *Kinyujiko Sankosho*, cited, 1932, p. 345.

effect of price fluctuation), also indicated a steady gain. The 1933 figure is more than four times the 1914 figure.

These statistical figures reveal in fact the nation's industrial achievements. Before considering in detail the industrial progress with reference to the number of persons employed, we may clarify two factors which are generally admitted as having great consequences upon the present and future of industrial development of Japan, viz. the prospect of foreign trade and the problems of mineral supply. In addition, a short review of the possibilities of further industrialization in general will be made.

C. PROSPECT OF FOREIGN TRADE

Japan's share in the international trade of the world increased in the field of imports from an average of 1·5 per cent during the 1911–13 period to 2·0 per cent in 1932, and in the field of exports it rose from 1·4 per cent to 3·2 per cent. Although the latest figures are far above those of average nations (less than 1 per cent), ranking with Belgium, Canada, or Italy, they are considerably lower than the figures of the United States, Great Britain, and Germany, which stand above 10 per cent.[1] Nevertheless, the ratio of exports to the total of manufactured goods of the nation was estimated in 1933 as 20·5 per cent. This figure is comparable with that of Great Britain, hitherto regarded as having one of the highest ratios in the world, and shows the relatively high concentration of Japanese industry on foreign trade.[2]

In Table VI, Chapter II, we observed that the gross value of foreign trade of Japan increased from 1,224,000 yen in 1914 to 2,383,000 yen in 1930, and that the *per capita* value also increased from 24 yen in 1914 to 38 yen in 1930. Export trade alone also increased correspondingly. Neither

---

[1] *Foreign Commerce Year Book*, U.S. Department of Commerce, 1933, p. 348.
[2] The percentages in 1929 and 1931 were 23·7 and 18·2 respectively. *Japanese Trade and Industry*, Tokyo, Mitsubishi Economic Research Bureau, 1936, p. 494 ; the corresponding figure for the United States was estimated at less than 10 in 1929. *Commerce Year Book*, U.S. Department of Commerce, 1931, Vol. I, p. 89.

one of the above data depicts the whole situation, however. We must call attention to the fact that the value of goods involving more technical manufacturing processes includes a relatively greater labour value than goods involving a lower degree of manufacture. Therefore, we may consider at this point Japan's foreign trade commodities classified according to the degree of manufacture. The following figures portray the percentage of commodities classified by the degree of manufacture of the total import and export trades in 1897 and 1933, the earliest and latest years for which such data are available.

TABLE XCI

FOREIGN TRADE COMMODITIES CLASSIFIED ACCORDING TO THE DEGREE OF MANUFACTURE, 1897 AND 1933 [1]

(Percentages of Total)

Year.	Food, Drink and Tobacco.	Raw Materials.	Semi-Manufactures.	Manufactures.	Miscellaneous.
	I. *Import*				
1897 . .	24·38	24·42	16·61	33·44	1·15
1933 . .	9·06	61·77	17·19	11·52	0·45
	II. *Export*				
1897 . .	12·89	10·35	50·84	23·03	2·89
1933 . .	8·62	4·03	29·40	56·29	1·65

The preceding tabulation reveals the significant fact that during the period from 1897 to 1933 Japan's exportation of raw materials declined from 10·35 per cent to 4·03 per cent of total exports, while the exportation of completely manufactured goods increased from 23·03 per cent to 56·29 per cent. The reverse is true in the case of imports and these figures together illustrate the increasing capacity of Japanese industry to furnish the national population with the services of the world to an extent more than proportional

[1] *Kinyujiko Sankosho*, cited, 1934, p. 383.

to the increase of total value of imports and exports. The following tables, citing the position of major import and export commodities, afford material for further analysis of Japan's situation in international commerce.

TABLE XCII

VALUE OF IMPORTS WITH CLASSIFICATION OF PRINCIPAL
COMMODITIES, 1929, 1931, 1933 [1]

(Unit 1,000 Yen)

Commodities.	1929.	1931.	1933.
Food, drink, and tobacco . .	*271,156*	*158,612*	*173,185*
Rice and paddy	22,782	6,973	11,521
Wheat	70,896	32,936	44,384
Beans	78,744	37,350	50,339
Sugar	31,160	15,603	12,794
Miscellaneous	67,574	65,750	54,147
Raw materials	*1,223,917*	*684,338*	*1,181,146*
Seed for oil manufacture .	30,777	14,549	23,292
Coal	42,979	28,268	36,657
Raw rubber	33,884	13,182	29,685
Sulphate of ammonia (crude)	48,086	15,861	9,420
Soy bean meal and cake .	75,919	44,349	41,169
Raw cotton	573,016	296,273	604,847
Wool	101,816	86,145	164,191
Lumber	88,838	43,379	40,585
Miscellaneous	228,602	142,332	231,300
Semi-manufactures . . .	*355,393*	*181,138*	*328,799*
Pulp	13,486	11,840	27,068
Woollen yarn	18,735	12,431	3,022
Pig iron	28,435	11,229	25,253
Other iron	131,286	36,798	111,388
Lead	15,036	8,129	11,901
Zinc	8,194	3,092	7,462
Others	140,221	97,619	142,705
Manufactures.	*345,913*	*197,534*	*220,328*
Petroleum	34,682	35,993	34,774
Woollen tissues . . .	19,941	9,943	7,213
Machinery	121,095	50,910	72,658
Others	170,195	100,688	105,683
Miscellaneous.	*17,044*	*10,115*	*8,672*
Total	2,213,423	1,231,737	1,912,130

[1] *Asahi Nenkan*, cited, 1935, p. 194 ; *Kinyujiko Sankosho*, cited, 1934, p. 383.

TABLE XCIII

VALUE OF EXPORTS WITH CLASSIFICATION OF PRINCIPAL
COMMODITIES, 1929, 1931, 1933 [1]

(Unit 1,000 Yen)

Commodities.	1929.	1931.	1933.
Food, drink, and tobacco . .	*160,118*	*120,297*	*157,988*
Beans	14,612	5,079	7,159
Aquatic products . . .	22,349	10,177	10,301
Flour	26,816	9,517	34,955
Tea	12,028	8,232	8,449
Sugar	29,975	14,861	14,909
Preserved food	25,683	18,947	46,984
Others	28,655	53,484	35,231
Raw materials	*88,739*	*44,802*	*73,765*
Waste silk	13,041	2,393	1,302
Coal	23,216	15,009	14,159
Lumber	21,138	9,954	18,639
Others	31,344	17,446	39,665
Semi-manufactures	*883,775*	*422,844*	*538,793*
Vegetable oils	9,120	5,227	8,330
Raw silk	781,040	355,395	390,899
Iron.	5,253	7,411	34,566
Cotton yarn	26,756	8,510	15,713
Braid	5,186	1,821	6,950
Others	56,420	44,480	82,335
Manufactures.	*937,307*	*532,930*	*1,031,576*
Cotton tissues	412,707	198,730	383,215
Silk tissues	149,954	82,766	140,928
Cotton hosiery shirt . . .	29,674	16,477	31,190
Glass wares	13,211	6,532	15,327
Machinery	13,617	13,641	25,857
Pottery	36,963	19,309	35,633
Paper	26,289	20,996	17,689
Others	254,892	174,479	381,737
Miscellaneous	*33,787*	*18,707*	*30,193*
Total	2,103,726	1,139,580	1,832,315

The above two tables clearly indicate the structure of
Japan's international trade. It may briefly be summed up
as follows : the nation imports the necessary food and raw
materials for industrial purposes by an exchange of raw silk,
cottons, silk tissues, and such manufactures as preserved

[1] *Kinyujiko Sankosho*, cited, 1934, p. 383 ; *Asahi Nenkan*, cited, 1935,
p. 194.

foods (mainly fish), pottery, and machinery. The tables further show that the great bulk of Japan's export trade consists of products of light industry or semi-finished goods such as raw silk. The high concentration of exports of raw silk and textile products hitherto constituted a weak point in Japan's foreign trade economy. The tables indicate the fact that there is a trend away from such extreme concentration. Exports of rayon and woollen products and miscellaneous manufactures such as drugs, boots, shoes and clogs, show a considerable increase in recent years.

With regard to the countries of destination, the exports illustrated a tendency toward a high degree of concentration. About 95 per cent of the raw silk exported is destined for the United States. However, there are two forces leading to a breakdown of this tendency toward centralization of exports, namely, the high protective measures adopted by many of the chief import countries against Japanese goods and the opening of new markets for Japanese products. A concrete illustration of this situation is afforded in the case of British India, where, due largely to the extreme protective measures adopted, Japan's export of cotton cloths declined from 644 million square yards in 1932 to 451 million square yards in 1933—a loss that was more than offset by the increase in the total export of that product by 100 million square yards during that same year. The actual figure of Japan's export of cotton cloth in 1933 was 2,089 million square yards, surpassing that of Great Britain, with 2,032 million square yards, which hitherto claimed the position of undisputed leadership in that particular field of exports. The shares of Japan and Great Britain in the world's export of cotton cloths in 1933 were 39 and 38 per cent, respectively. Whether or not these favourable tendencies will persist and whether Japan will continue to progress in its industrial development are points yet to be considered.

D. MINERAL RESOURCES

One obstacle which is usually regarded as most dis-advantageous to Japan's industrial development is the nation's limited supply of mineral resources. At the present time, Japan's output of important industrial minerals is confined to copper, coal, and stones. These are the only minerals produced in sufficient quantity. All aluminum, almost all iron ores, oils, zinc, lead, and tin, are, of necessity, imported.[1] Three minerals of vital importance, namely, iron, coal, and mineral soils, will be considered here in some detail.

Iron.—Japan supplies almost all the steel and pig iron which she consumes. During the past few years the annual demand for steel has exceeded 2 million tons (metric) ; of this amount between 10 and 13 per cent is imported. As for pig iron, Japan proper produced about 1 million tons in 1932 ; the consumption during that year amounted to 1·7 million tons. The remaining 700,000 tons were, for the most part, imported from Chosen (200,000 tons), Japanese foundries in Manchuria (300,000 tons), and British India (150,000 tons). It is said that the importation from India would have been unnecessary were it not for price and investment relations.[2]

In contrast to her ability to supply these necessary products, Japan lacks the supplies of iron ore, out of which pig iron and steel are manufactured. Although her present annual demand for iron ore amounts to almost 4 million tons, Japan can supply only 6 per cent of this demand. The output from Chosen (150,000 tons) is negligible, as is Manchuria's (20,000 to 30,000 tons). Therefore, most of the ore consumed in Japan is imported from the Malay Peninsula and from China. However, it must be pointed out that those mines in the Malay Peninsula which supply Japan with iron ore are operated by Japanese. Further, through various treaties, Japan has access to iron mines in China. Thus, in spite of the fact that Japan depends almost entirely upon foreign sources for her supply of iron ore, she has adequate control over the sources of supply. Furthermore,

---

[1] *Kokusei Zukai*, cited, 1933, p. 184.
[2] *Ibid.*, p. 192. Concerning the figures in this section, compare with *Honpo Jukyu Shigen Yoran* (Statistical Tables of Supply and Demand of 156 Commodities), Tokyo, East Asiatic Economic Investigation Bureau, 1931, pp. 54–72.

because of the accessibility of maritime transportation, the cost of shipping the ores to Japan is somewhat lower than the transportation costs in the United States and Germany, where the ore is produced within the nation's own or neighbouring territories.[1] Hence the cost of iron ore is lower in Japan than it is in these ore-producing nations.

According to the authorities of the Yahata Government Iron Foundry,[2] the Asiatic regions north of the Equator have mineral resources of 180 million tons of ore which possess more than 50 per cent of iron content. Japan can, therefore, import ore from these regions at a cost which makes it economically practicable. If resources of between 30 and 40 per cent content be added, the supply is practically unlimited. Thus, these authorities conclude, the supply of iron ore presents no obstacle to the industrial development of Japan.[3]

Coal.—Japan's position with regard to coal presents practically no problem. Japan is the fifth coal-producing country of the world, and, generally speaking, is self-sufficient as far as this product is concerned. In 1932 Japan consumed 29·4 million tons. This was balanced by the production of 28·1 million tons, the imports of 2·7 million tons, and the exports of 1·4 million tons. The chief sources of import are Manchuria (1·4 million tons), North China (Kaiping coal, *c.* 300,000 tons), and French Indo-China (Hongay coal, *c.* 400,000 tons). Both Japan and Manchuria lack deposits of coking coal. Chinese and French Indo-Chinese coal are imported to balance this deficiency in Japanese coal. On the other hand, Manchurian coal is imported because of the difference in production costs.[4]

---

[1] *Kokusei Zukai*, cited, 1933, p. 194.

[2] In January, 1934, the Yahata Iron Foundry was merged with some private iron works, and became the Japan Iron Manufacturing Company.

[3] *Ibid.*, p. 194 ; Bureau of Mines, Department of Commerce and Industry, Japan, during the period of 1929–31, conducted extensive investigations of the iron resources of Japan. According to this survey, the resources were estimated at 120 million tons. Of this figure 13 million tons are reported as definitely surveyed deposits. *Ibid.*, p. 195.

[4] The *per capita* consumption of coal in 1931 was 0·4 tons. This consumption rate is higher than Italy's (0·3 tons) but corresponds to only 21 per cent of Germany's (1·9 tons) and 11 per cent of England's *per capita* consumption (3·5 tons) in that year. However, the Japanese use wood

Mineral Oils.—Although about 70 per cent of the world's motive power is supplied by coal,[1] the importance of mineral oils in the field of industry is steadily and rapidly increasing. Japan is deficient in this vital mineral oil resource. In ten years the annual oil consumption of Japan increased from 142·1 million gallons in 1922 to 584·4 million gallons in 1932. The above is exclusive of the amounts used for naval purposes. Of the 584·4 million gallons consumed in 1932 only 58·4 million gallons, or 10 per cent, was produced in Japan. In addition to this, the Sagalin oil fields, to which Japan has access by treaty,[2] produced about 75·9 million gallons; thus 134·3 million gallons,[3] or 23 per cent of the total oil consumption of Japan in 1932, was produced within Japan or came from Japanese controlled resources.

The shale oil industry has, in recent years, been developed in Japan as a means of supplementing this deficit in the nation's oil resources. It is produced as a by-product of the coal-mining industry. The method involves the application of dry distillation to the shale which covers the coal layers of the Fushun coal mine. Excavation of oil shale layers of the Fushun coal mine amounts to between 6 and 7 million tons a year. As the oil content of these layers is about 5 per cent, the annual production of oil from these layers will reach about 330,000 tons, which approximates the amount of the annual oil production of Japan proper. It is estimated that the Fushun mine will continue to be profitable for the next thirty years.[4] The present annual capacity of oil production of the mine is 70,000 tons.

Of the 712·6 million gallons of oil imported by Japan in 1932, the United States supplied 387·1 million gallons, or 54·3 per cent of the total amount imported. The remainder was supplied by the Dutch East Indies, Russia, British

as a household fuel. The converted fuel value of wood consumed annually in Japan corresponds to 10 million tons of coal ; the fuel value of hydro-electricity (*c.* 10,700 million k.w. hours) annually consumed corresponds to 15 million tons of coal. *Ibid.*, pp. 198–9.

[1] *Kokusei Zukai*, cited, 1933, p. 200.
[2] Russo-Japanese Treaty of 1925.
[3] *Appeal by the Chinese Government*, League of Nations, *op. cit.*, pp. 84–5.
[4] *Manshu no Kogyo* (Mineral Industries in Manchuria), Dairen, South Manchuria Railway Co., 1928, pp. 362–3.

Borneo and other Asiatic territories. There is keen competition among the exporters of oil and in normal times, when international relations are amicable, there is no difficulty in obtaining a sufficient oil supply.

E. Prospect of Further Industrialization

The foregoing analysis of the mineral supply of Japan justifies the general view that Japan is seriously lacking in fuel and iron resources. However, it does not follow that the further industrialization of Japan is therefore impossible.

In this connection it is worthy of note that after a realistic analysis of the nature and source of national power, Bertrand Russell concluded that such power is dependent on two factors : the number of population and extent to which the nation's population is capable of public organization, and the mineral resources that the nation possesses. Russell further maintains that the importance of the possession of mineral resources is secondary to that of organization capacity, and that since the large population of Japan shows a high propensity for such capacity, the nation may remedy her inadequate mineral resources by acquiring control of such resources elsewhere.[1] Dr. Moulton observed that although Japan does not possess large ore resources within her own boundaries, this deficiency has obviously not proved to be an insuperable obstacle in the growth of industry.[2]

From the purely economic point of view it appears that demand is the controlling force in the supply of such necessary materials for industry as energy and mineral resources. Demand for industrial products is of course determined by the extent of the markets. It is the writer's opinion that Adam Smith's shrewd deduction that the application of the division of labour is limited by the extent of markets, may be applied in this connection, namely, that the supply of mineral resources is determined by the extent of the

[1] Russell, B. A. W., *The Prospect of Industrial Civilization*, London, George Allen & Unwin Co., 1923, p. 192.
[2] Moulton, H. G., *op. cit.*, p. 465.

demand for the industrial products of a nation.[1] This may be tenable in view of our highly developed techniques of transportation.[2]

After a careful survey of the conditions of markets in China, Manchuria, Hongkong, India, Dutch East India, the Philippine Islands, and the Straits Settlements, Dr. Moulton found that Japan is gaining markets in those areas more rapidly than are other countries. He further maintains that the steady growth of multifarious manufactured exports affords fairly conclusive evidence that in terms of cost· and quality Japanese products compare very favourably with those of other nations.[3]

It is at this point necessary to make some qualifying observations. It has been noted that light industries, of which textile manufacturing is typical, dominate Japanese industry. These enterprises are exposed to the competition of nations newly awakened to industrial interest. For this reason Great Britain is now experiencing pressure in her Oriental markets. In considering the industrial future of Japan it is necessary to study, briefly at least, the industrial situation of her neighbouring nations.

In 1932 India had more spindles than Japan. China had 4 million spindles in the same year although 40 per cent of this number were owned by Japanese.[4] Because of this rapid development of the cotton industry in hitherto industrially backward countries, Japan, in an effort to advance her industrial position, must strive to produce a

[1] In order to avoid the criticism that the author's logic rotates in a "vicious cycle," it may be added that the demand for products, other conditions remaining the same, is chiefly determined by the price and that the iron and energy resources are only small elements in the price determining factors. Moreover, it was already observed that the importation of these materials is a relatively simple and inexpensive process in Japan.

[2] Ichihashi, Y., *op. cit.*, p. 387. The cost of railroad transportation of freight for a distance of 4,000 kilometres from the western coast of the United States to the East is 350 per cent of the cost of ocean transportation for the distance of 8,500 kilometres from this same western coast to Japan. The railroad coast to the central part of the United States from the western coast is about 200 per cent of the shipping cost to Japan. *Kokusei Zukai*, cited, 1933, p. 346.

[3] Moulton, H. G., *op. cit.*, pp. 453–69.

[4] With regard to these statistics of China, Manchuria and Kwantung Province are included. The number of spindles are : India, 9,312,000 ; Japan, 7,798,000 ; China, 4,295,000. *Ibid.*, p. 106.

superior grade of tissue. This policy has necessitated various far-reaching innovations in her national economy and international trade relationships. For example, Japan, prior to 1926, imported almost all her cotton from India. In recent years, however, most of her cotton has been imported from the United States. In 1932, 72 per cent came from America, while only 21 per cent was imported from India. This reversal is indicative of Japan's attempt to place textile products of superior quality on the markets of the world, for American cotton lends itself more readily and more successfully to the manufacture of fine yarns than does Indian cotton.

However, there exist various and concrete obstacles to the industrialization and economic development of Japan. Typical of such elements is the protectionist policy of certain nations as manifested, for example, in the silk market. Here Japan is in a rather peculiar position. While fully equipped and well qualified to manufacture silk products, she is unable to do so extensively, owing to the tariff policy of the United States—a policy which closes that extensive market rather effectually to foreign producers. Hence Japan exports only raw silk to this country, and consequently the development of silk manufacture in Japan is automatically and effectively inhibited. In the face of similar economic policies by other nations, with the attendant tendencies toward national self-sufficiency, Japan's industrial development is considerably handicapped.

In addition to this protectionist tariff policy there is an increasing tendency on the part of various nations to apply a quota on imports. In this connection it must again be noted that various nations hitherto backward in industrial development are making efforts to achieve an economic self-sufficiency. Professors Thompson and Crocker summed up Japan's position when they simultaneously declared that in embarking upon a programme of intensive industrialization Japan is setting her face against the current of the times.[1]

In any event, the further industrialization of Japan must proceed along very carefully planned lines. The applica-

[1] Thompson, W. S., *op. cit.*, pp. 268–70 ; Crocker, W. R., *op. cit.*, p. 182.

bility of the theory of comparative costs in international trade becomes more and more limited as nations attempt to control their foreign trade by the dual system of the protectionist and mutual preferential policies. An unwieldy and over-optimistic industrial plan under such circumstances is dangerous to the stability of the country.

So much for precautions. The foregoing analysis of the various factors in the industrialization of Japan seems to indicate on the whole one significant point, namely, that despite the many difficulties suggested above, it is reasonably certain that the nation may be able to further her industrialization. However, it remains to be seen whether or not such industrial progress will be accompanied by a demand for labour sufficient to warrant national industrialization as an efficacious population policy.

F. Industrialization and Employment

The process of industrializing a nation carries with it wide social implications and profoundly influences the nation's population trend. In this section will be considered the effects of this process on the population employed in the manufacturing industries.

A study of the number of factories and factory operatives in Japan since 1900 revealed the data shown in Table XCIV. As indicated in this tabulation, the number of operatives in 1916 reached 1 million, and was doubled in 1929. Increases in the three ten-year periods ending in 1930 were 295,142, 769,281, and 318,439. From 1930 to 1933 the increase was 261,391. Number of the annual increase was more than 100,000 only during the Great War period and in 1929 and 1933. In some other years there were even actual declines. All these figures do not include miscellaneous factory labourers whose numbers were reported as 79,453 in 1930 and 95,485 in 1933.

The percentages of the regular factory operatives were 28·04 in 1920 and 31·67 in 1930 of the total number gainfully employed in manufacturing industry. Numbers of the population gainfully occupied in manufacturing industry in

TABLE XCIV

NUMBER OF FACTORIES AND FACTORY OPERATIVES, 1900–33 [1]

Year.	Number of Factories.	Operatives.			
		Male.	Female.	Total.	Annual Inc. or Dec. (–).
1900	7,284	164,712	257,307	422,019	—
1910	13,523	274,587	442,574	717,161	—
1914	17,062	318,667	535,297	853,964	—
1915	16,809	350,976	559,823	910,799	56,835
1916	19,299	458,632	636,669	1,095,301	184,502
1917	20,966	567,844	713,120	1,280,964	185,663
1918	22,391	646,115	763,081	1,409,196	128,232
1919	43,949	706,074	814,392	1,520,466	111,270
1920	45,806	700,124	786,318	1,486,442	– 34,024
1921	87,398	771,593	915,449	1,687,042	199,600
1922	46,427	834,314	856,705	1,691,019	3,977
1923	47,786	838,197	926,936	1,765,133	74,114
1924	48,394	859,783	929,835	1,789,618	24,485
1925	49,161	852,554	955,827	1,808,381	18,763
1926	51,906	893,834	981,361	1,875,195	66,814
1927	53,680	923,201	975,671	1,898,872	23,677
1928	55,948	948,876	987,373	1,936,249	37,377
1929	60,412	960,342	1,134,898	2,095,240	158,991
1930	62,787	893,036	911,845	1,804,881	– 290,359
1931	64,572	891,210	918,505	1,809,715	4,834
1932	67,448	971,100	924,200	1,895,300	85,585
1933	72,078	1,091,905	974,367	2,066,273	170,972

Figures cited are as of December 31 of respective years ; Miscellaneous factory labourers are excluded ; Government factories are included.

Up to 1928 factories are defined as workshops employing 5 or more operatives. Since then workshops with such capacity regardless of the actual number employed are included in this category.

1920 and 1930 were given as 5,300,248 and 5,699,581 respectively.[2]

From these data we may now observe that during the ten-year period from 1920 to 1930 the entire population gainfully engaged in manufacturing industry increased 399,333, a relatively small number, considering the vast number of the nation's total population. Of this limited increase, however, 318,459 or 79·75 per cent was contri-

[1] For 1900–25, *Tokei Zensho*, cited, p. 50 ; For 1926–30, *Rodo Tokei Yoran*, cited, 1932, p. 16 ; For 1931–3, *Kinyujiko Sankosho*, cited, 1935, pp. 241–7. [2] See pp. 77, 79.

buted by the group under regular factory operatives, thereby suggesting a greater increase in productivity as compared with the increase in number. More detailed analysis of the composition of industrial population in 1920 and 1930, shown in the table below, seems to coincide with such an inference. The table follows:

TABLE XCV

AGE AND SEX COMPOSITION OF POPULATION GAINFULLY EMPLOYED IN MANUFACTURING INDUSTRIES, 1920 AND 1930

Age Period.	Male Workers.			Female Workers.		
	No. of Workers.		Inc. or Dec. (—).	No. of Workers.		Inc. or Dec. (—).
	1920.	1930.		1920.	1930.	
14 and under	190,775	131,913	— 58,862	221,909	169,539	— 52,370
15–19	615,988	752,503	136,515	438,864	509,032	70,168
20–24	577,537	708,490	130,953	244,154	250,942	6,788
25–29	527,029	639,072	112,043	135,859	118,138	— 17,721
30–34	441,005	554,777	113,772	112,685	89,519	— 23,166
35–39	369,978	430,070	60,092	106,478	73,051	— 33,427
40–44	314,856	344,298	29,442	96,059	65,065	— 30,994
45–49	223,248	264,534	41,286	71,998	55,428	— 16,570
50–54	165,631	200,852	35,221	52,879	41,819	— 11,060
55–59	120,141	116,972	— 3,169	37,152	25,993	— 11,159
15–59	*3,355,413*	*4,011,568*	*656,155*	*1,296,128*	*1,228,987*	*— 67,141*
60 and over	170,166	125,670	— 44,496	65,857	31,904	— 33,953
Total	3,716,354	4,269,151	552,797	1,583,894	1,430,430	—153,464

We may deduce from the above table that during the ten-year period the structure of Japanese industrial population has undergone a significant change. That is, while the net increase is only 399,333, as has been noted already, this number was a result of an increase of 736,280 among the group of male workers aged 15–54 and female workers aged 15–24, and a decrease of 336,947 among the group of both sexes under 15, male workers over 55, and female workers over 25. This really is a significant change in favour of more productive groups. But this is not all; there is an accelerating mechanization of industry.

This aspect of the increase in the productivity of Japan's labour force was studied by T. Minoguchi in general terms. Mr. Minoguchi calculated the number of adjusted "complete workers" by applying certain weight values to the different age and sex groups. When the results were expressed in the form of index numbers, the figure for manufacturing workers was 108·43 in 1930 compared to 100 in 1920. By adjusting this first index number to that of the industrial outputs cited by the Industrial Research Office of Nagoya Commercial College, Mr. Minoguchi concluded that the productivity of a unit of the "complete worker" was 154·51 in 1930, in comparison to 100 in 1920. Similar figures for other industries were 150·1 in mining, 111·99 in agriculture, and 88·29 in aquatic industries.[1]

In further illustration of the tendency of labour intensification the following figures are cited :

TABLE XCVI

AVERAGE NUMBER OF OPERATIVES IN TEXTILE MILLS PER GIVEN NUMBER OF SPINDLES AND LOOMS, 1929–33 [2]

Year.	Number of Operatives per 20,000 Spindles.		Number of Operatives per 100 Looms.	
	First Half-Year.	Second Half-Year.	First Half-Year.	Second Half-Year.
1929	62	62	289	266
1930	59	49	252	217
1931	46	44	208	204
1932	44	46	204	198
1933	47	46	182	191

As depicted in this tabulation, the average number of operatives per 20,000 spindles decreased from 62 to 46, or 25·8 per cent, during the period studied, and the number of operatives per 100 looms decreased from 289 to 191, or 28·2 per cent.

That these tendencies toward an intensification of labour have broad social implications is clearly apparent in con-

[1] Ueda, T., Editor, *op. cit.*, Vol. II, 1934, p. 408.
[2] *Asahi Nenkan*, cited, 1935, p. 150.

sideration of the increase of the nation's population of working age groups. Hence, despite the steady increase in production, Japan is now face to face with a problem of unemployment. A brief consideration of this related problem of industrial concentration is expedient at this point.

G. Problem of Unemployment

Japan first experienced an unemployment problem in the modern sense of the term during the period following the post-Great War depression. This situation was particularly aggravated in the spring of 1922, when, as a result of the Washington treaty of naval limitation, the nation experienced its first large-scale dismissal of skilled workers.[1]

Dr. T. Nagai estimated the extent of Japan's unemployment during the post-War depression in 1920 at approximately 200,000. Dr. T. Fukuda of Tokyo Commercial College arrived at a similar figure in estimating the number of unemployed after the great earthquake in 1923. The first official report of unemployment statistics was based on the unemployment census which was carried out in conjunction with the census of 1925. Twenty-four commercial, industrial, and mining centres were covered and the official report placed the number of unemployed at 105,612. The figures of this unemployment census are cited below :

TABLE XCVII

Unemployment Figures of Twenty-four Industrial Centres, October 1, 1925 [2]

Gross Population in the Area.	Groups Investigated.	Number in Each Group.	Unemployed.	Percentage of Groups Investigated.
11,585,669	Salaried men . .	615,331	19,396	3·15
	Wage earners . .	1,533,433	46,278	3·02
	Casual labourers .	206,251	39,938	19·36
	Total . . .	2,355,015	105,612	4·48

[1] *Saikin no Shakai Undo*, Kyochokai, cited, pp. 845–9.
[2] *Rodo Tokei Yoran*, cited, 1932, p. 284.

In September, 1929, the Social Bureau of the Home Department organized the publication of a bulletin citing a brief estimate of Japan's entire unemployment situation. The extent of the nation's unemployment, as reported in the bulletin, is as follows :

TABLE XCVIII

UNEMPLOYMENT ESTIMATES OF THE SOCIAL BUREAU, 1929–33 [1]

Date.	Salaried Men.		Wage Earners.		Casual Labourers.		Total.	
	Number.	% of Group Inv'd.	Number.	% of Group Inv'd.	Number.	% of Group Inv'd.	Number.	% of Group Inv'd.
9/29	59,158	3·76	113,163	3·22	96,269	6·37	268,590	4·07
1/30	65,836	4·02	145,856	4·00	128,214	7·96	340,488	4·93
7/30	75,057	4·74	171,213	4·49	150,277	9·34	378,484	5·34
1/31	62,929	3·85	158,596	4·35	128,214	7·96	371,802	5·39
7/31	71,249	4·32	181,036	4·91	154,638	9·37	391,377	5·59
1/32	78,068	4·69	214,626	5·85	193,192	11·59	485,886	6·94
7/32	82,080	4·90	218,745	5·87	210,076	12·42	510,901	7·20
1/33	80,519	4·76	175,427	4·66	188,086	10·52	444,032	6·13
7/33	69,938	4·11	150,451	3·94	197,788	11·12	418,167	5·73

Date as of beginning of the month.

According to the above table, unemployment in Japan has never appreciably exceeded the half-million mark during the period here studied. In general it has remained between 300,000 and 400,000. The percentage of unemployed to the total number of employees remained at about 6 until July, 1933. Compared to the percentage of the Western nations, which vary between 20 and 40, Japan's percentage is very low.

The first organized unemployment census of a national scope was combined with the general census of October 1, 1930. The report of that unemployment census gives the figures shown in Table XCIX. According to this tabulation, Japan's unemployed in 1930 numbered 319,813. This figure is even lower than the estimate of the Social Bureau which placed the figure as of October 1, 1930, at 374,140. The estimates of the Social Bureau are

[1] *Shitsugyo Jyokyo Suitei Geppo Gaiyo* (Abstract of the Monthly Returns of Unemployment Estimate), Social Bureau, Home Department, Japan (mimeographed).

TABLE XCIX

REPORT OF THE UNEMPLOYMENT CENSUS, OCTOBER 1, 1930

Occupation.	Male.	Female.	Total.
Agriculture	11,880	3,153	15,033
Aquatic industries	2,196	39	2,235
Mining	8,291	1,436	9,727
Manufacturing	124,146	10,948	135,094
Commerce	24,615	2,012	26,627
Transportation	33,525	799	34,324
Official and professional services	42,592	5,274	47,866
Domestic	4,937	2,857	7,794
Miscellaneous.	38,555	2,558	41,113
Total	290,737	29,076	319,813

generally considered to be too low.[1] Such disparity in
results may be due to prejudice on the part of the Japanese public against an official unemployment investigation, and to confusion of the unemployed group with
that portion of the population which requires public
relief. These factors, it is believed, are likely to result in a
misleadingly low official estimate of the unemployment
situation. There are various unofficial estimates of the
number of unemployed, which place the total between
1 and 3 million for the years 1930 to 1933. However,
these figures are equally, if not more, unreliable than those
previously cited.

In the above unemployment statistics, the figures for the
so-called white collar occupations are especially unreliable.
Table XCIX gives the unemployment figure of those engaged
in official and professional services as 47,866, and
Table XCVIII gives the number of unemployed salaried
men as between 60,000 and 80,000. At any rate the number
is not very large. Nevertheless, the social significance of
unemployment among this group, in view of the fact that
they are more articulate in expressing their discontent, is
comparable with that of any other group.[2] The particular

[1] *Economist*, Tokyo, Aug. 1, 1932, pp. 11-17.
[2] Cf. *supra*, Chapter II, Section C.

problem of unemployment of the intellectuals, however, will not be considered here.

Other factors which make the Japanese unemployment statistics obscure and the reported figures generally low are the Japanese family system and the rural origin of industrial workers. Table XCIV revealed the fact that, due partially to the dominance of the textile industry, the majority of factory workers are females.[1] They are recruited from the rural districts to work in factories in the cities. Their work is of a temporary nature. When they are dismissed and return home, they do not, as a rule, register as unemployed. The majority of the male workers are also recruited from rural communities, and are usually skilled farmers. Thus, when they lose their jobs in the towns they have no difficulty in finding shelter and work in their rural homes.[2] Table C below statistically demonstrates this situation:

TABLE C

DISMISSED FACTORY WORKERS CLASSIFIED ACCORDING TO THEIR
DESTINATIONS, 1923–31 [3]

Year.	Total Number.	Percentage of Total.					
		I.	II.	III.	IV.	V.	VI.
1923* . .	1,064,393	21·4	12·9	34·0	10·6	6·9	14·2
1924 . .	1,044,409	24·2	12·9	30·9	11·6	6·8	13·6
1925 . .	910,305	21·4	11·3	33·8	12·4	7·2	13·9
1926 . .	842,204	20·8	11·4	32·6	12·1	9·8	13·3
1927 . .	684,568	18·3	9·3	36·1	10·8	15·2	10·3
1928 . .	655,096	20·3	7·8	36·6	16·4	10·0	9·0
1929 . .	671,936	17·0	8·0	39·0	12·0	12·0	12·0
1930 . .	569,433	13·6	8·0	39·0	14·1	10·7	14·6
1931† . .	656,114	12·0	4·5	43·3	16·3	12·3	11·6

* March–December, 1923.   † January–October, 1931.

I, Re-employed in the same field of industry; II, Employed in the different fields of industry; III, Returned to the farm; IV, Employed in miscellaneous works; V, Not employed; VI, Not reported. After 1926 only factories and mines employing 50 or more workers were investigated.

[1] *Social Reform*, Sept., 1929, p. 95.
[2] Takahashi, K., *Nihon Noson Keizai Kenkyu*, cited, p. 365.
[3] *Kojo Kozan Rodosha Idocho* (Investigation of Labour Turnover in Factories and Mines), Social Bureau, Home Department, Japan, March, 1923–Oct., 1932 (mimeographed).

The above statistical tabulation demonstrates the pertinent fact that between 30 and 40 per cent of dismissed factory workers return to the farms. It is noticeable that while the ratios of re-employment in the same or different fields of industry are diminishing, the ratios of settlement in rural and village homes are increasing. During the first ten months of 1931 only 16·5 per cent found positions in industrial fields, while 43·3 per cent returned to the farms.

This rural background of the Japanese factory worker is instrumental in minimizing the apparent extent and significance of the nation's problem of unemployment. An attitude, perhaps feudal in nature and heritage, on the part of employers further contributes to this effect. While wages are low as compared to those of other nations, the Japanese employer has a relatively high sense of paternal responsibility for his employee's welfare, thus contributing to some extent to economic security for the latter. The custom of paying dismissal wages in particular may be mentioned in this connection.[1] These dismissal wages usually are paid in addition to the regular retirement fund and amount to the equivalent of one or two months' wages, not infrequently reaching five months' compensation.[2]

This does not mean, however, that Japan can evade the social consequences of unemployment. Nor does this justify the backward condition of social and economic legislation necessary in an industrialized society, as for example unemployment insurance and old age pensions. Rather, a social structure such as Japan's, characterized by an extreme lack of specialization among the industrial workers, obscures the

[1] Another example of this paternalistic trait of Japanese capitalism is the payment of strike costs after a settlement of a dispute has been reached. It is the custom among the Japanese employers to meet this expense and make allowances to the strike leaders discharged, irrespective of the success or failure of the strike. This is done for the reason that, after all, employers are responsible for the conduct of their workers. For numerous examples, see Harada, S., *op. cit.*, pp. 225–34 ; *Saikin no Shakai Undo*, Kyochokai, cited, pp. 348–73.

[2] Cf. *Ibid.*, pp. 845–7 ; Moulton, H. G., *op. cit.*, p. 347 ; Kawarada, K., " Remedies for the Problem of Unemployment," *Keizai Orai*, April, 1932, p. 95. In June, 1936, a law which provides for compulsory payment of retirement allowance was passed. The minimum allowance to be paid is equivalent to 20 days' wages per discharged worker, when such worker has been in employment for 1 to 3 years.

cost of the branches of the nation's industrial life, and ultimately jeopardizes the general standard of living.

As a matter of fact, under the present state of Japan's rural economy and declining status of the family system,[1] the situation of those male workers who return to the farms is not a desirable one.[2] Moreover, the worker, having once experienced the advantages of town life, does not wish to settle permanently on the farm, and he eventually leaves again.[3]

In view of these facts, it must be added that the industrial and social problems which are the resultants of unemployment among Western industrialized nations, assume in Japan the form of a general low standard of living and a consequent inefficiency along all the lines of economic life. It has already been noted that the existence of a vast number of peasants with little or no land holdings, and the increasing number of small retail traders, constitute a more serious economic problem than does the acute but remediable problem of unemployment. In the industrial West the problem resolves itself into one of a redistribution of national wealth, while in Japan it involves a more fundamental revision of the economic and social structure, which, in view of the present increase of population, is a formidable task and one which is quite unlikely to be assumed for some time to come.

H. Conclusions

In concluding this analysis of Japan's present industrial situation and future economic outlook, it may be expedient to emphasize the several most salient points discussed. That Japan will continue to industrialize is a generally accepted fact. However, this industrial expansion, in view of the growing limitation of the fields of free competition, must be based upon a well-planned programme embracing both the economic and social patterns of the nation. More-

---

[1] Suehiro, G., " The Necessity and Possibility of Unemployment Insurance," *Kaizo*, Jan., 1932, pp. 41–8.

[2] Ono, T., " Outline of Agrarian Unemployment Problem," *Social Reform*, No. 108, Sept., 1929, p. 95.

[3] Harada, S., *op. cit.*, p. 101.

over, owing to the increasing emphasis on mechanization and efficient organization, industrialization is proceeding at a greater pace than is employment, thereby creating a labour differential which may assume serious proportions. The growing importance of the problem of unemployment testifies to the limitations in the possibilities of population absorption in industry, and thereby foreshadows changes and readjustments in wider economic and social systems.

CHAPTER XI

BIRTH CONTROL AND THE DISTRIBUTIVE SYSTEM

A. INTRODUCTION

THROUGHOUT this work, an effort has been made to emphasize the close relationship between the population trend and the economic situation. Further, and more specifically, the present tendency toward an increasing pressure of the population upon the national life of Japan has been noted. From these premises it may be deduced that eventually a new trend approaching a limitation of the increase of population will of necessity manifest itself.

This limitation may be effected either through an increase of deaths or by a restriction upon births. With regard to the former means, infanticide is not likely to regain a foothold in Japan. Moreover, the general death rate is steadily decreasing and is a causal factor in the present-day large natural increase. Therefore, the limitation of population numbers must be accomplished through the restriction of births. It is, perhaps, to be expected that, as man gains a new measure of control over deaths, he should also make an effort to regulate births.

There are several methods of restricting births: the postponement of marriage, the recourse to abortion, prolonged abstinence between married persons, and the use of contraceptives. It has already been shown that the Japanese marriage-age has been steadily rising, causing a decrease in the fertility of women.[1] However, the most commonly employed means of limitation are abortion and the use of contraceptives. The latter method is generally

---

[1] *Supra*, p. 104.

regarded as most effective, and is the only means advocated by proponents of the birth-control movement.

B. Movements for Birth Control, Legalization of Abortion, and Eugenic Sterilization

As early as the first decade of this century the birth-control movement of the West found strong allies and exponents in Japan among such scholars as Dr. K. Ukita of Waseda University and Dr. K. Katsumoto of the Kyoto Imperial University.[1] Nevertheless, not until the post-War period did the movement for the control of births assume the character of an important social movement. Even then, and for some time after the Great War, birth control was widely regarded as a " dangerous doctrine." The refusal on the part of the Government to allow Mrs. Margaret Sanger to land in Japan in March, 1922,[2] caused considerable consternation throughout the country and stimulated a widespread public interest in the problem. It is significant that the first birth-control association in Japan was organized in May of the same year.[3]

Although there was no statutory prohibition against the practice of contraception and the dissemination of such information, the suppression of public lectures and publications was carried out as a police measure. When in the early period of its existence, the Population and Food Commission considered the problem of contraception, the public was considerably surprised at this innovation. Nevertheless, the fact that the movement progressed steadily is indicated in the statement made by Professor Penrose, who, some time between 1927 and 1930, was invited by the Commission to submit a statement on the contraceptive appliances used in British birth-control clinics. He declared that when the list and specimens were examined it was

[1] Cf. Kawai, T., " On ' The Necessity for Contraception ' by Dr. Ukita," *Tokei Shushi*, No. 336, Feb., 1909.

[2] This was later revoked.

[3] Cf. Ishimoto, S., *Facing Two Ways*, New York, Farrar, 1935, p. 220 ff. ; Tsutsumi, T., *Ninshin Chosetsu no Igakuteki Chishiki* (Medical Knowledge of Control of Conception), Tokyo, Jitsugyo no Nihonsha, 1930, p. 72 ; Majima, Kan, *Haha yo Kenmei Nare* (Be Wise Mothers !), Tokyo, Jitsugyo no Nihonsha, 1931, p. 235.

found that all but one British contraceptive had a counter-
part of Japanese manufacture in Japan.[1] In 1928, Dr. H.
Shimomura, vice-president of the Tokyo and Osaka *Asahi*,
the largest newspaper companies in Japan, maintained that
the trend of the birth-control movement in Japan was well
indicated in the articles and advertisements of contraceptives found daily in Japanese journals.[2] The fact that
the Population and Food Commission in December, 1929,
favoured the " reasonable " practice of birth control has
previously been noted.[3] Since then such public officials
as the Minister of Education and Chief of the Bureau of
Court Physicians have openly advocated the public adoption
of birth control.[4] The latter official has published in one
of Japan's most representative magazines, an article on the
methods of contraception.[5]

In the summer of 1929 the Deputy Mayor of Tokyo
drafted a plan whereby municipal birth-control clinics were
to be established in the poor sections of the city. However,
the Home Department, the supervisory authority of the city,
exerted enough pressure to force the abandonment of this
plan. Nevertheless, there were by this time many such
clinics in the large cities of Japan. In 1930, according to a
report, Tokyo had between sixty and seventy birth-control clinics.[6] Unfortunately, however, very few of them were
properly and adequately equipped and in some instances
resort to them resulted in serious impairment to the health
of women who attended. Consequently, in December, 1930,
the Home Department issued an ordinance designed to
regulate the sale and distribution of contraceptive devices

[1] Penrose, E. F., *Food Supply and Raw Materials in Japan*, Chicago
University Press, 1930, p. 70.

[2] Shimomura, H., *Jinko Mondai Kowa* (Lectures on Population Problems), Osaka, Osaka Asahi Shimbunsha, 1928, p. 182.

[3] *Supra*, p. 45.

[4] Cf. Hatoyama, I., " The Prosperity of a Nation depends on how it
Controls Population," *Kenko no Hikari*, Jan., 1933, Birth Control Number ; " A Meeting to Hear the Opinion of Minister of Education Hatoyama," *Bungei Shunju*, March, 1933, pp. 50–66. The minister resigned
from the post in March, 1934.

[5] Irisawa, T., " Contraceptive Method of Periodical Abstinence," *Central
Review*, Sept., 1932, pp. 145–66.

[6] Majima, Kan, in, Sanger, M., and Stone, H. M., Editors, *The Practice
of Contraception*, Baltimore, William & Wilkins, 1931, pp. 284–7.

which had been proved harmful to maternal health. The main provision of this ordinance was the prohibition of the sale to laymen of any contraceptive appliances that were to be inserted into the uterus, or of any such materials judged by the Home Minister to be injurious.[1]

Interruption of pregnancy, or abortion, is prohibited by the penal code.[2] However, the attitude of the Japanese public toward voluntary motherhood and the regulation of births has been rapidly changing. The legalization of abortion in pregnancies of less than three months' development has been demanded by proletarian political parties since about 1929. Professor G. Suehiro of Tokyo Imperial University, the foremost authority on Japanese civil law, declared that the feeling of guilt concerning abortion is rapidly fading, and abortion is generally regarded with as little moral conscience as is contraception. He favours the abolition of laws designed to suppress the practice of abortion, and declares that if the Bill intended for this purpose which has been placed before Parliament is defeated, it will be due to sheer hypocrisy on the part of politicians.[3] Professor Suehiro's attitude is shared widely and is reflected in court decisions where persons convicted of performing abortions are given suspended sentences or placed on probation. This is fast becoming the usual practice.[4] In this connection it may be noted that in 1933 there were but 143 convictions under the first trials. There is no doubt that the general public condonation of the practice of abortion will vitally affect Japan's immediate population growth—despite the existing legal prohibitions.

The movement for eugenic sterilization is gaining momentum throughout Japan. In 1928 the Physicians' Association urged upon the Government the necessity of sterilizing the mentally abnormal, the feeble-minded, the criminally

[1] See the whole articles of the ordinance in *Annual Report of the Sanitary Bureau,* cited, 1930, pp. 26–7.

[2] Penal Code, Chapter 29. According to this code persons who undergo abortions may be imprisoned for a period not exceeding one year. The maximum penalty for the second parties who perform the abortion is imprisonment for a period of seven years.

[3] *Bungei Shunju,* June, 1932, pp. 190, 192.

[4] *Fujin Koron,* May, 1933, p. 142.

irresponsible, and those with inheritable diseases.[1] While
the special committee of the Board of Investigation of
National Hygiene in Japan has been deliberating this issue
since 1932, the Japan National Hygiene Association decided
to propose in the 1933–4 session of Parliament a Bill providing for eugenic sterilization.[2] In view of the present
trend of public opinion, the enactment of such a law within
several years is not wholly impossible. An incident illus-
trative of the nation's reversal of attitudes was the sterilization by a university hospital of a sexually abnormal
seventeen-year-old youth. The vasectomy was performed
with the tacit consent of the Tokyo Juvenile Court, under
which the youth was paroled, and thereby incited no
antagonistic police action.[3]

Evidence of the recent tendency of Japanese public opinion
regarding population limitation has been presented in the
foregoing pages. As far back as 1928, Dr. Y. Shimojo, then
the Director of the Bureau of Statistics, maintained that the
decline of the number of births in 1927 was partially caused
by the practice of birth control.[4] Later events proved this
statement to be premature as far as the crude number of
births was concerned. Nevertheless, it is quite certain that
the declining trend of the nation's refined birth rate [5] reflects
the effects of the birth-control movement.

C. Study of Differential Birth Rates

It is almost a sociological truism that a phenomenon of
differential birth rates based on social classes manifests
itself during the period of gradual penetration of the birth-
control movement. In Japan there are several factors which
may in the future result in a relatively uniform extension
of the practices of birth control among the different social
classes ; chief among these are the freedom from legal prohibition against the dissemination of birth-control inform-

---

[1] *The Osaka Mainichi*, Dec. 12, 1928.
[2] *The Tokyo Asahi*, Oct. 13, 1933.
[3] *The Osaka Asahi*, Aug. 1, 1931.
[4] *The Tokyo Asahi*, May 10, 1928.   [5] *Supra*, pp. 109–10.

R

ation,[1] the comparatively high literacy rate of the Japanese people,[2] and the widespread publication of birth-control advertisements and articles in the daily newspapers and magazines.[3] Differential birth rates, however, constitute a practically universal phenomenon, particularly throughout the Western world.[4] It is therefore premature at this time, in the face of the gradual adoption of contraceptive practices, to suppose that Japan will present an exception to such a universal sociological phenomenon.

We have already observed that the birth rates of large cities differ considerably from the rates of rural districts. Although these are crude rates the disparity in the figures is indicative of a greater fertility among the farming population as compared to that of city dwellers. However, this is not a differential birth rate as generally understood ; such a rate signifies a difference of birth rates among more rigidly specified social classes.

Pending the proposed inclusion of fertility statistics in the regular national census,[5] a definite statement on the subject cannot at present be formulated. Some statistical data has been compiled demonstrating the fertility of different social classes in Japan. It is doubtful whether these limited materials reveal an existence of definite tendencies toward a differential birth rate among social classes. Nevertheless, they will be cited here because they illustrate to some degree several interesting facts concerning the fertility statistics of Japan. A study of the fertility of women past forty revealed no differentiation along social lines other than the fact that such class distinctions affected the age of marriage ; nevertheless, among the younger group

---

[1] Were it not for the legal ban on dissemination of birth-control information, the practice would have spread more evenly throughout the United States. Cf. *Recent Social Trend in the United States*, Report of the President Research Committee on Social Trend, New York, The Commission, 1933, Vol. I, p. 53.

[2] Illiteracy rate in 1932 was estimated by the *Kokusei Zukai* at 8·5 per 100 population of ages ten years and more. Furthermore, since the illiterate people are mostly confined to the group of advanced age, particularly to that of over sixty years old, the rate will be reduced greatly within a few years. *Kokusei Zukai*, cited, 1933, p. 397.

[3] Maeda, T., in, *Bungei Shunju*, Sept., 1931, pp. 24–5.

[4] Cf. Thompson, W. S., *op. cit.*, p. 110.   [5] See *supra*, p. 51.

of women the tendency toward a differential birth rate is to some extent in evidence.

In 1924, Mr. Toshio Furuyama conducted an investigation into the fertility of 2,200 women aged forty or more in Niigata City ; this study demonstrated the fact that fertility is higher among wealthier classes. It is generally supposed that this is due to the earlier marriages of wealthy women.[1] A little later a similar investigation of 2,912 Tokyo women past forty resulted in identical findings.[2] However, a study,

---

[1] Statistical results of Furuyama's Study are tabulated (Furuyama, T., " Fertility and Age of Marriage of Social and Occupational Classes," *Shakaigaku Zasshi*, No. 13, May, 1925 ; No. 14, June, 1925) :

AGE AT MARRIAGE OF HUSBANDS AND WIVES AND NUMBER OF BIRTHS PER WIFE, GROUPED ACCORDING TO FAMILY INCOME, 2,200 COUPLES, NIIGATA CITY, 1924

Annual Income (Yen).	No.	Average No. of Births.	Age of Marriage.	
			Husband.	Wife.
Less than 100	8	4·50	28·38	23·67
100– 200	72	4·94	28·89	23·96
200– 300	289	4·12	28·02	24·98
300– 400	342	4·44	26·73	23·95
400– 500	163	4·82	26·36	23·29
500– 600	215	5·13	26·55	23·60
600– 700	176	5·05	26·07	22·63
700– 800	161	4·98	26·18	22·45
800– 900	112	5·29	25·81	22·48
900– 1,000	76	5·04	25·70	22·22
1,000– 1,200	140	5·35	26·20	22·25
1,200– 1,600	136	5·52	26·20	22·27
1,600– 2,000	95	5·50	25·50	21·22
2,000– 3,000	85	4·58	25·11	20·56
3,000– 5,000	48	4·58	26·56	22·02
5,000–10,000	41	5·00	25·16	20·92
10,000–50,000	35	5·03	23·55	20·15
Over 50,000	6	5·17	24·90	18·63
Average	—	4·85	26·47	23·02

[2] NUMBER OF BIRTHS PER MARRIED WOMAN OVER FORTY, CLASSIFIED BY INCOME LEVEL, 2,912 WOMEN, TOKYO, N.D. (*c.* 1933)

Annual Income (Yen).	Birth per Married Woman over Forty.
Less than 500	3·22
2,000– 5,000	4·00
5,000–10,000	3·88
Over 10,000	4·21
Average	3·69

Cf. *The Japanese American* (New York), Aug. 10, 1933.

R*

conducted by Mr. Eiichi Isomura, definitely established a differential birth rate among the younger women of Tokyo.[1] In 1926 the Tokyo municipality conducted a most comprehensive investigation of Japanese differential fertility rates. In the Borough of Koishikawa 5,506 women were studied, and the report of this investigation seems to coincide with the results of the three surveys referred to in the foregoing pages. Table CI shows the average fertility rate per 100 women, embracing five professional classes and covering nine divisions in the duration of the marriage relationship.

In reviewing this tabulation, attention is directed to some serious shortcomings in the figures which are noted at the foot of this page.[2] Even with such defects in consideration, we may still infer that in recent years the salaried men have a lower fertility rate than the wage earners.

It is admitted that the statistical data presented in the above study are in general too obscure to draw definite conclusions. Still, the study presented in Section B of this chapter at least justifies our observation that the practice of birth control has been gradually spreading among the Japanese in recent years. Some writers have observed

---

[1] NUMBER OF BIRTHS PER 100 MARRIED WOMEN AGED 19–30, CLASSIFIED ACCORDING TO SPACE OF LIVING QUARTERS, YOTSUYA BOROUGH, TOKYO, 1925

Space of Living Quarter (No. of Mats).*	Owned House.	Leased House.
Less than 10	311·1	347·1
11–30	252·3	318·4
31 and over	251·7	162·1
Averages	257·3	323·3

* Space of one mat in Tokyo area is 1·758 metre by 0·879 metre.

See *Saimin no Shissanritsu ni Kansura Chosa* (Investigation of Birth Rates among the Poor), Tokyo Municipality, 1927, p. 17.

[2] There is some doubt as to the method of this categorical classification of social classes. It must be noted that until recent years social mobility in Japan was quite simple, and, therefore, social capillarity proceeded at a great rate. Thus many of the members of the higher classes began at lower levels. Such facts make the division of social classes rather arbitrary and reduce their significance in this study. Moreover, some doubt exists concerning the advisability of categorically placing the small merchant and manufacturing classes in the second rank. Another point to be noted is that the duration of the marriage relationship, excluding a consideration of the ages, does not afford a satisfactory basis for the comparison of fertility rates, since, as already noted (p. 104), fertility in women declines rapidly after the age of prime, which, we observed, is 19.

TABLE CI

NUMBER OF BIRTHS PER 100 MARRIED WOMEN GROUPED BY SOCIAL
CLASSES AND DURATION OF MARRIED LIFE—5,506 WOMEN,
KOISHIKAWA BOROUGH, TOKYO, 1926 [1]

Duration of Marriage (Years up to 1926).	Big Merchants and Manufacturers.	Small Merchants and Manufacturers.	Pensioners.	Salaried Men.	Wage Earners.
Less than 5 . .	100	120	90	110	120
5– 9	170	230	150	220	240
10–14	290	320	290	330	320
15–19	370	400	350	390	430
20–24	410	440	450	420	490
25–29	490	470	470	470	480
30–34	530	550	390	480	520
35–39	—	570	180	530	470
Over 40 . . .	500	—	—	—	—
Average . . .	308	307	300	282	315

The divisions of the five social classes and the number of their members are
as follows : Big merchants and manufacturers, 184 (including owners of factories, merchants, head priests of temples, lawyers, physicians owning hospitals,
high officials, nobles, big landlords, members of the House of Peers, etc.) ; Small
merchants and manufacturers, 2,176 (including owners of restaurants and hotels,
physicians, contractors, etc.) ; Pensioners, 244 (including landlords, those who
depend on the interest of bank deposits, agents of landlords, etc.) ; Salaried men,
1,779 ; Wage earners, 1,123.

that one of the obstacles to the further penetration of the
birth-control movement is the Japanese method of house
construction, which impedes the utilization of some contraceptive devices.[2] However, in view of the fact that the
adoption of birth control is not merely a mechanical innovation but, rather, involves a fundamental revision of both
mental attitudes and social patterns, an obstacle of this
character is insignificant.

The prospect of a decrease in the fertility rate does not
solve Japan's present population problem. The imminent
decline of mortality rates, particularly that of the infant
group, which usually is attendant upon a decline of fertility,

[1] *Saimin no Shissanritsu ni Kansura Chosa,* Tokyo Municipality, 1927,
pp. 58, 66–9.
[2] Cf. Negishi, S., *Ninshin Chosetsu no Jissai Chishiki* (Practical Knowledge of the Control of Conception), Tokyo, Shibundo, 1927, pp. 192–6 ;
for data on the same subject in India, see the article by Pillay, Captain
A. P., in Sanger, M., and Stone, H. M., Editors, *op. cit.,* p. 282.

will serve to augment the nation's natural increase. In addition, because of the present large infant group, the number of future mothers is on the increase. Furthermore, as has already been noted,[1] the adequate disposal of that portion of the population which will, in the near future, constitute a potential labour force, is a matter of serious consequence not only to Japan but to the world at large.

D. System of the Distribution of Wealth and its Significance on the Population Movement

The foregoing study of the population problem of Japan rests upon the inviolability of the institution of private property, and the institution of the family as a basic foundation of the social order. It is generally conceded that under the existing system of capitalism, which is an outgrowth of the institution of private property, the utilization of the economic resources of a nation may fall short of the possible physical maximum. Also, under the system of private property and the co-existent institution of the family, the utmost social efficiency in child-rearing and in the general support of the population may not be fully realized. This situation is a concomitant of the inequitable distribution of wealth inevitable in the system of capitalism as we know it to-day. Reference may be made to Chapter II, in which the social organization after the Reformation of 1868 was traced with special emphasis on the effect of the changed social order upon the population trend.

It is recognized that limitations in the population capacity are inherent in the present economic and social set-up. It has also been pointed out that there exists a definite tendency toward the concentration of capital and enterprise in the field of industry and commerce, that there has been a rapid increase in the number of petty traders and professional people in urban districts, and furthermore, that there is a tendency toward an unfavourable distribution of land in the field of agriculture.[2] On the other hand, the wide diffusion of occupations, together with the influence of the

---

[1] See *supra*, pp. 135-7.   [2] *Supra*, p. 23 ff. ; pp. 81-2 ; p. 154.

family system and the paternalistic attitude of employers, modify the direct effect of the concentration of wealth.[1] However, the effects of such institutions as private property and the family on the population movement of a nation involve considerations too complex to be discussed in this present work. It must suffice merely to mention the importance of this angle of the problem in its relation to the population trend of Japan.

An equation set by Dr. Y. Takada, which was regarded as a unique contribution of the Japanese to the theory of population,[2] illustrates the position of the distributive system as follows : [3]

$$dp = BS$$

B $=$ Number of population
S $=$ Standard of living
d $=$ Distribution coefficients *
p $=$ Productivity

* Actually the percentage of the total annual national income which is distributed among the low-class groups which comprise the major part of the population.

Dr. Takada believes that the above equation demonstrates the fact that a combination of the productivity and the distributive coefficient balance the combined weight of the population and the standard of living. The " distributive coefficient " is not defined satisfactorily, however. Nevertheless, the equation is important in that it suggests the relative influence of the system of distribution in determining the social effects of productivity.

In a country such as Japan, where the natural resources are limited and the population density is high, special attention must be accorded to the creation of a well-balanced and a more or less equitable distribution of the national wealth. To this end, the promotion of international co-operation for freedom of trade and for access to certain essential natural resources (within or without the nation's boundaries) must be accepted as the fundamental basis of Japan's external policy. Finally, the promotion of maternal

[1] *Supra*, pp. 84–5, 234.   [2] Nagai, T., *op. cit.*, p. 307.
[3] Takada, Y., *Jinko to Binbo* (Population and Poverty), Tokyo, Nihon Hyoronsha, 1927, p. 181.

and child welfare, the enactment of laws safeguarding tenantry and peasant proprietorship, and the enactment of effective labour legislation, are but a few of the policies which Japan must incorporate into her domestic programme.[1]

[1] A report of the Population and Food Commission of 1927–30 stated that the improvement of the methods of distribution of the national income and the manner of consumption of this income was one of the most vital issues in the nation's population problem (see *supra*, p. 46). The policies suggested by the commission attacked many of the most obvious maladjustments of Japan's distributive and consumptive system. The chief points of the report will be cited below :

1. Persistent searching studies of the cost of living and the formulation of its index numbers.

2. Reorganization and extension of relief measures for the poor and, further, the adoption of social insurance plans designed to promote the security of the nation's population.

3. Adoption of unemployment insurance and other measures to increase the security of the nation's employable members.

4. The limitation of dividends on corporations and the bi-annual bonus of the directorates of these corporations, and the institution of similar means necessary to create a more equitable distribution of the benefits of industries.

5. Revision of the system of taxation so as to limit, on the one hand the extent of unearned incomes, and to prevent on the other, unwarranted expenditures on luxuries.

6. Extension of government supervision over monopolies and inter-company price agreement on articles considered necessities of life.

7. Regulation of housing conditions in urban areas. The revision of lease and tenant laws in order to protect the interests of the lease-holders and tenants.

8. Improvement of the systems of short distance transportation, public and private marketing, and such popular financial organizations as banks, pawn-shops, loan societies, and the like.

9. Encouragement and protection of both consumers' and producers' co-operatives.

10. Study of adequate and modern methods of economy of consumption. Also, the encouragement of an abandonment of formalism in the social life of Japan and the superfluous expenditures attendant upon it —hence the creation of a general social acceptance of the value of saving.

SUMMARY AND CONCLUSIONS

THE first part of this study was devoted to an examination of the early movements and trends of the Japanese population. One of the most pertinent facts demonstrated in this connection was that from very early times Japan has been densely populated, particularly when compared to the density of Western nations. Perhaps the factor most contributive to this density of population has been the Japanese system of small farming. This system, which is more or less prescribed by the mode of living prevailing in temperate-subtropical climes, has been discussed in detail in a late chapter.

During the early Tokugawa Era, about the seventeenth century, following the widespread devastation wrought by centuries of warfare, an attempt was made to rehabilitate the lands devoted to agriculture, which policy was conducive to a rapid expansion in the nation's population. However, within a century a change was manifested, and a period ensued in which the population barely maintained its level. This situation was attributed by the writer to the practices of abortion and infanticide. These practices, in spite of legal prohibition, were prevalent among all classes in Japan's social structure, and represented an effort on the part of the nation's population to establish a balance between population numbers and means of subsistence.

The Meiji Reformation, in 1868, under the influence of Western capitalistic industrialism, precipitated many far-reaching social and economic changes. The first national policy of the post-Reformation Government aimed at the suppression of family restriction as it was then practised by means of abortion and infanticide. This policy demonstrated its effectiveness particularly at about the end of the

nineteenth century when Japan began to industrialize.   The
increased demand for labour thereafter warranted, and
rendered socially acceptable, the government policy of
suppression of family restriction.

Since then the population has increased rapidly and
steadily.   Not even during the Great War, when Japan was
faced with the difficulty of maintaining an adequate food
supply, was the nation's population increase considered a
problem or in any way related to the shortage of supplies.
In fact the problem of over-population has arisen only since
the War ; during this latest period, Japan's rapid economic
expansion has come to a halt, and a series of developments
have forced upon her the cognizance of certain limitations
in her national development.   It was pointed out that this
recent reversal in attitudes regarding population expansion
is a fairly universal development.

Before undertaking a detailed examination of demographic
trends, attention was called to the fact that prior to 1920
the nation went through several systems of census-taking
and recording.   The writer pointed out that a thorough
knowledge of these changes in census systems is essential
for a critical examination of Japan's population.   One of
the outstanding features of the present trend of the Japanese
population is the predominance of minor age groups.   This,
implying a large proportion of future potential mothers, is
of great significance in the compilation of the future population figures.   Another feature is the dual movement of
industrialization and urbanization.   The urbanization, by
affecting the marriage, birth, and other demographic rates,
produces a counterbalancing force to the above-noted age
factor.

The marriage rate, which is regarded as one of the most
stable elements in vital statistics, has experienced a considerable decline since the post-Great War period.   In view
of the rapid fall in fertility after the prime of fertility is past,
the effect of this decline on the nation's population trend
cannot be overlooked.

Beginning at an unusually low level, the birth rate has
gradually risen since the Reformation.   At about the be-

ginning of this century Japan's rising birth rate crossed the declining rate of Western industrialized nations. The death rate has also risen steadily, thereby negating, in considerable measure, the increase in the birth rate. Statistical evidence shows that since the post-War period the trends of the refined birth and death rates have been downward. At no time have these rates in Japan reached the high level they attained in Western nations.

In spite of the declining refined birth rate, the Japanese population is steadily increasing. Two factors, considered individually and in combination, are contributive to this imminent increase, namely, the general diminution of the death rate and the changing age composition of the nation's population. Without exception, all studies undertaken by experts in this field point to the fact that by 1960 the population of Japan will reach somewhere between eighty and ninety million. If we apply the present ratio of occupational figures to this population estimate it will be necessary for Japan to provide, annually, about half a million new positions in her economic structure for this additional population. Such disparity, even temporary in nature, between a nation's economic possibilities and its population trends, may be considered a causal factor in the nation's problem of population.

In the last five chapters of the thesis the possibilities and limitations of proposed remedies for Japan's population increase have been considered. An examination of the situation in rural communities revealed the limitations of further absorption of population in these quarters. More than that, the tendency toward land consolidation and the general improvement of agricultural methods tend to encourage the city-ward movement of the rural population. Rural Japan is a great reservoir of the nation's surplus population.

A study of the food supply of Japan revealed that the nation's food problem is not intrinsically a problem of merely feeding the increasing millions, but rather it resolves itself into questions of the relationship between the urban and rural districts, and between Japan proper and her colonies. The question is, in essence, one of values and distribution.

It directly affects the general population in that the food producers, should they find themselves unable to cover their costs for a long period of time, may thereby bring ruin to the rural districts (which at present contain nearly one-half of the entire population) ; the nation would thus be faced with a serious problem of over-population.   On the other hand, if the present high cost of Japanese agriculture were to be fully met, the cost of food would oppress Japanese industry and lower the real wages of labour.   How can the cost of food production in the nation be reduced to the level of world costs, or at least to the level of costs in Japan's colonies ?   This is a question of paramount importance in the nation's population problem.

Japan legalized freedom of immigration as recently as 1885.   The slowness in overseas expansion which then ensued may be attributed to the prevalence in Asiatic areas of a high density of population on a lower standard of living, and to the exclusion of Japanese in the New World under White domination, particularly in territories predominantly inhabited by Anglo-Saxon peoples.   Lack of a tradition of overseas expansion, due to the prolonged seclusionist policy under the Tokugawas, may also be partially responsible for the indifference of the Japanese to migration in modern times.   However, the considerable degree of success achieved in the Japanese migration movement to Hawaii, the United States and Brazil is testimony to the potentialities of Japanese as colonists.   The establishment of peace and order in Manchuria will gradually encourage settlement of that region by Japanese farmers.   Nevertheless, the very nature of the colonization or emigration movement precludes its efficacy as a solution to the problem of over-population.

At the present moment hope seems to be centered in plans for the further industrialization of the nation.   Japanese industry has progressed phenomenally.   As demonstrated in the present study, the deficiency of natural resources within the domain may not prove a serious handicap in the nation's industrial development ; modern transportation facilities, and the influence that Japan enjoys in East Asia, combine to create a counteracting force to her natural handicap. However, in view of the present universal tendency toward industrialization, further industrialization of Japan, calculated to expand the export of manufactured products, must proceed within the limit of a well-measured plan. Moreover, the rapid improvement in industrial organization and technological development results in proportionately less utilization of man-power. Thus it is likely that further industrialization will serve to stimulate an interest in the problem of a re-evaluation and re-distribution of wealth, rather than to accelerate the demand for labour.

The problem of unemployment does not in Japan assume the serious proportions which it has in many Western nations. This is attributable not only to the lesser degree of national industrialization, but is also due, in some measure at least, to social patterns peculiar to the Japanese family system, and to the feudal heritage of responsibility on the part of the employer for the care and protection, to some degree, of his employee. Hence capitalism has been blended with old feudal patterns, alleviating, at least to outward appearances, the difficulties inherent in a general unemployment problem. Capitalism as it has developed in Japan, and the industrial and social problems which are concomitants of unemployment in the West, assume in Japan the form of a general low standard of living and a consequent inefficiency along all lines of economic and social life.

During the past decade the birth-control movement was introduced in Japan and has gained considerable headway. Moreover, there is now a tendency toward a relaxation of the law regarding abortions, and a strong movement for eugenic sterilization has sprung up. Notwithstanding the ultimate significance of the birth-control movement, there are various factors which contribute to a minimization of the immediate effects of this movement as far as the present population growth is concerned.

Finally, the writer suggested that since it particularly affects maternal and child welfare, a re-evaluation of the social system, looking toward an improvement in the distribution of the national income, is essential in adequately attacking Japan's population problem.

Our study of the Japanese population showed that, generally speaking, the trend of population growth followed the trend of economic development. Public regulation of population was effective only when the economic situation warranted the policy advocated. In other words, the population trend is influenced chiefly by conditions and desires of individual families, and only very slightly by public dictation. The essence of population movements is self-interest, whatever may be the degree of enlightenment. Attempts rationally to control the birth of that portion of the population generally regarded as undesirable will gradually gain in prestige and effectiveness. In view, however, of the factors controlling human birth, the prevailing policy of *laissez faire* with regard to the general population will probably continue indefinitely.

Another point to be noted here is the nature of age composition of the population, which impedes, and in some measure circumscribes, group adaptation of the population to changing environmental situations. Hence at the present, despite the fact that the true (refined) birth rate is in the downward trend, the actual number of births is increasing in Japan.

In conclusion, it can be said that in spite of the long run adaptation of the population trend to economic conditions, the total social situation of any given period is conditioned by the population movement. The future of the Japanese population problem does not warrant an optimistic outlook any more than does that of other nations.

INDEX OF SUBJECTS

n. *indicates footnote references*

Abortions, 14–16, 31–7, 237, 240
Abstinence, 237
Adopted son, institution of, 32 n.
Age distribution, 89–92
Agricultural Bureau, Department of Agriculture and Forestry, 142, 145 *et passim*
Agricultural incomes, 145–8
Ainu, 1, 58
Anglo-Saxon people, 195, 209
Australia, immigration policy of, 194
Autonomous Rice Control Law, 174–5

Banks, concentration of, 23, 26
Birth control, 33, 46, 237–40
— statistics, 43, 105–13, 124–6
Brazil, 195, 199–201

Calendar, revision of, 48 n.
— age, system of, 6 n.
Canada, immigration policy of, 195
Census, 2–3, 5–7, 48–56
Charter Oath, 18–19
Child Labour, rate of, 84 n.
Chinese in Japan, 206
Chosen, 27 ; Japanese in, 190–4, 202 ; rice, 169–72
Chosenese, in Japan, 207–8
Class system, 6, 14, 17
Coal supply, 221
Colonial Militia, system of, 189
Colonies, 27, 190–4
Colonization, 188–211, 213
Comparative cost theory, applicability of in international trade, 226

Concentration of capital, 23–30, 246–7
Control economy, in foreign trade, 226
Corea, see Chosen
Corporation capital, 23

Daimyo (feudal lords), 15, 19
Death statistics, 113–21, 124–6
Debts, of farmers, 145
Density of population, 3, 5, 8, 62–4, 140, 247
Differential birth rates, 241–6
Diminishing returns theory, applied to Japanese agricultural economy, 148–53
Diseases, 119–24
Distributive system, 246–8
Division of labour theory, of Adam Smith, 223
Divorces, 99–100

Earthquakes, 12–13, 22, 41
Epidemics, 12–13, 114
Exclusion of Japanese, by the United States, 41–2 ; in general, 194–5

Family, size of rural families, 141 n.
— system, effect on population growth, 37, 246 ; declining state of, 235
Famines, 12–13
Farms, statistics of, 142–4
Fecundity, definition of, 103
Fertility, census proposed, 51 ; definition of, 103 ; differ-

ential, 241–6 ; relationship to marriage, 100–5
Fertilizer statistics, 149–51
Feudalism, fall of, 19 ; influence of, 29, 234 ; rise of, 2
Food problem, significance of, 42, 161–2
— supply, condition of, 161–87
Foreign loans, 21–2
— trade, 215–19
Formosa, see Taiwan
Future population, estimation of, 126–37

" Gentlemen's Agreement," 195
Gold standard, 22, 213

Hokkaido, acreage in, 143 ; colonization of, 67, 68, 189

Illegitimate births, 94–6
Illiteracy rates, 242 n.
Immigration, 41, 45, 188–211, 213
Imperial Economic Conference, 29, 41
Industrial policy, 21, 44, 212, 225–6
— revolution, 9, 21–3, 206
— workers, statistics of, 226–30 ; future increase of, 135 ; rural origin of, 233
Industrialization, 212–36
Infanticide, 14–16, 31–7, 87, 210 n., 237
Informal marriages, 92–6, 109
Intermarriage movement, 37–9
Iron supply, 220–1

Japan-Manchoukuo Treaty, of June 10, 1936, 202
Juvenile Court, Tokyo, 241

Karafuto, 27, 190–4, 202
Korea, see Chosen
Kwantung Leased Territory, 190–4, 202–6

Land, concentration of, 246 ; hunger, 157 ; periodical redistribution in early period,

3 ; property, restriction of, 14, 154 ; values, 151–3
Landlords' unions, 158
Living cost, survey of, 173 n.
Longevity, 116 n.

Mabiki (thinning), 31
Malthusian theory, 12, 39, 47
Man-land ratios, 12, 159
Manchoukuo Treaty, see Japan-Manchoukuo Treaty
Manchuria, crisis in, 46 ; Japanese policy toward, 183 ; immigration in, 202–6, 210–11
Marriages, 237 ; statistics of, 92–9, 243
Mechanization of agriculture, 159–60
— of industry, 213, 228–30
Mineral resources, 219–23
Model factories, 20
" Money economy," 17
Morbidity surveys, 121–2
Mura (village), 68 n., 69 n.

National Hygiene Association, 241
National incomes, 26 ; distribution of, 247
— strength, factors analysed by Russell, 223
Natural calamities, 12–13
Necessites of life, international trade in, 161
Newspaper editorials, 44 n.
Nutritive values of foods, 184–7

Occupational statistics, 76–85
Oil supply, 222–3
Oriental culture, its effect on agriculture and population, 140
Overseas Affairs, Department of, 44, 177
Overseas expansion, in sixteenth century, 188–9, 210

Parliament, elections for, 27 n. ; members of, 28
Paternalism, in industry, 234, 247

Peasants' unions, 155
Pederasty, 12
Philippine Islands, 201–2
Population and Food Commission, 44–6, 238, 239, 248
Population Research Institute, 46
Private property, system of, 19, 246–7
Prostitution, 12
Public health, condition of, 121–4

" Rationalization " of industry, 22, 213
Reclamation programme, 180–3
Reclamation Subsidy Law, 169, 173, 182
Reformation of 1868, 17–21
Regional classification, 64–5
Rice, colonial, 169–72 ; Japanese, 167–9 ; policy on, 172–84 ; relationship to general food problem, 162–4 ; riot, 40, 42, 166 ; supply of, 164, 178–84
Rice Control Law, 173–7
" Rice economy," 17
Rice Law, 173

Samurai, 6, 14, 20, 189
Sanitary Bureau, Home Department, 121–2 *et passim*
Seclusionism under the Tokugawas, 14, 17, 188–9
Sex distributions, 87–9
— ratios, definition of, 87
Shogun (military regent), 5, 10, 15
Small-farming system, 140–2, 145–8
Social legislations, 29–30, 234–5, 247–8
— mobility (social capillarity), 28, 244 n.

South Africa, immigration policy of, 195
South Manchuria Railway Company, 192, 204 n.
South Manchuria Railway Zone, 190–4, 202–6
South Sea Mandatory, 190–4
Southern Sakhalin, see Karafuto
Special Rice Account, 173–4
Statistical Bureau, Cabinet, 55, 185 *et passim*
Sterilization, 240–1
Sumptuary laws, 14

Taiwan, 27 ; Japanese in, 190–4, 202 ; rice, 169–72
Tariff autonomy, acquisition of, 21
Tenancy problem, 153–8
Territory, area of, 58, 63 ; expansion of, 27, 39
Textile industry, 213, 224–5, 229, 233
Tokugawa Era, 3 n., 11, 17
Transportation cost, land and ocean freight rate compared, 224 n.

Unemployment, 28, 41, 77 n., 230–5
United States, immigration policy of, 41–2, 195
Urban-rural districts, definition of, 68–9
Urbanization, 21, 68–76, 190

Washington Conference, 41–2, 230
Western penetration of Orient, 18

Yamato Race, 1–2

Zodiac, 6 n., 32, 61

INDEX OF PERSONAL NAMES

n. *indicates footnote remarks referring to persons in question and*
b. *indicates simple bibliographical references at the foot of the page.*

Akiyama, Onosuke, 206 b.
Allen, George C., 37
Alsberg, C. L., 159 n.
Ando, Hirotaro, 179, 180
Andreades, A., 8 b.
Asami, Noboru, 191 b.
Ayusawa, Iwao, 44 b.

Beard, Miriam, 29 b., 144 n.
Bisson, T. A., 213 b.
Bowley, Arthur Lyon, 130
Buchanan, D. H., 145 b.
Burke, Edmund, 210 n.

Cannan, Edwin, 130
Carr-Saunders, A. M., 38 n.
Crocker, Walter R., 108, 109, 149, 225

de Gobineau, Joseph Arthur, 38 n.
Dennery, Etienne, 203 b.
Droppers, Garrett, 8, 12

Egi, T., 40
Eto, Tsuneji, 14 n.

Fairchild, Henry P., 206 b.
Fujiwara, Gingiro, 212 b.
Fukuda, Tokuzo, 230
Furuyama, Toshio, 243

Gide, Charles, 159 b.
Gondo, Seikyo, 12 n.
Grey, Egerton C., 184–7

Hara, K., 17 b.
Harada, Shuichi, 44 b. *et passim*

Hashimoto, D., 74 b. *et passim*
Hatoyama, Ichiro, 339 b.
Hijikata, Seibi, 80 b.
Honda-Masaharu, 17 n.
Honjo, Eijiro, 7, 8, 10, 12, 14, 15
Horie, Yasuzo, 7
Hughes, Charles E., 41 n.
Hume, David, 210 n.

Ichihashi, Yamato, 13, 209
Inagaki, Otohei, 129
Ino, Hidenori, 4 b.
Inoma, Kiichi, 73 b.
Irisawa, Tatsukichi, 239 b.
Ishihama, Chiko, 17 b.
Ishimoto, Shizue, 238 b.
Isomura, Eiichi, 244
Ito, Hirobumi, 18 n., 38

Johnson, Albert, 41 n.

Kanaji, Ichiro, 191 b.
Kaneko, Kentaro, 18 n., 38, 181
Kanno, Wataro, 2 b.
Kato, Hiroyuki, 38 b.
Katsu, Kaishu, 7, 8
Katsumoto, Kanzaburo, 238
Kawada, Shiro, 153 b.
Kawai, T., 238 b.
Kawakami, T., 3 b.
Kawanishi, S., 13 b.
Kawarada, K., 234 b.
Keller, A. G., 203 n.
King, F. H., 158
Knapp, A. M., 18 b.
Knibb, George, 126–7
Kobayashi, Ushisaburo, 21 b.

Kuczynski, Robert R., 47, 110, 111, 112
Kume, Kunitake, 1 b.
Kuroita, Shobi, 1 n.

Maeda, Tamon, 242 b.
Majima, Kan, 238 b.
Minami, Ryozaburo, 43
Minoguchi, Tokijiro, 229
Miura, Shuko, 18 b.
Miyakuni, Chiyokichi, 40
Moulton, Harold G., 20, 223, 224
Murdoch, James, 5
Mywatt, Paul, 154

Nagai, Toru, 20, 230
Nagaya, Toshio, 69, 89
Naka, Tsusei, 1 b.
Nakabashi, Tokugoro, 39
Nakagawa, Tomonaga, 76 b.
Nasu, Hiroshi (or Shiroshi), 69, 171
Negishi, S., 245 b.
Nikaido, Yasunori, 36, 121
Nishikawa-Kyurinsai, 4 b.
Nitobe, Inazo, 206 b.

Okajima, H., 13
Okawa, Shumei, 17 b.
Okazaki, Fuminori, 50 b.
Ono, Takeo, 15, 36
Orchard, John E., 11
Ota, K., 26 b.

Pearl, Raymond, 129
Penrose, Ernest F., 206, 228
Perry, Matthew Calbraith, 17
Pillay, A. P., 245 n.
Pitkin, Walter B., 148 b.

Ro-Tozan, 15
Russell, Bertrand A. W., 223

Sanger, Margaret, 40, 238
Sawada, Goichi, 5 b.
Sawamura, M., 184
Shimojo, Yasumaro, 128, 241

Shimomura, Hiroshi, 239
Shiomi, Saburo, 153
Smith, Adam, 223
Soda, Takeo, 111, 112, 130–7, 178
Spencer, Herbert, 18 n., 38
Suehiro, Gentaro, 240

Taguchi, Ukichi, 5 b.
Takada, Yasuma, 183, 247
Takahashi, Kamekichi, 13
Takahashi, Yoshio, 37
Takano, Iwasaburo, 49 n., 50 n., *et passim*
Takekoshi, Yosaburo, 12 b.
Takimoto, Seiichi, 141
Takizawa, Matsuyo, 17 b.
Tanaka, Giichi, 44, 45
Tanaka, Kogai, 12, 16
Taniguchi, Yoshihiko, 65 b.
Thompson, Warren S., 44 b., 76 n., 82 n., 225, 242 n.
Tokugawa-Iyeyasu, 11
Tokugawa-Yoshimune, 5
Tsuchiya, Takao, 15
Tsuji, Zennosuke, 12
Tsurumi, Yusuke, 30 n., 42 n.
Tsutsumi, Tatsuo, 238 b.

Uchida, Ginjiro, 1 b. *et passim*
Uchida, Kosai, 20 n.
Ueda (or Uyeda), Teijiro, 109, 130–7
Uehara, Tetsusaburo, 189 n.
Ukita, Kazutami, 238

Wilkinson, H. L., 127
Wolfe, A. B., 47 n.

Yagi, Yoshinosuke, 171 b.
Yamamoto, Jotaro, 212 b.
Yamamoto, Miono, 190 b.
Yanaihara, Tadao, 194 n.
Yokoyama, Yoshikiyo, 3
Yoshida, Togo, 3, 8
Yoshikawa, Shuzo, 31 b. *et passim*
Yoshio, E., 207 b.
Yugi, Juzo, 7

Printed in Great Britain by
Butler & Tanner Ltd.,
Frome and London